W9-ACG-934

At the Turn of the Tide

At the Turn of the Tide

A BOOK OF WILD BIRDS

Richard Perry

FOREWORD BY ROBERT ARBIB

ILLUSTRATED BY NANCY LOU GAHAN

Taplinger Publishing Company   NEW YORK

First published in the United States in 1972 by
TAPLINGER PUBLISHING CO., INC.
New York, New York

Illustrations copyright © 1972 by
Taplinger Publishing Co., Inc.
Foreword copyright © 1972 by Robert Arbib
All rights reserved.
Printed in the U.S.A. by Vail-Ballou Press, Inc.

Published simultaneously in the Dominion of Canada by
Burns & MacEachern Ltd., Ontario

Library of Congress Catalog Card Number: 74-179950

ISBN 0-8008-0506-2

Designed by Mollie M. Torras

CONTENTS

FOREWORD

It is now almost three decades since Richard Perry's first book was published. A study of bird life in Britain at the lonely rim of the sea, it was full of treasure. But the world was in the grip of war; hearts and minds were consumed with the deprivations and agonies of the times. A less fortuitous atmosphere for the arrival of a philosphical book of bird observations could scarcely be imagined. Limited by paper rationing and the lack of outlets for critical notice, *At the Turn of the Tide* never won the acclaim it deserved, nor the audience it warranted. Across the Atlantic it went completely unnoticed; in fact it was unobtainable.

But the talents so abundantly promised in this work were not to be denied, and its author went on to become a well-known and respected member of that select group of naturalist-authors who can turn hands to any subject, and turn them well. The list of his previously published works is testimony to the author's versatility and his professionalism. The books are carefully researched and engagingly written, filled with legend, fact, anecdote, and science. The style, especially in the later works, is more reportorial than literary. But they are good reading.

At the Turn of the Tide is of a different *genre* entirely. It is a very personal and subjective work, an evocative appreciation of a special environment and its inhabitants that is an almost lyrical testament to the beauty and mystery of the salt-marsh. The writing is elegant: in these pages Richard Perry is an artist of the *chiaroscuro* school, painting images of light and sudden shadow, of mood and motion, of air and water and land that merge in an ever-changing panorama—now desolate, now pulsing with life. There is writing here that reminds us of Elliott Coues, W. H. Hudson, Thoreau. The reader who listens with the inner ear, and sees on the screen behind the closed eyes, will find pure delight in page after page of images more akin to poetry than prose.

This is a book painted in earth colors and moody skies, in the grays and ochers of the salt-marshes (the "saltings") of Britain, in all seasons, all weathers, and every time of day. Here is a late autumn sunset, filled with music:

> The sun is setting a fiery golden behind a bank of cloud over the hidden sea in the west. Gulls, pale kings of the sunset, are forever drifting idly over the flats, and from far out on the sands come laughing cries of herring gulls and deeper barkings of great black-backs; a cormorant swishes low over the marsh, soaring away from me in a desperate hurry; and all part of the blessed peace are the plaintive cries of a startled redshank, the strong, hoarse croaks of gray crows, and the lovely quavering call of a pack of curlew.

Good writing, of course, is more than merely a way with words. It is, first of all, *seeing*. And Perry sees the world with a truly perceptive, even imaginative eye. Then too, it is *hearing*, and Perry has an ear equally sensitive to the music of bird calls and the inner rhythms of English prose. But writing is even more quintessentially *thinking*. Since every sentence is, or should be, a thought, if you cannot think lucidly you cannot write at all. Perry's senses, and his thought processes, are beautifully in harmony in this book.

The art of describing a bird, precisely, so that we can see every detail of its plumage, visualize it in its natural setting, observe its smallest and most typical movements, and even hear its call—without sounding like a textbook—is one given to few writers. Perry does it repeatedly. Of the fulmar:

> The fulmar is not the gull-like bird I pictured before seeing him. In close flight his dove's head seems large out of proportion to his plump, cylindrical body and narrow wings, which are unexpectedly dark, a patterned sooty-gray in strong contrast to his snowy head and breast, and very straight and angled at their tips, like a gannet's. Planing interminably over the bay, he beats his wings at irregular intervals, with the quick motion of a swift or a shearwater, in between long bouts of gliding and soaring. The grace of his flight grows on me until it becomes a beautiful and essential part of the seascape. He seems in perpetual motion —I wonder to what purpose, for, since he feeds only at night, there is nought in his ceaseless circling and planing but pleasure. But fulmars slanting athwart the colossal white crests of the surf-breakers are as vital to the perfecting of their beauty as gannets plunging into tempestuous seas . . .

Of the dunlin:

> Diminutive dark knots, dunlin, only, on an average, seven and a half inches in length, are most perfectly proportioned, with the neatest figures imaginable: shaggy bellies, black in breeding plumage, pale silver in winter. Their spread wings unexpectedly disclose a black rump, when they *tizzee* up and away in simultaneous flight: many hundreds swarming up and down the creek in intricate evolutions, with an impressive rushing of wings beating in perfect time. They dwell upon their whispered notes, caressing them to a twittering song: beautiful when its melody is lost and heard in swiftly changing flight. . . . they alight with an inexpressibly graceful butterfly gesture, common to many small waders before and after flight: arching slender, tapering

wings vertically above their backs, revealing the soft white silk of their undersurface: a lovely movement suggestive of an infinite luxury of physical contentment.

Birds swarm in these pages; their personalities and individualities are observed, organized, and presented to us alive and bright of eye. This is not simply lyrical description, this is the reflection of sensitive and questing observation.

Beyond the felicity of expression, this is careful and intelligent field work, and the ornithology it records is as valid and fresh today as it was when first set down. Many of the birds that swirl through these pages—the geese and ducks, the herons and gulls and terns and shorebirds—will be familiar to readers on the western side of the Atlantic, from much the same, if not identical, habitats. Canadian and American devotees will find many of their favorite species here, better delineated than they have ever been before. Here, too, they will meet and know species unfamiliar to them, but no less fascinating.

Perry does more than look and listen and record. He ponders, deduces, and theorizes. Anyone who has watched a school of fry darting in seeming computerized unison, like cells of a single organism, or marveled as a flight of sandpipers flashes from sand bank to sky in mass flight, will be intrigued by the author's hypothesis on how synchronous movement in animals is accomplished.

On the ever-intriguing origins of bird migration, Perry may be open to question, but even here the reader must carefully weigh the lines of reasoning and the evidence for the hypotheses offered. Little real progress has been gained in these last thirty years in explaining the origins of migration, although we know much more today about its mechanics.

In these pages, too, the reader will enjoy provocative discussions of protective coloration of birds and their eggs, of injury-feigning and the broken-wing act, of instinct and emotion in birds, and everywhere, reflections on the how and why of migration. There is even a "new" theory on the eclipse plumage in waterfowl.

This is a literate bird book, but it is something more. On a canvas of infinite horizons, Perry weaves a tapestry of sea and bay, estuary and marsh, and of the interdependence of all life in this special world of daily ebb and flood. This is a book about ecology, long before the word came into common usage. It leaves the reader with an indelible awareness of the richness of this little-known, seemingly desolate environment. And although it was written at a time when other concerns, seemingly more dire and more urgent, were convulsing the world, it has a powerful implied message for all of us today.

For of all the world's habitats, most particularly in North America, none have been so ravaged, depleted, wasted, and despoiled, or under such destructive pressures today, as the tidelands and wetlands that are the special concern of this book. *At the Turn of the Tide* was written long before anyone was fully aware of the precious nature of these places—and before the threat to their existence was evident. But no book could be more timely today in reminding us of the importance and special beauty of the wetlands—so fragile, so coveted, and so irreplaceable.

If the beauty and the science that join here so harmoniously serve to open our eyes and reinforce our resolve to battle against the forces of ignorance and greed that seek to destroy our tidelands, then this book has served a far more important service than its author, so many years ago, could have ever dreamed.

Now turn the page and meet the eye and ear and mind of Richard Perry, at the turn of the tide.

Robert Arbib

INTRODUCTION TO THE
SECOND EDITION

This is a book about the wild birds that frequent the tidal lands and islands of England—such places as Braydon Water, Brancaster Staithe and Scolt Head, Holy Island and the Faeroes, Rockcliffe Moss and the Solway Firth. I wrote it soon after I first discovered that these wonderful places were as typical of English country as the woods and fields and hedgerows of village England.

Three months before he died fighting with the Eighth Army at Mareth, Lieut. Alan Richardson, a Devon man, who was at once the youngest and promised to be the most notably original of English bird-photographers, wrote to me from the desert:

For the first time, I think, I realize that I am in an army, and understand the meaning of a soldier's job. I have thought on the events that have brought me here and the reason why I am ranged among the leading participants of this madness of war. It

13

is not that I like being a soldier, nor that I hate Germans or Italians, nor that I fervently wish to reap honor and glory in battle. No. My wish is to help to turn back history a few years—to bring back the days when one could roam the countryside in peace, and when it was only the beautiful things in life that seemed to matter, sunsets over the estuary, the wild birds, and the friendship of the children I used to teach.

Should any of us with similar ideals survive the holocaust, it will be our bounden duty to those who have died, to ensure the preservation unspoilt, of such few wild places as are yet left in England. Let us, however, be watchful. We do not want a regimented Nature. We do not want reserves bristling with keepers who have no spiritual or intellectual awareness of the treasure they guard: but wild places, where those who come back can be in the sun, free to observe, meditate and create.

Richard Perry

Holy Island, 1943

I

THE CHARM OF THE MARSHES

In the first days of September I came to rest at last in a black
cottage at the foot of a black windmill with white turret and
gray-slatted sails. A strangely desolate place, only six minutes
from an East Coast holiday resort by the rail running past the
windmill, and yet in some ways the loneliest of the many
lonely places I know—no road, no water, no milk, no lighting, no living beings but an occasional wildfowler or marshman; noise only in the trains thundering past to the Races, in
the distant sirens of beet factories, in the chugging of the
pleasure-boats and tramp-steamers up and down the river
that cut through two thousand acres of bare, tidal mud flats.
Its loneliness bit deep into me.

The windmill stood on a fifty-yard strip of green, between
the mud flats stretching away beyond my eye's discerning
and the endless fresh-marshes on the other side of the railway
track. The track, the mill, the cottage and its outbuildings, its
little garden and scanty trees, formed an oasis for small birds.
Pied and yellow wagtails, whitethroats, and those boon migratory companions, wheatears and redstarts, flirted along the

rails: a motley company; a chiff-chaff crept through the bushes in the garden, and shy blackbirds and song thrushes scolded from the stunted trees; house martins and sand martins twittered briefly on migration, but never stayed; yet thirty or forty swallows perched on the handrails over the millstream every morning singing their twitter-songs with great gusto, the brows and throats of the adults vivid burnt sienna, of the young but yellowish. Under the casing of the mill wheel a resident swallow had built her nest, and the first of her five young flew on September 16. Swallows, linnets, starlings and an occasional lark were all our songsters: this was no country for singing-birds.

The fresh-marshes were squared up by innumerable dykes; their relief was the jigsaw of gates leading from marsh to marsh: each standing alone, with dykes as fences, a long-shanked heron gaunt on each top rail; they were softened by far oases of farms in their several emplacements of apple trees; twenty-four windmills spanned the marshes in a half seen, half imagined arc; and all the world was grazing cattle —once experienced, who can live a full life without the distant, day-long lowing of cattle in his ears? My mind finds great peace in their straight backs and sloping necks silhouetted against the ground mists of autumn evenings, after days of hot sun, windmill sails crossed above the long white swathes.

The place had held vague romance for me since childhood. A rough, wild spot I had imagined it: Valhalla of "John Knowlittle" (A. H. Patterson), who, in his life, attracted there all the rarest wildfowl and wading birds, drawing oddly humorous cariactures of those who studied them. When I saw the little square houseboats permanently anchored in the mud, I knew his spirit to be housed in one. I could see him sweeping the flats with his telescope, and then pushing off in his punt to the blue-stilted avocets probing with their "cobbler's awls" on the hummocks, or to the great white spoonbills dredging in the ooze. They still come every year: where-

Avocet in courtship dance

fore I had come too. The previous autumn there had been
three spoonbills and fifteen avocets here in September.

Wherever I go in the British Isles there is always some bird
whom, afterwards, I associate especially with that place,
however common he may be elsewhere. At twilight, the first
evening, I strolled along the sea-wall that holds back the salt
tide from the fresh-marshes, and saw the *genus loci* of this
strange place, the short-eared owl: most amusing of birds.
Though some nest in the British Isles and many winter, most
of the short-eared owls I have seen have been on their spring
and autumn passages. Resting and roosting on the ground,
solitary owls often rise from some marsh or fen or salting, to
float leisurely over the reed-beds and slant down in some
more secluded fastness; but here they were in twos and threes
and in packs of eight or ten: twenty-five in an evening.

During the day I flushed them from rocky sea-wall, from the long grass of the marshes, or from tumble-down cottage: for, while hunting at all hours, the gloaming was, owl-like, their preference. In the soft autumn dusk their flight was exquisitely buoyant, when dipping disdainfully with slow, irregular wing-beats, they dropped like sycamore seed-wings to the hayfield behind the sea-wall, to stand with wings a little unfurled and pushed forward, revealing their white shoulders. All British birds of prey have beautiful plumage, but none more lovely than the gray, black, and silver mottling of the short-eared owl at this season: his long, straight wings copper-shafted. Athwart a rainbow in a stormy sky he falls silver, for the black edges of his wings create an illusion of white latticing, by reason of the gray margining to each feather.

I found them entertaining and companionable birds, because of their intense curiosity (another owl trait), for they hovered and wheeled with angry *zew-zewk,* just over my upturned face which was white in the dim light, watching me intently with bold gaze of light-brown eyes in small, turning bullet-heads. More accustomed to the rushing stoop and upward swish of enraged, nesting tern or black-headed gull, the noiseless swoop to and up from my head of these soft-feathered owls was uncanny, but exhilarating.

They stooped continually, with staccato *quick-quick-quick-quick,* at the unfortunate kestrel swaying on his telegraph wire, though not more often than that arch-pest, the rook; nor is the lapwing, himself plagued by black-headed gulls in other parts of the country, guiltless of skua tactics with kestrels. Sometimes they quarreled with drawn out *ew-ew-ewch;* but it was the packing of these owls that most fascinated me: a dozen twirling out over the flats like falling lapwings, wheeling away, higher and higher on their autumnal migration, in soft, disembodied flight—gone so leisurely, so softly.

If the inimitable short-eared owl was perhaps the spirit of these marshes, it was the kestrel who here revealed himself in a new light. Everyone knows the "wind-hover" hawk: indeed I believe there is no country place in the British Isles where I have not seen him fanning the wind in searching hover, or swaying on a telegraph wire. He is territorially conservative, working some special field or marsh month in, month out. But never anywhere knew I so many as on these fresh-marshes. From dawn to dusk three or four hovered over every marsh, stooping like gannets to successful capture or, much more often, swinging sideways in long glide after unproductive hover; sometimes cutting out over the water, in guise a cuckoo, with narrow, curving wings quick-beating. Indeed so rarely do I see a kestrel in successful hunting that it is always a mystery to me wherewith he fills his craw. This particular summer there had been a plague of field voles and, consequent upon this, an invasion of kestrels, short-eared owls, and —does it sound strange?—herons. Mice and voles are the kestrel's staple food, though beetles are not overlooked, and I have seen two quarreling, with shrill *kreek-kree-kree-kreek*, over a pipistrelle bat, which escaped in the confusion. Though often mobbed by small birds and buffeted by larger, the kestrel is no great enemy to the fledglings of either.

What surprised me most, here, was to find him a noisy bird; hitherto I had found him exceptionally silent and, though seeing a kestrel almost every day of my life, heard but seldom his shrill cry. But here I heard the *skee-ee-ee* of two quarreling or playing, separate *dik-dik-dik* calls of two chasing some yards apart, or a single *zee-tew* of alarm; and all day long the marshes were noisy with his indefinite *kee-lee-lee*—usually denoting piracy on the part of two or three rooks: an incident of quarter-hourly occurrence.

Third characteristic bird of the fresh-marshes is the little green sandpiper—indeed he is as characteristic of autumn migration as the wheatear of spring. How often have I not strolled up a dyke or approached a hidden pool, for a tiny black-and-white wader to tower up almost at my feet, with alarmed *toos-leep toos-leep*. Mounting swiftly and erratically with soaring, twisting flight, the white rump to his black back is as salient as a house martin's. He goes away with a clear, trippling *tzwee-wee-pee-zee*, to return again and again to the shallow pool from which I have disturbed him. How pearly-white are his underparts! His black back is green or blue or brown at the play of light, and his white tail is edged with a dark green lacing. He bobs about like the common sand-pipers, who were constantly skimming out over the mud flats from the sea-wall, with clear *pee-pee-pee-pee*, circling back, five or six together, on vibrant, hesitant wings, pearly under-sides silver in the sun.

For no good reason another autumn migrant is often con-fused with the green sandpiper, the white greenshank. Al-though nesting on Scottish moors, the greenshank is essentially an autumn bird of passage, visiting at odd times, even during the hardest winter, any water or oozy habitat in the British Isles; seldom, however, do I meet with him going

Kestrel with its prey

north in the spring.[1] As with the short-eared owl, so these fresh-marshes and tidal flats attract more greenshanks than any other place I know, for he is a solitary species. One evening, after flushing a green sandpiper, I lay on the sea-wall, when the tide was going back off the mud to the river, watching and listening to as many as twenty greenshank calling everywhere, nine or ten often flighting together: a strange thing to see! His clear *tew-tew-tewk* is one of the most distinctive of wader's cries, and was to be heard a mile over the flats at all hours of the day and night. Some of the older birds were still calling *chewvee-chewvee:* a nesting call, hardly to be distinguished from that of the male roseate tern.

In late summer some passage greenshanks—the early-coming birds of the year—have rump and underparts obscured by drab edgings to their feathers, but in the autumn every part of their plumage except the drab-olive wings is an ashy white; in flight the white back is striking, and facing me on the ground the greenshank seems a white wader. Long, sharp, straight and fast in flight, he has at rest an irriating habit of feeding in little drains and sunken pools on the flats, which wholly or partially obscure him. Glimpsing him thus at a distance, bobbing at the edge of a creek when the sun glimmering upon the wet mud dispels all color, I might mistake him for a redshank; but he is distinctly a higher-standing bird, his bill markedly uptilted. His method of feeding, when I can observe it, is delightful, for he dashes through a shallow pool with bill and half of his head immersed; pushing forward with a smooth, slightly impeded action, as if forcing his coulter bill through the ooze or water—as no doubt he is—after small marine game and stranded fishes, perhaps, isolated in tiny pools by an ebbing tide: a most energetic, forceful motion. Whereas the redshank feeding in the same pool, immersing delicate, sharp bill and three parts of his head, dibbles from side to side, with equal energy and extraordinary rapid-

[1] For explanation of which see remarks on red godwits in Chapter XIII.

ity, often gyrating body about bill in a whole circle; though more usually he probes his beak only in a hundred different places in the ooze.

Searching the flats every day for avocet and spoonbill, I pushed the little flatbottom that served me in lieu of a punt vast distances over the sticky ooze when the tide was out: often stepping unwarily into drains and filling my gum boots with a chilly, viscous composition of ooze and water. One morning I pushed off, with much sweating and cursing, to await at what I thought would be a likely rallying ground for waders from all parts of the flats, when the flowing tide gradually pushed them on to the higher mud of the "hummocks" —only to be caught by a whole gale that continued the day long, so that I had some difficulty in rowing back to the mill, the mud being so lightly covered and the wind approaching hurricane force in squalls.

On another very calm day I sat for six hours in the flatbottom, without anything startling happening. The flats were so extensive and the tide varied so much from day to day that it was not easy to adjudge, on a particular day, which would be the last dry mud where all the waders would gather before high water. The problem was no less acute when the tide was ebbing. One lovely day, with a fresh wind from the southeast, I wasted the best of it rowing two miles against the tide, to find that all the waders had gone in the opposite direction to that I had expected—the truth of the matter being that they, rather naturally, prefer that mud from which the tide has most recently gone back, or over which it flows most slowly, bringing new life to the myriad small animals that bury themselves in the mud between tides.

But, in all this tribulation and toil, there were compensations for the avocets and spoonbills that never came. Twice those once-nesting, spasmodically-wandering waders, ruffs and reeves, dropped over the sea-wall from the fresh-marshes, with clear *knut-knut* and loud *scree-oo:* a cry I have known wildfowlers to mistake for the mellow whistle of a widgeon.

Dusky redshank excepted, winter ruffs and reeves are the only waders that may forgivably be mistaken for redshank, and the only wader in whom the female is so much smaller than the male. Though actually a smaller bird than the redshank, the ruff appears larger, thicker at the shoulders, and stands higher on the legs; the reeve smaller and shorter on the legs, which, in my experience, are invariably a pale green, whereas those of ruffs vary from bird to bird, some being that bright orange-red of the redshank. The most absolute distinction between the two is the nebulous, yellow back-margining to the wings of the ruff, so different to that broad white edging to the wings of the redshank.

Better than ruffs and reeves was another common bird of the Dutch pölders, the black-tailed godwit.[2] There were, strangely enough, few bar-tails present. Almost every day I watched a little bundle of a dozen or more black-tails on the flats. On the wing they can in no wise be mistaken for their bar-tailed relatives; my first impression was of oyster-catchers: both in the straight, quick-beating flight and in the salient black-and-white striping of their wings. A third sure distinction is their trick of flying with long legs stretched out far behind their tails. But at rest the differences are subtle when the two species are not together, for the black or barred tail is not an obvious sign of identity. Together, the immensely long legs of the black-tails stand them an inch or two higher than the bar-tails, though even so it must be remembered that the bills and shanks of the latter vary enormously in length from one bird to another. However, when the black-tails are feeding, probing and rotating in the ooze in the usual godwit manner, they give little fluttering jumps every now and again, with wings at half-cock, revealing snowy rumps, which are whiter than those of most bar-tails, in whom I have not observed this habit. Moreover a bar-tail is just another long-legged wader among other long-legged waders, whereas the

---

[2] It must not be thought that he is a rare bird. I have observed him on the West Coast from the Solway to North Devon.

redder-headed black-tail stalks gigantic, with majestic curvings of swanlike neck: a grand bird.

Every morning, when I climbed the mill to inspect the flats, there were gryphonesque cormorants standing immobile, with outstretched wings bent at the elbows, on the channel stakes of the river: heraldic figures straight from *Alice in Wonderland*. Sometimes they vibrated and flapped their wings vigorously, choosing usually to face the wind, sitting back on their stiff tails. This I have found to be an infallible distinction between shag and cormorant, for the former spreads his wings only when swimming on the sea, a thing I have never perceived the latter to do. In winter, too, when his "top-knot" crest is not in evidence, another distinction is the shag's habit of "snaking" his periscopic neck up and down when in flight.

One morning there was the delightful picture of nine heraldic cormorants standing stiffly on nine adjacent stakes. When taking off into flight, they preferred to drop to the water and paddle-plash for some distance, before gathering sufficient impetus to project their ungainly bodies into flight, although they *are* capable of launching into direct flight.

There was, too, an afternoon when I watched five cormorants circling higher and higher from the flats, until some greater black-backed gulls accompanying them were no longer visible without the binoculars—which would be at about five thousand feet—at which altitude the cormorants headed seawards in file. At first sight this seems an odd thing for cormorants to do, but all manner of birds orientate thus before moving off to feeding grounds or on migration.

To these flats at low water in the late afternoon—as to other flats all about the British Isles—began to stream in endlessly from the northwest the black-headed gulls. It is a familiar phenomenon, like the sunset gathering of starlings, yet ever wonderful. They congregated in their tens of thousands on the mud beneath the windmill. For as long as four hours, depending upon the flow of the tide over the flats, they stood about aimlessly or bathed in shallow pools, maintaining the while as unceasing clangor, comparable to the din of the starlings at their roost. Then of a sudden, with the water making fast, there would come an abrupt and universal silence, and I, watching the owls, would look up, wondering what change there was in the world. The gulls had moved away silently to another part of the flats still dry. . . .

The quiet evening is suddenly full of the *curee-cu-curee* of curlew coming over from the marshes, and in the twilight I know the waders only by their cries: whispered *tissee* of dunlin, mellow *phooee* of ringed plover, *peeeeder-peeeeder-peeeeder* of redshank, explosive *pip-pep* of black-tailed godwit. At this hour, when the west is layered in pink and white, orange and gray, herons sail over the sea-wall, with harsh *waak;* a tramp-steamer, showing ruby lamp, tows a K-rigged sailing-barge down the river; gunshots reverberate along the woods the other side of the flats; kestrels give up their day-long hovering, to perch on telegraph wires, dipped at by irascible owls; a little owl calls; cattle graze in the evening mists. . . .

When darkness has fallen, and the marshman is out feeding his pigs by lantern, I sit alone in his tiny kitchen, writing— alone, that is to say, but for the cheery fire gleaming on the polished brasswork, two kittens tumbling together, a cat, and two dogs curled up on their chairs. At this hour there is a great peace over the flats and the marshes, and it is the night-sounds coming to me through the open door that sealed my memory of the place: the mill sails creaking, the chugging of a boat up the river, the lowing of distant cattle, small pigs grunting and squealing, the sear *pee-it* of a late plover, and especially, in such a place, the clear, wistful *phwuee-phwuee/phwee-phwee-phwee-phwee* of curlew flighting in to their night feeding on the mud in scattered fifties and hundreds. In the exuberance of their feeding hour, they fall to the flats in the moonlight with an abandoned rocking of sickle wings.

But most characteristic and most forcefully rugged of all night-sounds is the explosive *watch* of heron, flapping heavily over from fresh-marsh to creek, rasping the night at minute intervals at the full moon. Fat herons are shot only after the full moon. When there is no moon they cannot see to spear fish or eel, and their best fishing is at night.

A bird of distinction and dignity, and, like the barn owl, to be thought of only amid his characteristic surroundings, there are few marshy places or rivers in the British Isles without their gaunt fishers. But the heron is essentially the gray spirit of quiet, remote, desolate places, and his discordant *krank*, though heard often in the day, belongs to the dark hours. How many herons fished on these fresh-marshes and mud flats I do not know, but it was not possible to go outside the mill without seeing three or four beating slowly away on great convex arches of wings, long necks hunched back into shoulders, long shanks stretched far out behind short, square tails; or one here, another there, perched long-stilted, on gate or gatepost: or peering, white-necked, over the bank of a distant dyke. Often there were as many as twenty in a single gathering—in the Hebrides, where they nest solitarily, I have seen seventy-five together on the brackened cliffs of a sea loch.

Once I walked up under cover of a fat, black Aberdeen-Angus bullock and stood nine feet away from one gobbling a field mouse; so intent was he watching it run, bent forward for the spearing, one leg "akimbo," that it was a minute or two before he sensed the presence of an alien in his customary element, despite the fact that I had come up downwind, and he was away with outstretched neck and hanging shanks.

Another time I was curious to know why a heron squatting on the side of a dyke never stirred at my approach, not even when I was but three feet from him, and saw how beautiful was the lucent, yellow iris about the black pupil of an eye that seems so glassily basilisk at a distance. Two bloody shanks, broken at the knees, and a lacerated wing was the answer—the unclean work of a careless gunner.

The heron fishes only in quiet places: a grave, slow-moving bird—until a fish swims into the ken of that keen eye, when, with lightning thrust of spearing bill, the sinuous yellow neck uncoils . . . a little excited lifting of the great wings . . . and a slapping fish is writhing between the sharp mandibles mashing up the small bones . . . tilting back his snaky head, he swallows it with sudden gulp. If it be a large fish, he stalks thoughtfully from the water and beats it two or three times upon the bank before swallowing. Then, very carefully, he cleans his dagger beak on the grass before striding down to the water to drink.

Gray (or common) heron

Squatting in a punt on the flats, I learned the value to a heron of his long shanks, for standing breast-deep in the middle of a creek—twelve of them in one creek!—he caught fish at minute intervals. The popular conception of a heron motionless the day long in one place, spearing fish from hour to hour, is wholly false. Rather does he work fast, often stalking along the creek from one fishing place to another—ornithological literature is full of such fallacies handed down from one generation of lazy observers and hack writers to another. Superficially this particular fallacy seems plausible no doubt, for my first and last views of a heron are identical: a thin yellow head, with black plumes and black-and-silver filigree at the scrawny throat, peering over the tufted spikes of the reeds, apparently eternally watchful. But sometimes I catch him off his guard, falling to his feeding pool like a sportive curlew or a whiffling gray goose, turning almost over with an astounding rocking of wings from side to side: an impressive spectacle in so huge and broad-winged a bird, but a motion of abandon hardly in keeping with his natural dignity! No more so than that of a heron sitting down, which he does in the manner of a kangaroo, with long shanks stretched out to one side; or of those gray old gentlemen hunched up behind stone walls when gales lash the barren coast of Northumbria.

There is something intensely individual about the uncouth, explosive cries of heron in the night silence of southern estuaries and saltings, northern sea lochs and lagoons. He warns me at midnight of the otter bringing his kill to the shallows where generations of otters have eaten, or that the poacher is abroad with his salmon nets. Watchful and ever suspicious of danger, he is the true spirit of marsh and mud flat. Moon, tide, sunrise, and sunset: these are the gods of the birds of the saltings. At the full moon, when the tide begins to flow, at the first light, and at the darkening, I see and hear things that others perhaps do not see. That is, if I have a mind to be patient with an elusive beauty, for here are not the warm, intimate, vivacious creatures of hedgerow and woodland; birds of the saltings owe nothing to Man: they distrust his presence, retaining their unapproachable freedom. To know them I must become an accustomed part of their environment: a marshman or a fisherman, an unobtrusive entity of sea boots and guernsey and tattered oilskin; moving about my business quietly and secretively at dawn and at moonrise, when the tide is making over the endless flats and the waders are mad with the spell of the moon and the racing waters. It is then . . . when curlews are "bubbling" and oyster-catchers piping . . . if I am a shapeless bundle in an old flatbottom or just another clump of *sueda*, that I learn the spirit of the saltings. It charms me back year after year, although on a hundred previous occasions I have endured a hell (to me) of physical discomfort of aching cold and cramping wet, of loneliness, and of a desperate weariness of mind and body. The same elusive charm that takes me from soft living to tramping the mountains as a shepherd at all hours of the day and night, in all weathers; that draws me from my warm bed at dawn, when my vitality is depressed to its lowest ebb, out into the bitter cold and drenching of a North Sea fishing; that keeps me out all night huddled in a trench of ooze and half-frozen water, waiting, interminably waiting, for the gray geese to gaggle out from the potato fields, where they have been guzzling in the moonlight, to the island sand banks where they rest during the day.

This is one aspect of that hackneyed expression, "the charm of birds." Perhaps because of its physical discomfort, the charm of the saltings goes deeper than the gay beauty of a goldfinch or the fluted notes of a blackbird.

When I am thinking life grim and colorless, I find it salutary to remember that the key to a wealth of color and rich experience is in my own pocket.

II

FLIGHTING AT MOONRISE

Layman, gunner, artist, and naturalist alike find ducks among the most fascinating of birds. Poets write clever poems about them, capturing for me the piquant charm of their pathetically comical spirits. The layman delights to feed them and is amused by their quaint antics. Few pass by the lakes in the London parks without a smile at one, up-ended, busily exploring a watery underworld in search of succulent snail or submerged weed, maintaining his inverted posture the while with smoothly paddling webs.

There are two classic prose descriptions of ducks, wild and domestic: the late Lord Grey's beautiful account of a pintail, Elizabeth by name, who, bred of a wild mother at Falloden in 1921, nested there in four successive seasons. Although migrating at varying dates every year, she returned each time, after weeks or months, to feed from his hand. And in *Lorna Doone* there is a charming passage concerning the disaster that overtook an old white drake, father of the farmyard, in a time of flood; and how he was rescued from his dangerous and ignominious position between the bars of a swing-hurdle across the stream in full spate by wayward Tom Faggus on his gentle mare Winnie, and restored to his anxiously quacking wives, none the worse for his adventure by reason of the warming potency of a peppercorn! More recently, Peter Scott and Lord Kennet have introduced us to Florence, a wild duck who nested in Kensington.

Those landlocked or city-bound can enjoy endless hours studying the wildfowl of the city parks and acquainting themselves with the habits and forms of those rarer duck they may be fortunate enough to encounter in some future excursion into wilder country. More often than not, when in London, I turn into St. James's Park, where are a multitude of curious wildfowl. Almost every British duck is there, some pinioned, most free to come and go, and some that I may not meet wild in this country once in a lifetime.

The cantankerous little tufted duck, persecuted by greedy black-headed gulls, cuts through the water at his best speed, silver belly lifted far out in his hurry, long black crest all askew, an expression of intense anxiety in his round yellow eye. Finally, with tiny spring, he vanishes beneath the surface with scarce a ripple. Under water he propels himself along with both webbed paddles rowing together, almost at right angles to his body, his head much lower than his tail. He emerges with a resilient bob, like a rubber duck in a bath, to the surprise and annoyance of waterfowl in the vicinity, so that he is soon fleeing to more peaceful waters again.

Who can suppress a chuckle at the engaging confidence of a mallard who, waddling up on bright pink webs, bluff tail awag, gazes knowingly up with head on one side? I shall find it a sad world if I cannot appreciate the humorous side of its many tragedies, great and small. Birds and beasts are often a source of mirth. One winter's day the lake was frozen in St. James's, but a small sheet of water had been kept clear of ice and was crowded with a varied assortment of waterfowl. An old mallard came flying into the lake to alight, in the usual manner, on his webs, placed forward to take the strain, and the undercoverts of his tail. Expecting to land on the water, he received the shock of his life when his outstretched webs met, instead, the firm, slippery surface of the ice and he found himself skidding along on his tail! I should like to have believed that he wore an expression of sadly injured dignity as he slid smoothly, with impromptu skill, the twenty or thirty yards to the pool of water, powerless to arrest the even tenor of his way. Possibly he enjoyed the new sensation; possibly his discomfiture was not unmixed with satisfaction at the considerable stir he caused among his fellow ducks.

But though, like the red-headed pochard who winter on the Round Pond, Kensington, many of these park ducks are genuinely wild birds nesting on the continent of Europe, their slavish allegiance to the crumbs of nursemaids and ham sandwiches of city lunchers outrages my natural sensibilities. Surely these ornamental duck have not the wild flight of those clear-cut against the orange dawn of the flat lands! Nor the free motion of a mallard checking in full flight, swooping grandly upwards, with convex wings pushed forward and half closed! Nor of a spring of teal streaking downwind at one hundred miles an hour, corkscrewing from five hundred feet in a "falling leaf," with a wild abandon that stirs my blood; or a thousand, sharply turning and stooping as one, silk-tearing the air with musically cutting wings; butterfly-dusted emerald wing-slots exquisitely a-sheen, glancing in the sun! Can that placidly purring widgeon be the cousin of a golden-crested drake motionless at the margin of the reeds when the crimson of the sunset fades on the still waters of some marsh-broad? And that pintail: did I see him with his duck a few evenings ago, upright and watchful, breast and striped neck so white on the pink-stained mere?

Seeing a mallard among the ornamental waterfowl in some city park, I am prone to exclaim sadly that, for once, Nature has created the inartistic. Against such a background his gamboge bill, scintillating bottle-green head, and bright salmon-pink legs are gaudy and flamboyant as he waddles, ungainly, up the grassy bank. The canvas is not big enough for such bold painting. But to see him with his brown duck on some cold, gray pool lost in the brown and dull green sweep of a salting, when a misty ray of morning sunshine from the gilded edge of a rain-cloud dusts with gold his sparkling velvet head . . . that is beauty!

And so, too, the brilliant green head and bright orange-red legs of a shoveler are surely artistically incompatible with dazzling white breast, chestnut flanks, and misty-blue wings. His huge, spatulate bill draws attention to his gaudiness, riotously gorgeous enough to leave me a little breathless at each new ornamental encounter: he is impossible! But off the stern coast of Northumberland there is a tiny island, shelterless from the fiercest gale and often shrouded in cold, damnable mists; a drake shoveler wheels around the gray lough once and twice, brakes with webs wide-splayed and drops almost vertically, hovering above the water, bringing sudden warmth and color into a cheerless day.

The true wildfowler finds unequaled sport in the long vigil or grueling stalk, and in the swift flight and canny ways of duck and geese. No other birds test so surely his endurance and skill. Compared to the bloody massacre of a big pheasant shoot, with its perennial attendant evils, wildfowling is almost an art. I regret the loss of beautiful life: I admit that the true wildfowler, the old sort, the countryman, goes out for the love of the thing, for the thrill of the thing; he can no more resist the call of the flighting than I can the call of the hills, of the sea, of any wild place. If he is of the true breed, a night without a shot means little to him; he is content to watch and wait and see things that the modern slaughterer has not the understanding to see, because he is not a countryman, knows nothing about the country, cares less, and is intent only on securing a record bag by fair means or foul— mostly foul. For such men your old-fashioned wildfowler has the utmost contempt and reserves his strongest language . . .

men who shoot barnacle geese with modified machine-guns, or widgeon with adapted repeating-rifles!

Let me write of pleasanter things. Widgeon, teal, and mallard must always be the wildfowler's first love, from the very nature of their habitat; shoveler and swift pintail often cut into the salt-marsh, but these three are the true flighting duck: spirits of the saltings. Mallard (wild duck) we call "gray duck" on the Solway; and widgeon, "loughs," from their habit of frequenting loughs in the hills, just as on the Northumbrian coast they are "hews," because of their musically whistling calls. The mallard may be *the* English nesting duck and the widgeon only a Scottish nester, but it is the latter which is the wild duck of the gunner.

From Scandinavia and the Baltic and from the Arctic tundras comes in August the advance guard of the hundreds of thousands of Continental nesting-duck who winter in the British Isles. Young birds these first arrivals, for it is likely to be October and November before the main army crosses the North Sea. The harder the winter on the Baltic, the greater the numbers of duck and geese seeking shelter in these islands. I can bring forward tolerably intelligent theories to explain some of the mysteries of migration, but the behavior of these wintering geese and duck seems to provide an insoluble problem. For, on rare occasions, when a hard bout of weather on the Continent freezes the waterways, driving the wildfowl westwards to these islands, a thaw may set in and open them again, whereupon these obvious auxiliary armies of wildfowl vanish from their haunts in this country, to reappear on the Continent. How am I to explain this phenomenon? Can it be that they are conscious of the warmer currents of air hundreds of miles away? Can they smell open water at that great distance? It almost seems as if they can ("X-rays of odour," Fabre), for, locally, I know that when a spring tide covers a marsh thousands of duck appear at the flighting that night, where none have come on previous nights; and at high water duck and curlew flight down from the hills to the es-

European widgeon

tuary, although they cannot possibly have *seen* the bore coming.

In late autumn and early winter widgeon and mallard stream up northwest from the North Sea for weeks on end. Some days I watch them coming up in little close-flying bundles of twenty and fifty every ten or fifteen minutes; on other days a flight of a thousand flies in irregular chevrons strung out over the sky: the spearhead of the van ever shifting, as one duck after another falls back into the lee of a companion who breaks the wind resistance; circling wide, the thousand drop down to rest on the mud flats, only to rise again, onward, north and west, at the roar of a punt-gun. The punters, hurrying down from half-finished crab pots, have pushed off from the shore, up the shallow winding creeks, when rumor reaches them that the duck are down on the mud. If the ducks stay, the boxes sunk in the mud far out on the slakes have each its occupant that night—the shoulder-gunners awaiting their chance at moonrise, when the hungry immigrants flight down to the green *Zostera* freed by a falling tide.

Once they are settled in their winter quarters, the duck adopt a more or less regular routine of life. During the hours of daylight they pack on the wide waters of the estuary, or a mile out to sea, or on a secluded lough on the hills, where they can sleep and preen safe from the man with the gun. When the light begins to fail they flight into the marsh or flat where they feed during the night: white-bellied widgeon grazing like gray geese, heavy mallards and little teal guzzling at the grass roots in the slushy marges of the pools. At first light in the morning they flight out to sanctuary again, over the shoulder-gunners hidden beneath the brow-edge of the marsh, to the estuary where the punt-gunner awaits them in the lee of a sand bank.

On the Northwest Coast I know a desolate salt-marsh of two thousand acres jutting out onto the broad mud flats and sand banks of a great estuary. It is the Valhalla of all flighting duck. Periodically covered by the tides, it is also one of the richest grazing grounds in the country, where a thousand cattle fatten in the summer and fifteen hundred little Herdwick sheep from the Cumberland hills in the winter—strange, furry, brown or cream primitives, said locally to be of Spanish origin from the Armada, and ancestors of all modern breeds of English sheep. Nor cattle nor sheep, nor gray geese nor duck, can check the luxuriant growth of grass strengthened by the salt deposits of the tide. In years gone by, seventy cartloads of mushrooms have been taken off it in a season; and thousands of plovers' eggs, skillfully interlarded with well-inked redshanks' and gulls' eggs—equally acceptable to the gourmand—were marketed in London at three pence an egg. Now only herds and rare wildfowlers visit its creek-cut wastes. Some years ago they built a viaduct across the estuary, and many of the duck coming up to the marshes from the sea lifted at it and returned whence they had come, but now that it has been destroyed the numbers of duck seeking sanctuary on the marsh are prodigious.

In the late autumn the flats about the marsh are a staggering sight in the evenings. As far as my binoculars can carry, and farther, every square yard of mud and sand bank and creek and pool is black with birds: aswarm with gulls and lapwings and curlew, mainly, but also oyster-catchers, crows, geese, and duck. The babel is fabulous, the wealth of life not credible. And then, as autumn draws on into winter, there begins in the early afternoon the familiar gathering to communal roost of the gulls. For more than three hours I watch them stream endlessly down the river from the plowlands: black-headed, common, herring, and greater black-backed; there are unbelievably more gulls wintering on these flats than anywhere else I know. In hard winter, when the snow is falling, they forego their customary pleasure of playing over the winding river on the way out to the estuary, and cut straight across the marsh. In the course of their passage over it they halt at the flushes (as do starlings and lapwings) . . . whitening the green plains under . . . whitening the marshes like flowers in hundred-yard blocks and slashes: to take flight ever and again, careening onwards in masses of twirling ghost-birds scurried by the blizzard, silent as the snowflakes.

Although the duck-flighting tends to be at its best for the gunner on windy evenings of rain, most beautiful are those rare, calm evenings of unspoilt sunset, when a sharp frost comes down at the darkening and the tide comes up with the moon. On the short days of winter I must go down to the marsh early in the afternoon if I am to choose a good site for the night's flighting. There are so many factors governing the movements of duck. Their natural flighting time to their feeding pools is at the darkening, but if there is a good moon they prefer to flight on with its rising. If the tide is late at the full moon the bulk of them will come up the estuary when it flows, at ten o'clock or midnight; on the other hand, if it has been a very high tide (which comes at the time of the full moon at this season), they wait until some of the water has run off the marsh, baring the slushy margins to the pools. If a marsh is over-shot or dry of flushes they do not come at all, so long as there is any feeding to be had elsewhere. If there is snow on the hills, with the loughs frozen, and a dry, neglected marsh has recently been covered by the tide, the flighting begins in the early afternoon, and some duck stay on the marsh all day. There are always units of gray duck and teal and widgeon in the creeks and pools by day throughout the winter. And when the marsh is entirely flooded by tempest-blown spring tides, and quite unapproachable, widgeon in thousands and teal and mallard in hundreds bob about on the waves just out of gunshot of the sea-wall.

Those afternoons and evenings and nights waiting for the duck to flight have given me hours of peace not paralleled by any other experience of natural life. Squatting with my dog in a creek, smoking, my sense of contentment is complete. The loneliness on the marshes is absolute. As far as I can see are acres and acres of creek-cut marshes, dotted with Herdwick yearlings and occasional brown hares, and the tide-wet sands stretching away to eternity. The sun is setting a fiery golden behind a bank of cloud over the hidden sea in the west. Gulls, pale kings of the sunset, are forever drifting idly over the flats, and from far out on the sands come laughing cries of herring gulls and deeper barkings of great black-backs; a cormorant swishes low over the marsh, soaring away from me in a desperate hurry; and all part of the blessed peace are the plaintive cries of startled redshank, the strong, hoarse croaks of gray crows, and the lovely quavering calls of a pack of curlew. A right and a left rumble around the mountains and die in the sunset, but the curlew still live. Two loughs circle blackly, sharply etched against the exquisitely ethereal blue of this northern evening sky, and a tiny dunlin, flighting like his betters, rustles past with sibilant call—for duck and geese are not the only birds that flight to the marsh. Golden plover and dunlin, absent during the day, whisper over it at night, the latter flashing whitely when their bellies turn in the fading light, vanishing at another turn of their backs. For a while they skim low over the flushes, banking like courting ringed plover, as if hawking insects. They settle at length on the water, apparently swimming, though actually they are standing on submerged shanks; for, after minutes of immobility, they begin to run through the water, feeding.

Then, too, from two o'clock in the afternoon onwards little bundles of curlew flight in from every quarter of the surrounding hills and fields, with strange, inward chatterings; their hurrying, sharp-winged flight shooting them past the gulls idly drifting down the course of the river. They move up into the marsh creeks with the tide, but only at moonlight do I find them actually on top of the marsh, dibbling in the oozy margins of the flushes with huge sickle bills. . . .

Lying half in and half out of a water-hole—a very cold and cramping business—looking onto the rippling, tarnished waters of the northern river, I can make out a great, black bunch of a thousand curlew, and, feeding with them at the edge of the river, some fifteen hundred lough ducks. Time and again they rise instantaneously, with a thunderous clap of wings, to settle on the water with a roar of surf. Further out in the tide gray duck quack heartily. A little before the darkening, at their last settling on the water, the loughs begin bathing and courting, with a mighty din of plashing and whistling . . . to grow suddenly quiet with the deepening dusk.

When it is neither night nor day the flighting begins with a bundle of gray duck coming in high from the estuary. A little later the loughs flight from the river in small bundles, but only about ten bundles go into the flushes on the marsh; the bulk of the fifteen hundred gradually accumulate well in on the sandy marsh across the creek a few yards from me, and I can hear the silken rustling of their grazing bills. By nightfall, when a new moon has Venus in her arms, a sparkling golden cross, there are hundreds of loughs there, who rise as I do, with much purring of alarm by the ducks. After a high tide there is too much water on the marsh for good lough feeding. Is it coincidence that they flight onto this dry, sandy marsh at the water's edge first, or are they instinctively aware of the unsuitable nature of the inner marsh, onto which they tend to move as the water drains off?

Every wildfowler remembers one flighting that far excelled all others, and though I have been seeking beauty and not sport, I also have that memory of a December afternoon when, for a mile down the sandy marsh bordering the northern river, lough ducks were feeding solid, fifteen abreast. While I lay and watched them, amazed, I totted up what I thought they might number, and by no means could make it less than twenty thousand, the which was mildly astonishing. . . . I moved away to get myself into position for the flighting, thoughtfully. It was a calm afternoon; the moon was nearly at the full, and the tide would be coming with it; the marsh was thick with droppings from the night before; there were exactly the right number of flushes suitably slushy round about; and there was that great mass of duck at the edge of the marsh: obviously hungry immigrants just arrived. . . .

I duly installed myself in a creek by two adjacent flushes, with a wispy, white moon in the southern sky and a pink sunset at my back, and puffed peacefully at my pipe in the great silence. It is only on dark nights, when there is no moon, that the loneliness of the marsh sometimes plays on my imagination, my stomach being empty, especially on those moonless nights when I am continually being forced away from my correct line off the marsh by the necessity of going back and around flooded creeks impossible to jump in the darkness— an interminable and exasperating process. If perchance there

is a little fog about, I remember how, in the old days when
the herdsmen watched their flocks on horseback, a three-day
northeasterly gale piled up huge seas outside the bar far
down the estuary, and they woke in their little hut at the far
end of the marsh in the early hours of the morning to a distant, thunderous hiss. . . . The bore was coming—two hours
before its time. Racing for their horses, they strove desperately to get their scattered flocks on the move, but in a few
minutes the sheep had been abandoned, and the men were
galloping for their lives. They got off the marsh with the tide
swirling above their horses' girths, but eleven hundred sheep
were drowned that night. Only once or twice in a century
does the unexpected happen, but it is well to know your
marshes.[1] . . .

As the light fades I strain every nerve, involuntarily, to
catch that well-remembered, silk-tearing cutting of sharp
wings; continually thinking to hear the sudden, heavy swishing of a bundle stooping to its pool, I peer into the twilight
for the little flights whose speed is too swift for my eye to pick
up, my heart thudding painfully at its suspended breathing.
So finely alert, there comes to me suddenly, from very far
away, a rhythmic clangor: almost it might be the baying of
geese. It seems to come momentarily nearer and as quickly
fades away again, but after that first confusing with geese, I
know what is coming to me out of the twilight, and stiffen ex-
pectantly. And then, when apparently the music is dying
away instead of crescending, they suddenly appear out of the
dimness . . . *hompa-hompa-hompa*—only a thousand times
more musical . . . up to me and past me on a level with my
eyes, forging onwards with magnificent straightness of eager,
out-stretched necks and heavy bodies, rhythmical wings beating one against the other: a glorious, strident, contrapuntal

[1] Curiously enough, there was an exact repetition of this phenomenon
in November 1938, when again eleven hundred sheep were drowned;
while at Christmas 1942 an even bigger bore swept up the firth and
flooded three thousand acres on the Scottish side.

music firing my blood . . . and then they are gone and their music with them, caught for a flash by the last light when they swoop whitely up at harrying gulls. No other sound of Nature holds for me the emotional appeal of this forceful, primitive wing-music of wild swans.

At half-past four o'clock, when there is still light, and the colorless moon stands out from the sky as a stereoscopic globe, two teal come in, traveling faster, it seems, than I have ever seen duck travel before: one hurtling into me like a shell, to vanish in upward swoop; the other swishing rocket-like past my head, to plow up the right-hand flush, making no check in his terrific stoop down and through its smooth waters, swimming away to the edge to guzzle in the slushy grass.

A quarter of an hour later, when it is moonlight, though still red and orange in the west, the flighting begins in astounding reality, and for seventy-five minutes the night is hardly quiet for two minutes at a time of the musically-beating wings and melodious calls of rocketing, dimly-seen forms whirling across the moon.

They come, not only in ones and twos and sevens and dozens, but in scores, all with that same devastating momentum of speed: teal as rockets, widgeon whistling round and round the flushes, gray duck heavily swishing. Even with that splendid, lambent moon it is hard to pick them up against the black heavens, but all about me is this weird hush of purposeful wings. In quieter minutes I hear soft calls and musical wings from the outer darkness, but I never really see them coming. The most vouchsafed me is a sudden cutting of sharp silhouette across the moon, and then perhaps a dim, hardly-seen form tense and motionless upon the water, or a sudden circling of black figures athwart the pale west.

This hour of the darkening and moonrise is the ducks' hour of life as surely as dawn belongs to songbirds. I sense it in the terrific speed of their coming out of the north: not as a mass flight, but concentrated in these little bundles traveling

with bullet directness to their objective; I hear it superbly in
the trilled, dynamic *wr-r-r-r-ee-oo* from the blue bills of the
Titian-headed widgeon wheeling around the pool with their
mates: a mad ecstatic minute!

These minutes of passion are all in the lightning flight:
once they have landed, the cries of the drakes are soft, in answer to the laughing *chockaw-r-r* of the ducks. It is then that
I hear the loveliest musical note, instrumental or natural, that
god Pan ever created. While the loughs have flighted in their
thousands, little teal at the edges of the flushes have whispered their customary medley of uncouth harshnesses and
bleating whistles. Now, with the flighting nearly at an end,
there comes from a drake teal in the right-hand pool the most
wonderful fluted piping with a fluted grace-note, to be an-
swered by a drake on the other pool. The double piping is so
musical, so tonally pure, so mellowly open, that I seem to
hear the plangent note on either side of the reed.

By six o'clock this rare flighting has ended. Clambering
stiffly out of my hole, wet and frozen, I trudge home across
the bright marshes, crisply white with sudden frost, kicking
golden phosphorescent sparks out of the tide-flooded pools. Is
there anything more beautiful than moonlight on calm water
or on the *sastrugi* of tide-wet sands?

III

DEATH OF A GRAYLAG

I often go out with wildfowlers. I like their company—if they
be countrymen; their wildfowling lore is full of interest for
me; and sometimes my inherent love of sport whispers that I
will have a more obvious goal in life to aim at by shooting
birds than merely by watching them. But, as yet, the shooting
has always spoiled a perfect experience; not yet have I shot
any wild bird. Stray hours with wildfowlers do, however, give
me "atmosphere." Out of many such, there is one day of
which I have an especially vivid memory.

We went down-river at six o'clock of a mid-winter morning, when green and golden plover were flighting from their
shingle banks with sear *peeit* and thin *phee:* five thousand
dipping as one over the water. Little bundles of goldeneye
duck came lifting over our heads, the wings of the splendid
white drakes whistling musically; and a *tew-tew*king greenshank went away noisily.

By eight o'clock it was growing light, with a crimson dawn
presaging frost at night. A charm of goldfinches colored the
edge of the marsh in black and gold and scarlet, but the

marsh itself seemed bare of geese or duck. A kingfisher shot bluely up a creek, to perch on its bank: a most ungodlike place for halcyon fisher!

Cormorant

Drawing blank two miles out of the far end, we walked up along the brow-edge of the northern river, but saw nothing but one hundred pinkfeet coming in west from the hills, and a drake goosander, magnificently hooded in dark green, splashing and diving in a foot-deep flush. Later, another two hundred pinkfeet settled on a sand bank in the river. For an hour we sat in a creek, waiting for the tide to push them off; but, when it did, they moved away (with typical goose contrariness) to a dry bank farther out, with a musical baying and a mighty roaring of wings, like the rumbling of a train over the distant viaduct.

Disgusted, we plodded back to the far end again, noting only little flocks of linnets and an occasional lark, and had lunch beneath the brow-edge. It was as warm as a humid day in May, and I discarded two sweaters. Right along an almost high-tide-line for half a mile stretched a single rank of some two thousand curlew. The roar of their wings, when tier after tier rose into sudden flight, was hardly less resonant than that of the two hundred pinkfeet, and their concerted babel of staccato, musical chatter was not unlike the hound-baying of distant geese. Beyond the curlew was a little pack of fifty oyster-catchers and a score of cormorant statuesque on the sands, among them white-bellied birds of the year; with them were odd great gulls, whose deep cries we heard all day long. Afloat were loughs and gray duck.

After lunch we went away to the northern river again, on whose banks and waters were some two thousand loughs—the edge black with them—a sprinkling of gray duck, and another pack of a thousand curlew. Walking a mile out onto the sands we put up the pinkfeet, who alighted on the marsh on a flat, creekless plateau, impossible to approach . . . put them up again, equally unluckily . . . a third time, and they gaggled right away back to their old place on the sands. At this point, it being two o'clock, we lay back against a flood-jettisoned tree-trunk in the middle of the marsh, snoring pleasantly in a hot sun.

An hour later I sat up and had a look around with the binoculars. There might, or there might not, be a little gaggle of geese on the marsh a mile away—for gray geese are remarkably difficult to pick up at any distance in certain lights. Sheep dotted about: high-tide drift; hummocks of turf broken off creek banks and deposited upon their brow-edges; thistles, indistinguishable from the forest of poppynecks, and heads of geese over a mirage of atmospheric waves: all these things they resemble very closely; grazing, their bent necks plucking at the grass, they are shapeless lumps, for their colossal wings cover them like beetles' shards; on the *qui vive*, upstretched thin necks are lost in a gray background.

Making a long detour right across the marsh, we crawled up over the tide-wet sands, beneath the crumbling, turfy brow-edge, to a creek which we believed would take us in to them—if they were geese. Eventually, gliding up my head with infinite caution over the brow-edge, with a sinking doubt at the pit of my stomach, I espied them in the gloom some three hundred yards distant, against the twinkling lights of ——, four miles across the marshes: thirteen grazing with rounded backs and snaky necks.

For an interminable hour we waded and squelched through the water and oozy mud at the bottom of the twisting creek, cautiously popping up our heads from time to time, to see the geese feeding steadily away from us, as is their way when they are a little suspicious, but uncertain of any real danger. When we were within forty yards of them I lay down beneath the brow-edge with the Labrador, leaving my companion to stalk on round a bend in the creek. For half an hour I watched them feeding steadily away. . . .

Graylag goose

It was almost quite dark when my companion eventually got in his shot: dropping five—an exceptional shot, only possible under some such conditions as these—one of which the Labrador retrieved when it dived in a flush. They proved to be graylags: four of them young birds and one an old gander splendidly barred and mottled on breast and belly with black and brown and gray. I held them up by their fine necks, and my emotions were perhaps those of others before me. There was no fear in their brown eyes, nor were they expressionless like those of gulls; they were soft, beautiful, and absolutely calm. I find it repugnant to suggest that there was any human reproach in their depths. If I sought an anthropomorphic parallel, it would be that of perfect resignation to their fate. I have seen domestic geese with glassy, basilisk eyes; it was the soft tranquillity of these wild eyes that stirred me deeply. Here were five splendid birds, grand birds, beautiful, full of a great vitality of life: one paddling in the air pathetically with his webbed legs and retching with his yellow beak, the other "reacting" with feebly threshing wings; when at length they lay still, their brown eyes remained open. . . . And there remained for me, always, a profound impression of waste, unnecessary waste, of beautiful life.

We went home across the marshes with our heavy loads, flushing little bundles of musically whistling widgeon from the pools. The night was very lovely: a golden moon shimmering in the clear, dark depths of every creek: a momentarily-seen golden fire. Later, Mars was strong enough to throw his baleful glow across the river. . . . But these things are sometimes too lovely.

IV

GRAY GEESE OVER ENGLAND

During the late summer and early autumn a strange phenomenon occurs on the illimitable Siberian tundras. It is reputably affirmed that before attaining to their full powers of flight, the young gray geese of the year forsake their nests and the old birds, and *walk* in the direction of their ancestral wintering grounds thousands of miles to south and west. The peasants, awaiting their perennial coming, net them, and salt them down for the cold, dark months of a long winter. Pulled by some inexplicable instinct, which I conceive to be part hereditary memory, part magnetic attraction perhaps, the survivors, and later the older birds, arrive every autumn in western Europe. I believe that on an average less than sixty thousand of these—pinkfoot, bean, and white-fronted geese —winter in the British Isles. The pinkfeet come only from Iceland and Spitzbergen.

Hundreds of miles of green sea-walls hold back the hungry sea from her rightful heritage. Behind these walls are leagues of brown potato fields, where the pinkfooted geese and the heavy mallard love to guzzle on the mushy potatoes left from the lifting. But still there are acres and acres of saltings, over whose splendid creek-cut grazing the sheep browse in the winter and fat cattle in the summer, where no men go but herdsmen and stockmen and occasional wildfowlers. And yet more acres and acres of bare mud flats, where tens of thousands of golden-crested widgeon and thousands of little black brent geese feed upon the green *Zostera* grass waving in an ebbing tide. Out here on the mud banks the geese love to rest, a mile away from Man, their only enemy. This world belongs to them and to the wildfowler gliding silently down with the tide in his long gray punt, or lying out in his coffin-box hide sunk in the mud. No other men but fishers venture onto these wastes, where the mud is soft and the channels of the sea constantly shifting.

Out there it is the moon and the tides and the winds that count. More often than not it is dreary to the spirit and intolerably numbing to the body; but I forget the physical hardships in retrospect, and remember only the shimmering mud I have seen stained with the crimson of frosty dawn or the orange of stormy sunset, and the exquisite beauty of a broad swathe of silver moonshine over wave-rippled sands where giant curlew "bubble": these memories all the dearer for the rough edge of bitter nights and freezing waters.

The coming of the wild geese and duck over the North Sea is for me the supreme moment of the Nature Year . . . sometimes thousands of feet up, at others only a hundred or two: now a thin black line, now a little black cloud athwart a red sunset over the black whale-bone ridges of the Cheviots. The little black brent come up in slow, easy flight, long wings decurved, with high metallic cries. White-cheeked barnacle geese, their cousins, come in on the same line of flight. Year in and year out it is always the same, for both duck and geese, from southeast to northwest. They alight on the mud banks, with a holding back of dusky body against curving black wings: to watch awhile in characteristically upright at-

titude, and then to walk fast and easily down to the creek for
the blessed drink and bathe.

Barnacle goose

Finest are the gray geese, nearly all pinkfeet, beating up
slow and heavy against the gale, their formation changing
from second to second, from line to chevron, and from chevron to double chevron, and back into wavering line again.
They pass low over the brown cliffs, with the clamorous clangor of young hounds in full cry: a musical and lovely diapa-
son that rises and falls, and is lost to me and heard again at
the fitful whim of the gale. Their pink bills and legs and
snowy tails are wonderfully bright in the fickle sun, their
heads, by some trick of lighting, deep blue, and the plumage
of some so dark as to seem a steely gray-black. They do not
drop down to the wide mud flats, but carry on steadily northwest, shortly to bear southwest to their West Coast sanctuary.
Down there, by the great flats margining a salt-marsh, a
wildfowler sits in his lonely cottage, cleaning his gun by the
yellow light of a guttering lamp, after the evening's duck

flighting. A Labrador, stretched out on the rush mat before the range, raises his head, suddenly alert, whines and wags his tail. The fowler considers him speculatively, and then, his eyes turning to the much-thumbed calendar on the wall, lays his gun on the table and lounges over to the door.

The moon is on the wane. Curlew shriek in the oozy creeks, a gray duck quacks harshly, and there is the explosive *watch* of an old heron disturbed at his night's fishing; but all these sounds he has heard a thousand times before, and he turns to go in. The dog at his side growls throatily and wags his tail again, so that the man stands poised in his stride, listening intently, inwardly cursing the noisy waders, aware of the thudding of his heart. At length he looks up at the skies beneath shading hands. From somewhere high up in the heavens there drops faintly to his ears a high-pitched *gug-gug*, and then another and another: *gug/gug-gug-gug/gug-gug-gug*. Across the face of the moon is etched a dark irregular skein of arrowheads. . . . The gray geese have come back to their winter feeding grounds, punctual to the very night: September 22.

All night the geese are passing high over the village, their metallic *gug-gugs* remote in the lonely heavens. . . . The next morning there are eight hundred out on the sands. Night and day, for three days, they gaggle in from the northeast, down the line of the Cheviot Hills, their eager, staccato cries sounding clearly long before I can pick them up with the eye: *gug-gug/gug-gug-gug,* and then the high-pitched calls of the geese: *queek/queek-queek/quick-quick-quick-quick,* followed by the deep *quank-quank/gug* of the ganders . . . strong, virile, musical calls that set my blood racing madly at their first hearing each succeeding autumn, as no other sound can but the wing-music and honking of wild swans.

At all hours of the twenty-four the geese are dropping into the marsh in their fives and tens, twenties and hundreds and even two hundreds: increasing by a thousand a day for the first three days, and then more gradually for another three or four weeks, up to seven or ten thousand. Lying out on the marsh, awaiting their homing, I seldom see them coming from any great distance: first warning of their return is a faint *gug/gug-gug* sounding very clearly yet elusively out of the silent heavens, and after a minute or two I pick up the skein against the blue sky, or it eludes me until right overhead.

Nearly all end their long flight by gliding, with never a beat of broad wings, from a mile or so distant of the marsh, at a thousand feet or more, in no regular formation: in continually shifting V, in line, in single file, individuals *gug-gug*ing repeatedly. A very fine sight it is to see the unhurried, even tenor of their long, wing-silent, downward glide. Some rocket down with a leaflike falling: a fantastic motion that has not the mad abandon of the ecstatic twirling, stooping to their feeding grounds at dawn. They are tired, thirsty, and hungry. The glide is unbroken until the newcomers sail into their fellows on convex pinions, like giant mallard, legs wide apart pushed forward in the braking: to hover finally, with quick-fanning wings, before alighting buoyantly.

For a few weeks the ten thousand stay about the marsh, and then gradually drift away to other feeding grounds down the estuary, until only a thousand odd are left to winter with me, although if the feeding prove extra good, three or four thousand stay. In the spring they gather here once again, before their return passage north. But it must not be thought that they pack on this marsh to migrate *en masse*. On the contrary, whereas in the winter they like to feed in gaggles hundreds and sometimes thousands strong, in the spring ten thousand pinkfeet scatter from end to end of the marsh in pairs and threes and small gaggles, gradually vanishing away to their nesting territories in April and May.

In these first days they are restless, constantly getting up in a swirling babel of din, and gaggling round the adjacent fields and hills, undecided where to feed, suspicious of all life and unfamiliar movement in these strange, new winter territories. They sound constantly the warning *ge-ge-ge-ge-ge*, and the sudden alarm: a querulous *gar-gar-gar*—sure signal to me, hiding my white face, that I have been discovered. So shy, they at this time feed in the dim light of early morning and evening, and, when not prowling the sky uneasily in noisy little gaggles, pass the day right out at low-tide-line on the wide sands, where I cannot approach them within a quarter of a mile.

Geese have comparatively poor sight, very poor in a dim light—or, rather, I am a mildly suspicious, but not actively dangerous, object until viewed at close range—and to voices and sounds they are quite indifferent, though they are quick to take warning from other birds, such as herons, who invariably manage to get themselves in between me and them; but their scenting powers are acute, and strongest defense of all, they have a still more acute telepathic awareness of any foreign, and therefore inherently dangerous, element entering their accustomed environment. I can crawl them upwind along an amply concealing creek, guided by their noisy chatter, to halt eventually beneath the brow-edge a few yards from them. For half a minute I do nothing, and then, just as I am preparing to raise my head cautiously between the two lumps of turf placed on the brow-edge a previous day, there comes suddenly that infuriating sound I get to know so well chasing geese: the stiff-quilled, swishing rattling of three thousand broad wings beating furiously, as gray wave after wave of grazing pinkfeet break suddenly away from the creek into mysteriously alarmed flight, with a mighty metallic baying, that still comes faintly to me when they pitch a mile away on the wide sands; for it is always to the safe harborage of the flats that they retreat when disturbed. And all I have seen of geese that day has been a wonderful-to-see tautening, reaching, upward *dive* of pale bellies colored by the setting sun—from nail of beak to pink legs stretched back against snowy tails double-chevroned in gray, perfectly streamlined bodies shooting up at an angle of sixty degrees, in the manner of teal rising from a pool in sudden alarm: an astounding acceleration for such large birds, impressing me with the immense power of wings able to project half a stone's weight into the air without preparatory run.

Walking athwart and in full view of the geese, they tolerate me without undue suspicion up to one hundred and fifty yards; crawling on my belly, I can approach them to forty or even thirty yards. But if I vanish suddenly into a creek, before I have crawled up the other side, they are up and away: their delicately attuned sensibility of me, as an object to which they are slowly becoming accustomed, suddenly upset by my disappearance. There is only one way to stalk them in daylight, and that is to lie out and wait for them; and come some time they surely will, for they are very faithful to their especial feeding and resting grounds.

Until they are immediately overhead I am seldom sighted; though, however well hidden, I am usually picked up then. But they have no conception of distance. Sheering up and away, with rustling pinions and urgent *gar-gar,* they will pitch within fifty yards and feed up to me again, although I lie out in the open only part hidden by some miserable tufts of grass. They will even allow me a certain liberty of wriggling movement; but if I abuse this liberty by slithering back into the concealment of a creek, they are away at once. It pays to be honest with geese.

Lying out there alone, in the middle of thousands of acres of salting and mud flat, listening to the far, metallic *gug-gug* of pinkfeet and the deeper clanging *owch-owch* of scattered graylags, I sense, momentarily, the supreme thrill of wild geese, that makes me ever ready to endure hours of hellish wind, numbed by the half-frozen water of some slimy creek, for a mere sight of them a couple of hundred yards distant. Although there may be a hundred or more graylags on the marsh, rarely do I chance upon more than a dozen in a gaggle; whereas farther down the Solway, where there are as yet no pinkfeet, four hundred of these splendid massive gray geese graze together a few yards from the road, and fifteen hundred thrive in the seclusion of a protected fresh-marsh a mile or two inland. The graylag tends to fly and feed silently, so that I can work around a gaggle all day and not be aware of their presence. That is where he scores over the pinkfoot, who bays continually on the wing and keeps up a constant chatter when feeding. The smaller pinkfoot, too, like all successful species, does things on the grand scale, and delights to feed and bathe and rest in the company of hundreds or thousands of his fellows. Yet he is ten or twenty times as numerous as the native graylag: mainly because, like the starling and black-headed gull, he is aggressive, adaptable, and gregarious; partly because he is less delicate in his feeding; and a little because he is quicker off the mark than the graylag. . . . The split second's delay of the gunner, allowing the pinkfoot to stretch into flight, may still wing the heavier, slower graylag. . . . The huge size of the pinkfoot gaggles and their restless natures make it almost impossible for me to approach them at all, which, within limits, is never a very difficult matter with graylag.

Although liking to associate in these huge gaggles, pinkfeet are very independent birds. In no gregarious species have I seen so much splitting of flocks when in flight, or of sudden departures of single geese or of small bundles from a gaggle feeding or at rest. Little units are constantly getting up for a prowl round the marsh, and when the main body takes flight it almost invariably leaves behind scattered, small gaggles; it is not at all unusual for three to five thousand pinkfeet to get up when I am a hundred yards distant, leaving behind them a gaggle of three, two old birds and a young one, who take no notice of me until I am twenty yards from them. Such familiar instances must not be confused with the phenomenon of the solitary goose. Particularly noticeable of such large birds as wild geese is the shunning of wounded birds by their fellows, even when fully recovered from their wounds and able in every way to conform to the physical requirements of their fellows. A goose, a duck, or even an oyster-catcher solitary is, in ninety-nine cases out of a hundred in the winter season, certain to be a pensioner, or merely pricked. It is as if their fellows scent the taint of the shot.

But never was there any wild bird less likely to respond to the influences of sentinel or leader commonly attributed to geese and rooks and such popularly sagacious species. Indeed, I have yet to see any species of wild bird respond intelligently to the actions of his fellows; I have seen only instinctive reactions—void of any semblance of logical deduction or intelligent premeditation—which are very much swifter in their response to external stimuli than the reasoned actions of a brain, and therefore infinitely more suitable to a wild bird's physical requirements. . . .

I have run down the crippled birds for the pleasure of examining and handling a live wild goose, but the result has always proved so aesthetically mortifying that I do so no longer. What a damnable heritage is mine that Man must always induce in a wild beast a spontaneous paralysis of fear, deriding and annulling my first pleasure at being close to it. Quickly, as if aware of being in the presence of a stronger, more implacable magnetic force than his own, the crippled pinkfoot gives up all attempt to outrun me and flattens to the ground, whether it be bare sand or concealing long grass. A most humiliating experience I find it, aware of a bird's normal and instinctive supreme confidence in his physical powers. While I stroke his head he lies motionless, long neck stretched out on the ground, lifeless but for the shifting brown eye. Picking him up, I place him in a shallow creek, along which he swims very swiftly, clambers out, and scuttles away low to the ground. When twenty yards away, he makes hastier progress, flapping his great wings, before settling down to a walk once more, until I turn and go on my way. Most marked in this low, creeping gait is the extraordinary breadth and weight of the great wings, as to make him seem top-heavy and overweighted. In body, length of wing, and leg this young goose was smaller than a greater black-backed gull, but in breadth of wing must vastly have exceeded him.

More times than I like to think I have seen this same distressing effect of the human hand and eye, or merely presence, upon wild bird or beast, inducing a physical paralysis akin to that from which a rabbit suffers when hunted by a stoat—it is a pleasant memorial to Man's relations with animals since the beginning. I have no desire to tame a wild goose—God forbid! for that would destroy his supreme attraction, his wildness—but I should be happier were I not inevitably a fearful object of suspicion. Alas, I cannot have my cake and eat it. I can have my wild goose wild, or I can have him captive, but I cannot normally enter, unheeded, into his wildness—which would be my natural Utopia.

Geese, like other animals, enjoy certain physical sensations, and one is to feel the incoming tide swirling higher and higher about their webs and legs. For such large birds, their webs are exceedingly sensitive, and they dislike feeding on stubble and potato fields when the ground is frozen and the hard, irregular crust and furrow jar their feet. It is at such seasons that they tend to be especially faithful to their marsh grazing grounds. Examining the webs of young gray geese, I am always astonished to see how pinkly translucent and uncalloused these are. The tide flowing swiftly over the sand banks provides an exquisite sensation when it coldly tickles their feet, and they stay out on the banks until actually swimming. Previous to the coming of the tide the geese have been resting. That is to say most of them have been standing on one leg with their heads tucked back in their scapulars; but there always are some geese on the move: dibbling in the mud like shelduck; flapping like farmyard cocks; preening, luxuriously spreading broad gray, white-flecked wings over bright puce legs—a delicious motion; flipping a few feet up into the air with supple pinions; and constantly uttering their sharp, staccato cries.

With the flowing of the tide, the excitement becomes intense, and punctuated, individual calls swell into a sudden colossal clangor that sweeps me up and leaves me helpless at its magnitude of sound: its babel of baying din. Gradually this dies down to an extraordinary but wholly satisfying humming, signifying their complete contentment: a remarkable sound heard only at such moments, or when, momentarily unsuspicious, all the thousands are grazing to their hearts' content—especially when they are feeding by moonlight. It is as if, there being no bees here at this season, the geese are replacing them, for, if I shut my eyes, my impression is of the droning of innumerable gigantic bumblebees. Ever and again the even hum rises into quarreling crescendo, when little swarms of geese run at each other, with necks "snaking" or outstretched poker-stiff, and hissing bills. Everywhere there is movement: swimming, bathing, dabbling, drinking, walking down to the water—erect, graceful, easy—walking up from the water, walking to and fro . . . I am conscious of being in the presence of intense social aliveness. At such moments of revelation—for not often can I watch several thousand unsuspicious geese at close range—I hear strange, intimate, unexpected sounds: a metallic, high-pitched *gee-gee*, a plaintive wader's whistle; and high-pitched, conversational noises: the *chuck-chuck* of chicks, the gobbling of turkeys, and, indeed, a whole gamut of farmyard and anserine modulations, uttered apparently with closed bills, which is no doubt responsible for the far-carrying powers of goose calls.

When the tide begins to ebb, the geese begin to fly or walk up to feed on the marsh. One lot after another at irregular intervals; it is an hour before the sands are finally bare. It is a strange sensation lying out there waiting for them to pitch in near their fellows who are already feeding fifty or sixty yards from me—for, with their intensely gregarious proclivities, I can be certain that the fifty or one hundred pinkfeet already feeding will soon be joined by hundreds or thousands of their fellows still out on the sands. As many as a thousand come in together, and it is grand to see how, coming up from a mile or more distant, they change in a minute from a dim, black

line to exciting reality. They come in downwind, and thus, to
alight with their fellows against the wind, they have to turn
at right angles to glide down, so that there is a continual
swimming up of one line behind another, stretching out in
the gradual forming-line far behind me; yet even then, intent
on pitching in, and assured by the presence of their companions beneath, they do not distinguish me. I find a new sensation in suddenly being swept up amid a swarm of fast-flow-
ing, low-flying geese, their droppings hurtling all about me,
and immediately overhead that all-enveloping sound of stiffly
swishing wings. Never, or very rarely, do incoming geese
pitch outside the ranks of their grazing companions, but manage to find space to plump down amid them, little notice
being taken either of their distant cries or of their actual ar-

Graylags in flight

rival; indeed, I do not remember seeing a goose looking up at his fellows in flight, as I have so often done other birds.

Gray geese, black barnacles, and even brent on occasions, graze; but whereas graylags neatly snip the grass short like a lawn with their long beaks, the short-billed pinkfoot plucks up the grass by the roots, pitting the marsh with deep, round holes in his guzzling for plantains, in the manner of a gray duck; so that a marsh which has been worked for a few hours by pinkfeet looks as if it had been upsnouted by a swarm of small pigs. Thus they favor, but by no means monopolize, the feeding in the slushier depressions, like teal and gray duck; whereas the graylag grazes in the orthodox manner, like a widgeon, on the drier plateaux and brow-edges of the marsh. The drier the winter, then, the fewer the pinkfeet feeding on a salt-marsh, if there are stubble or potato fields in the near vicinity.

On the Solway the pinkfeet move spasmodically backwards and forwards between saltings and exposed grass hills on the lower slopes of the Cheviots and Pennines, and, when suitable, corn and potato fields backing the marshes. The hill sites, having no cover, are quite unapproachable, and tend to be resting rather than feeding grounds, from which the birds may return at three or four o'clock in the afternoon. Thus there is no regular pinkfoot flighting to the Solway saltings, as on other coasts of the British Isles. They feed by light, and when there is no moon they are likely to feed during the day, and if there is much shooting, probably in the semi-light of dawn or dusk. There are other factors regulating their movements: tides, punt-gunners, food supply, snow on the hills, frost on the marsh. On the Wash, with its leagues of potato fields, there is commonly a morning and evening flight from feeding fields to sleeping mud flats; at Holkam there is the same shuttle-movement between preserved fresh-marsh and wide sands. On the Solway external factors are less constant: morning and evening flights are less strongly marked, often nonexistent; and little and large gaggles of geese are roving to and fro about sands and marsh at all hours of the twenty-four. It is very rarely possible to go onto these Solway saltings and see no geese—in fact I have never done so yet.

My common experience is to find them feeding steadily away from me, shuffling away in droves, without my ever getting any closer to them, however far I wriggle on my belly through the slushy, oozy, sodden grass which is likely to edge the higher plateaux over which the geese graze. But on rare occasions I have found myself lying only forty or fifty yards from a three-sided gray phalanx of perhaps five thousand pinkfeet, all unsuspicious or indifferent to my presence, for some momentarily inexplicable reason. Such occasions, together with certain miracles of duck-flighting at the full moon, I recall as among the richest experiences of one side of

my life. It is then that one realizes that these great masses of
pinkfeet hide in their ranks certain other goose personalities.

A rain-washed, gray-backed goose on gray days, the slender pinkfoot is essentially a brown goose in the winter sun,
with a misty lavender iridescence at his shoulders, for his
gray feathers are edged with copper, which gleams bronze
when the sun strikes it, the seemingly white bellies of five
young birds out of every gaggling hundred shining brightly
in the sun; while in the spring every feather of back and wing
is new-barred and scalloped in china-white.

But if the slender pinkfoot is, severally, the brown goose or
the gray goose, the heavy graylag is often the blue goose, for
on days of sun and rain there is a blueness about his great,
rounded wings when he spreads them in flight, and at his
flanks and the chevron on his snowy tail the lovely pale blue
of old English chinaware. . . .

Among the brown-necked pinkfeet nearest to me, I am suddenly aware of a single graylag, his long flesh-yellow beak
most obvious among the stubby pink and white bills of his
companions, with their black tips and bases; his long, flat,
grayish-brown head making one straight line with his beak:
contrasting strongly with the thin, conical, chocolate heads of
the pinkfeet; his pink legs much duller than those bright puce
legs of pinkfeet: so unbelievable a coloring for such large
birds! By the working of his bill he is, clearly, chattering
querulously, stimulated by his noisy fellows. He prowls backwards and forwards unceasingly, being chivied a little;
among the beautiful, graceful pinkfeet, he seems an ugly, ill-
shaped, ponderous bird—which is a gross libel, for graylags
are grand geese.

There is, too, thirty yards from him, the inevitable white
pinkfoot. Most large gagglings of pinkfeet seem to harbor a
white goose in their midst. He is not really white, but more a
very pale buff or cream (like most albino wild birds), with
the characteristic darker, browner head of a pinkfoot, and
conspicuous from his fellows at a great distance. My particu-

lar white goose, living on very good terms with his neighbors, is a gander, who has appeared in his winter territories for three or four seasons now. (Alas, news comes to hand that, inevitably, he has been shot and sold for £5—It is always so —But in the spring came three more, all in one gaggle: a gander and a goose paired up together, and a gander with a gray goose.)

When the albino and the grazing thousands of his fellows had taken to sudden flight with a thunderous roar of wings, leaving behind them the inevitable small gaggle of fifty odd geese hardly disturbed by the mass retreat of their fellows, I found that I was looking at, of all unexpected geese, a barnacle! A single black barnacle among all these thousands of gray geese! Busily cropping like his companions, his intensely velvet-black neck was in strong and lovely contrast to snowy white cheeks and the remainder of his plumage beautifully vermiculated in varying shades of gray and white.

On another occasion, when the pinkfeet got up from a sandy sward below the marsh proper, they left behind them three little black brent, who had deserted the succulent widgeon-grass on the mud flats to graze at this short, sandy grass. The white nicks at their sooty necks flashed momentarily when they bent and unbent in their grazing. When they rose into silent flight at my too-near approach, there was revealed that double chevron upon the snowy tail: hallmark of every wild goose. Actually only one gray chevron is patterned on the tail; the second is the gray or black of the upper back overlapping onto the snowy white of the lower back; but, out of the hand, the illusion is perfect. The breadth of wing of these small geese is remarkable, and any sinuosity of their beating wings hardly noticeable, so that they seem to fly straight-winged, like a fulmar petrel.

The truth of the matter is that wild geese, persecuted like other wildfowl, among whom it is not so noticeable, are continually changing their habitats. Prior to 1918 there was a hiatus of several years in the winter coming of the pinkfeet to

the Northeast Coast; forty-five years ago there were no pinkfeet on this part of the Solway, which was the sanctuary of
the graylags—silent, peace-loving, ponderous birds—who
nested on Scottish moors not far north, and of the black barnacles yelping cheerfully in the moonlight, with mellow
owoo, around every tump of samphire or short grass. But
today the noisy, gregarious pinkfeet—with their occasional
companions, white-fronted and bean geese—restless and aggressive, push ever farther west, like all adaptable, successful
species, and crowd out their black and gray relatives, who retreat steadily westwards. Where there were six thousand barnacles on a Solway marsh, there are now six hundred; where
four hundred graylags, forty. The punt-gunner has had much
to do with the decrease in barnacles, but little with the graylag, who is, rather, the shoulder-gunner's victim, and who,
disliking and upset by the garrulous pinkfoot, gives way before him. The little brent, too, is pushing west, partly no
doubt because the east and south become ever more indus-
trialized. Until 1936 my landlord, who had been wildfowling
for forty years, had never shot a brent goose on the Solway.

V

WINTER ON THE SALTINGS: AN IMPRESSION

In winter easterly gales tear in from the North Sea down either side of the sand hills of an island off the East Coast, sweeping across the broad creeks and bare saltings that join it to the mainland at low water, bringing with them sharp, sudden blizzards, through which I grope a stumbling way over frozen creeks—all about me soft calls of ringed plover and dunlin and raucous *quark* of shelduck—to plunge home in a dinghy kicking like a broncho. But yet I love the dreariness of winter saltings, where I may wander all day and have none for company but great-chested curlew, mighty of sickle bill, towering from hidden creek with shattering cry of alarm; and hold converse with no man but a solitary fisher scraping at mussel-bank or cockle-lay and he bitter at "them danged sea-pies," for in the early hours two hundred new-painted oyster-catchers, pleasantly piping the while, have littered the floor of his "lay" with opened shells, and well I know he paid £100 for it.

I can picture them about their unlawful business: alighting

from curving black-and-white-winged flight; running swiftly
on to the "lay," bowing forward so that snowy undersides and
carmine shanks are hidden in little pools; probing with orange bills and levering sideways with immense energy; a single bird motionless in that tense attitude peculiar to his kind,
ready to shuffle sideways, crabwise, if danger threatens; a
watchful curlew with them perhaps, his indeterminate olive-
gray plumage ringed and spotted like a civet cat's, magnificently slashed with golden lacing at his flanks, with Elizabe-
than arrogance; and then, their sport at an end, the two
hundred of them packed head to wind on the side of a mud
bank, their black mantles rendering them invisible.

Observing his rueful expression, it occurs to me to wonder
idly what would be my companion's comments could I take
him with me to the great flats of the Solway to be a witness
of one of the many miracles of bird life—for in autumn and
winter most oyster-catchers indulge their wading proclivities
to the full and like shelduck betake themselves out to the vast,
tidal mud flats of such pleasant wastes as Humber or Solway
or Fenham Flats; and there, waderlike, mass in thousands: de-
lighting their colorful souls in the small tidal game, mussels,
and cockles alive-o in the mud.

It is a little after noon, and the tide is sweeping over the
flats at great speed, for there is a bore running up the estuary
today. Packed on a grassy sand-rig, close-cropped by fifteen
hundred barnacle geese, are some three thousand oyster-
catchers. . . . But this is nothing: for, with the tide rapidly
covering the mud, the sky from southwest to north is etched
with long lines of oyster-catchers, strung out right across the
horizon and farther back in depth than my binoculars can
pick them up, converging on this sand-rig from every quarter of the flats. In many of these widely-spaced skeins there
are one thousand or two thousand birds. For an hour they
come up in their long lines: massing on the sand-rig, until
there cannot possibly be less than twenty thousand in a black
carpet that hides the sand. And as the tide swirls higher and

higher the thousands at the outer edge keep flying up over their fellows still high and dry, until the black carpet stretches away and is lost in the haze, though I can see the farthermost birds rising time and again in starling-like swarms. Once the half of them rise together, with a thunderous roar. And what a piping there is! Like black-headed gulls, the clangor endures, while they stand about and bathe . . . until the tide begins to ebb: when the silence is absolute. I find it impossible to believe that, hidden in the shimmering lightwaves of the sun there is a great army of birds less than one hundred yards distant. When the mud is uncovered once more, one little bundle after another takes off for its feeding grounds. . . .

A flight of white knots skim over us with musical, twittering chorus. Knot, godwit, and gray plover cover the world almost from pole to pole in their vast migratory flights. Hundreds of thousands skim British mud flats during their passage movements in spring and autumn, thousands stay for the winter. At every airplane over the flats there rise smoky clouds of godwit and knots, twisting and turning and falling, with perfect cohesion, in their packs of thousands—a peregrine falcon stooping into them. It is remarkable that such large and angular waders as godwit can keep such perfect flight order, often in the company of swiftly evolving dunlin. Their sharp *pip-pep* is a familiar cry out on the mud flats and sometimes in a sandy bay, where they probe the tide-wet with a musical chorus of *oo-yah* cries, sounding like little owls. Their pink and brown uptilted bills are a perpetual delight to me, when they come slanting over the creeks to alight, with long stilts hanging free, at a shallow pool on the flats. Running their long beaks in up to the hilts in the ooze when the sensitive tips locate worms, they rotate them slightly, as shelduck do, in wide sweeps.

Even in winter the gray plover is beautifully plumaged. Seldom can I approach to within forty yards of so wary a bird, but at that distance I can see the ashy streaks on his white breast and the intense black of his legs and beak and about his eyes. Only on the ground does he seem a plover: in the characteristic, still, watchful pose of a lapwing. Then breaking suddenly into superbly wild flight, revealing the broad black bar slashing his snowy tail and the unexpected flickering of black axillaries against white flanks, he cuts through the air at tremendous speed with the sharp wings of a wader. When three or four fly with dunlin or ringed plover —commonest flight association of the saltings—I hardly connect them with a sad, soft *phee-ee-ee:* so remote is this, the only cry they utter in winter.

How can I associate these gray, furtive, winter waders with those wonderfully plumaged red and silver birds that speed over these same saltings in May, when flying in line down the creek, as they are wont to do, come sixteen bar-tailed godwits? They tilt when they approach me, so that the sun burnishes the glowing fiery orange of their heads, shoulders, breasts, and bellies, as bright as golden carp: an amazing, inspiring picture, wholly unexpected in such long-legged wading birds. And that revelation of supreme beauty, the silver plover of May: loveliest, thus, of all British birds! In bright sun snowy cowl and forehead and the S-shaped broad margining to his neck and breast are dazzlingly silver against intensely black cheeks, throat, breast, and belly; the black and ash-white lacing of his back beautiful beyond description. In this glorious breeding plumage he seems twice the size and has ten times the majesty of that dull, gray bird of winter. Only the velvet-black axillaries denote that both are gray plover. . . .

A startled redshank, uttering plaintive *tew-phew-phew,* dashes over with occasional wing-beats and long glides, outstretched pink shanks flushing his undertail-coverts rosily. Out on the shore he associates with a motley company of various small waders; in a single group are redshank, knot, dunlin, sanderling, purple sandpiper, turnstone, and ringed plover, chasing minute marine game deposited on sand or great

heaps of oarweed by a flowing tide. From the flooding surf of
each breaker the waders hurry back to the heaps of seaweed,
and the redshank's manner of retreat is the loveliest gesture
imaginable: a fairylike dancing, as if he were a-tiptoe on his
bright vermilion stilts, with an inexpressibly graceful arching
of pale, slender-pointed wings high above his back that lifts
him forward a foot or two, his shanks still tripping it lightly
on the sand and in the air. A wonderfully delicately-propor-
tioned bird—bill so sharp, shanks so slender, plumage so
sleek and softly brown—the varnished pink-vermilion of a
redshank's legs is the brightest color in Nature; when their
background is brown rocks, only pink shanks remain: their
bodies vanish.

Regular habitués of the shore are gulls and gray crows.
When winter tides are small, five hundred greater black-
backed gulls and the smaller French-gray herring gulls pack
along the tide-line, moving up with its flow. The bloody
daubs on their cruelly hooked, yellow beaks might have been
imprinted there by natural selection, as warning of their pi-
ratical "nature." [1] All along the drift mark, as far as my eye
can see, are gulls, interspersed with occasional hooded crows,
somberly handsome in gray and black, quarreling over the
giant horse mussels cast up by the breakers. These both gulls
and hoodies carry to a height, soaring up with quick-flapping
flight, before letting them fall onto sand or shingle. This they
do again and again if the shells are not shattered at the first
attempt, and if, blindly, they choose sand instead of shingle,
eventually abandon the unbroken mussels in disgust. Their
harvest is rich: along some half-mile of tide-line one morning
are only three whole mussels, made too heavy by clusters of
whelks' eggs attached to them.

Mussel breaking is beyond the powers of the smaller gulls,
though common and black-headed gulls drop the tiny cockles
from a height. Although there are always some on the shore,

[1] In actual fact there is evidence suggesting that the red daubs attract
the gull chicks to the vital spot when soliciting their parents for food.

these small gulls are much more often to be seen inland, following the plow—as indeed do all gulls but kittiwakes—streaming down to the flats in their thousands at noon on Saturdays when the plowmen knock off early; but the old adage of a gull inland portending bad weather at sea dies hard. Both roost with the larger gulls on sand and shingle spits: sometimes as many as two thousand common gulls massed on a single sand bank.

Greater black-backed gull
upon its nest

I have grown weary of hearing that the common gull would be more correctly entitled the *uncommon* gull. I suppose that that is so. All I can say is that I have been continually associated with him in such scattered localities as Cambridgeshire, Sussex, London, Devonshire, Hertfordshire, Norfolk, Lancashire, the Lakes, the Highlands, the Hebrides, Northumberland, and the Solway. In the last seven localities, mature common gulls are to be seen in every month of the year but May and June: their extensive migrations taking

place in March and April, and July and August. And a very
pleasant sight it is to see the common gulls going out northeast to sea from the coast of Northumbria, in the customary
little bundles of forty at a time, with a great clangor of their
harsh, half-laughing cries. Going out high in irregular V, their
white wings with soft black shafts are beautiful to see against
a bright blue sky. Thousands upon thousands, too, roost and
rest on the Solway flats, feed on the plowlands, and nest on
the hills and merses. There, in the first days of February, I
hear the mating cry, that harsh *gee . . . yah/gee . . . yah*,
five times repeated: higher-pitched than the herring gull's. In
the middle of March, ten days or so after the curlew, begins
that streaming up to nesting territories at dawn, and streaming back at the darkening—though there are gulls on the
move at all hours of the day—with the familiar *eeeeyou* and
barking *ew*.

Out on the far sand-spits, in bright sun, pale pink shanks of
giant greater black-backed gulls are in strange, but lovely,
contrast to snowy breasts, intensely black mantles, and
white-mirrored pinions—for these colossal gulls are as huge
as gray geese. Where there is an estuary winding in through
remote sand banks, I meet of a morning an astonishing variety of birds: gulls, merganser, goldeneye, oyster-catchers, redshank, curlew, gray crows, merlins, cormorant, ringed plover,
dunlin, sanderling, brent geese, and shelduck, I have found
out here at one time.

The wonderful shelduck is the *genus loci* of the saltings.
True it is that in the late summer he holidays on the mud
flats, and that in March there are still many thousands dibbling in the mud; but early in December the trek back to
sands and salt-marshes nearer their nesting territories begins,
and early in the New Year the resident pack of four hundred
are once more about the island. I know them so well—a pair
had ducklings in a creek at the bottom of my garden—that
sometimes I forget to give them that second glance their magnificence warrants. The truth of the matter is that I cannot

accustom myself to regarding such dazzlingly ornate ducks as belonging to the drabness of winter saltings. Crawling painfully through sharp marram to the ridge of a dune on rare fine mornings, I find a score or so sunning themselves on the marsh below: the smaller ducks sitting, the drakes standing and *seep*ing conversationally—*tsew/tsew/tsew*—with constant "snaking" up and down of glossy velvet-black heads and arrogant shaking of water-glistening bills. Proudly they curve their heads and necks into the chessboard question marks of swimming sea horses. Broad chestnut sashes are bound across their dazzling white bellies, and black martingales pass between pink legs. Though they feed chiefly at night, one or two are sifting the ooze with rotary sweep of magenta bills: their long necks extended gooselike, their scapulars gleaming with the vividly coruscant green of a teal's speculum, broad tails depressed.

One pair each of four different birds of prey are wont to quarter the saltings at this season, taking toll of small birds and beasties, and of the hordes of starlings and lapwings. Of the kestrel and short-eared owl I have already written. Fiercest of hawks, the blue tercel merlin, hardly bigger than a blackbird, comes down from nesting territory on northern moor, with his bright squirrel-brown falcon, to hunt for miles over the winter marshes. Singling out her pipit or starling, the falcon flies him fairly down, eating, where she kills, the brains and perhaps a little of the breast—for a starling, at any rate, is too heavy for her to bear away in flight. Hunger satisfied, she takes up her position on the bank of a creek, flying reluctantly and heavily a few yards only at my approach. But supreme is she in full flight after tiny wader: flattening gloriously at her victim down along the tide-line; cutting at terrific speed through a rainbow of spray blown back from the breakers into the sun; throwing up a hundred feet in a single swoop twenty degrees back from the vertical: a most glorious thing to see! Her magnificent fire of life demanding release, a merlin must ever be harrying some bird, whether a-hungered or not: stooping, with the side-slipping glide of a swift, at an irritable peewit, who, entering into the spirit of the thing born of a mutual antagonism and the pleasurable sensation of speedy flight, gives her a long and menacing chase; swooping, at one hundred miles an hour, at a pair of carrion crows, with kestrel-like squeals of delight, to their squawks of annoyance: and they harrying her in turn, so that often in a moment attacker and attacked change roles, stooping, as it were, together.

Magnificent, too, is the hen harrier who crosses from Continental nesting territories to hunt English marshes through the winter. A great pearl-gray kestrel, the white-bellied tercel sails, with black-shafted wings slightly uplifted at their tips, along the line of dunes—a gigantic dragonfly (for the soft slender wings splayed at tips seem long out of all proportion to his body), he quarters low over the *sueda*, with characteristically buoyant, leisurely flapping, and the quick banks and turns of a lapwing. For so large a bird, the hen harrier is remarkably difficult to locate. The dark plumage—especially the rich chocolate of the falcon, with its yellow moons and unexpected (in a bird of prey) broad white band at the base of ring-straked tail boldly outlined by an edging of one black strake—is lost in the dead-brown *sueda* over which she quarters fast and low; and her ability for disappearing a mile away, only to reappear, unheralded, close at hand, is uncanny.

Skylarks, meadow pipits, linnets, and a few pairs of anxious reed buntings, perpetually jerking black heads and white collars, are on the island marshes all the year. The singing of the larks on these bare saltings is inferior to that of those inland. There are so few singing birds here, whose notes they may acquire, wherewith to make more beautiful the pattern of their own songs. Nor do they sing with the zest of other larks: their home is ever wind-swept, and there is little shelter from the fiercest storm.

In winter, when linnets flock together, greenfinches come

over from the mainland to join them in their endless hunt for seeds in the dry waste of old tide-lines. Ordinarily, the golden bars and slots of greenfinches' wings and tails are so bright that I am ever, at their sudden opening, imagining some rarer bird; but, against dark mud and *sueda,* their gold is paler than the primrose. In like manner, salting meadow pipits are olive-black: because of the constant soiling of their feathers by tide-wet mud and weed.

Two species of true migrant *passeres* winter on the island: shore larks and snow buntings. Both are attractive species: the shore larks sufficiently rare and elusive (running as fast as sanderling, stooping like larks) and the weather usually bitter cold enough to make long observation an act of some merit. Six, or perhaps only three, crouching forward like skylarks, feed, day after day the winter through, in a tiny marsh. Dry, except at spring tides, it is sheltered from the tempest in an amphitheater of the dunes and affords a generous measure of tide-layered plant waste, where hide insects, minute crustacea, and other small game. In this little world that they know well they are silent and least suspicious, their pinkish-gray backs difficult to pick up against the pinkish-gray *obione* and loamy mud. Troubled by sudden eddies of wind, they look up often with puzzled expressions: for the intensely black banding about their vivid mustard foreheads, temples, and throats (the eye hidden in the black cheeks) makes them seem to frown, bewildered; in a good light the little black horns of the male bird complete a Mephistophelean guise. Conservative and somewhat shy birds, a redshank noisy or a foot crunching the gravel, and they are away of a sudden with that slanting ground-flight of all larks: silvery-gray undersides pale in the winter sun. So plump upon the ground, their wings are unexpectedly long and tapering when they bound in desultory, linnet-like flight, chattering shrilly like titmice.

Snow buntings, or, more perfectly, "snowflakes," are everywhere in winter: straying from seashore to saltings, and into cottage gardens beyond; but they love best the island marshes, where most I like to see them. On a dull day the continual rising of "snowflakes," with harsh chatter and airy, bell-like rattlings, from muddy inconspicuousness, is a constant revelation of dazzling whiteness—the large and handsome cock-birds, strikingly black and white, brilliant among the smaller ruddy females: the ocher of the necklaces circling their breasts and of the crowns dividing their heads clear upon their white fields against dark-olive mottled backs.

There is a gap in the long backbone of dunes fronting the sea, where smugglers once unloaded from their ships at high water into boats that poled up the twisting creeks in the saltings. Now a dry marsh, the winds have swept white sand about clumps of rabbit-nibbled *obione*, forming little tumps a yard across and a foot deep. When northerly gales have blown with spring tides, the sea has broken over the gap, contouring the tumps at varying levels, so that looking through the wrong end of a telescope I find it easy to imagine that here is some hummocked Arctic tundra, where the "snowflakes" crouch, sloping forward, larklike, in the litter of dead *obione:* pecking vigorously at various small game whose world it is, and making themselves little sheltering hollows in the process.

VI

EIGHT LITTLE WADERS

True spirits of the saltings are the waders. Every square yard of mud is latticed with their three-pronged slots: from diminutive dunlin to giant curlew. Oyster-catchers, curlew, ringed plover, redshank, and dunlin I have with me always—though, alas, few dunlin nest on Yorkshire moors and Solway merses these days—and there is a host of Arctic-nesting waders on passage at most seasons. But there are eight little waders on English coasts who are responsible for much confusion in men's minds, and I wager that few can correctly identify them at all seasons by their plumages in the field, let alone by call or flight or peculiarity of habit.

After some weeks I learn to differentiate various species of wader by distinctions of size and plumage; but it is months, or years, before I enjoy the supreme satisfaction of recognizing my wader at any distance by some idiosyncrasy of flight or behavior. However, almost perfect in my art in one environment, I may yet be all at sea in another, when the normal adjustment of bird with customary background is out of joint. A knowledge of what, for want of a better definition, I term ornithological ecology is more vitally important to accurate identification of birds than is perhaps obvious. On the sea-shore of certain saltings, for instance, I know that any small waders are almost certain to be sanderling or ringed plover. If the unexpected happens, and dunlin intrude, my idly roving eye is arrested by distant dots probing around and about in one place, instead of racing along the tide-line in the manner of sanderling; or "twinkling" in short rushes, bobbing forward at every halt to seize a sand hopper, as do ringed plover. While a turnstone runs along, belly close to ground and legs set far back so that most of his plump body seems to be carried fore, in the style of a red-legged partridge; and a purple sandpiper is here to be found only in the creeks and

Turnstones with
a sanderling

on the flats, running swiftly but deliberately over the mussel-banks.

When I approach more closely, a turnstone, loath to move from a productive patch of seaweed, sidles away uneasily, with a sideways motion—as indeed do most small waders to a lesser degree—and, when finally he breaks into low, strong flight, reveals a strikingly bold black-and-white echeloning upon purple-brown back, distinct from that of any other wader. The smaller, straight-flying purple sandpiper, darker than any other small wader, seems almost black in flight, especially down the tail; the sanderling white, black stripings on wings; the dunlin gray-brown; and the tawny-olive ringed plover, with his black yoke, distinctively striped on wings only in gray and white.

Stints and curlew sandpiper probably do not appear at all; if they do, then I know the little stint by his resemblance to a tiny dunlin, with short beak and unexpectedly round head, like a ringed plover: his plumage pearly under, and black, brown, and white marbled on the back; he rises, with a *sweet-tweet-tweet,* and mounts higher into the air than other small waders. If it be his rarer cousin, Temminck's stint, then I catch a glimpse of his white outer-tailfeathers, when he towers with a sharp, spluttering call; but I do not really expect to see either of these little waders on the shore, but rather on sewage-farm or muddy estuary. If, as is more probable, a curlew sandpiper makes his appearance, looking very like a sanderling, he is obviously longer in the leg, bigger of body, and far longer of sharp beak, which is slightly curved at the tip. The curved beak, from which he gets another name, "pygmy curlew," is not a reliable sign of identity. And I know him for certain by the sudden revelation of white uppertail-coverts, rounded by a dark edging, when he breaks into flight, with soft *twee-twee:* a buoyant, flippant flight—his white coverts as conspicuous as the white rump of green sandpiper. But again, rather than in packs on the shore, I expect to meet him solitary at salting pool or sewage-farm.

For all practical purposes I have five small waders to consider—most attractive little birds—and their ecology is, roughly, this: on the beach at the edge of the tide are sanderling; on the rocks and sometimes on mussel-banks, purple sandpipers; on the mud and heaps of seaweed, turnstones; a little higher up, but still on wet mud or sand, dunlin; and higher still, often on tide-dry sand, ringed plover.

Although he is especially an habitué of rocks, I yet find the purple sandpiper, locally, on any type of coastline, and though all small waders are fearless, his confidence in Man is supreme. In a sandy cove, on one occasion, I came upon a flight of turnstone with a single purple sandpiper, who remained when his companions broke into flight. He stayed, moreover, to feed up the tide-line and past me within a yard, his white-rimmed black eye slightly apprehensive. Such an experience is extraordinary, when one reflects upon the wild, free life of the far-flying wader, who covers twenty thousand miles in one year. At such close quarters his head, breast, and shoulders are a drab gray, his lower breast freckled, his back and wings a purple-black, much laced with white, with two white slottings at an angle of forty-five degrees to his tail. Larger and more heavily built than a dunlin, than whom he stands more upright, his stouter bill has the upper base-half dotted in dull orange. His legs are of the same color, and, like a turnstone's, are shortish and set far apart on very large feet, so that feeding on a sloping sand shelf, picking up minutiae invisible to me, he almost sits on the sands. His calls are quiet, grating trills, between dunlin's and turnstone's, and a soft *tweet* or *sweet,* sharper than a sanderling's.

In the company of other small waders, or more usually in little flights of their own kind, are larger turnstones. In breeding plumage the males are superbly colored, and I do not know any other species with that same rich tortoiseshell mottling and shading on the back: another of those thousand tints of Nature that never fail to thrill me, no matter how often seen. In strong, unique relief are the black line-markings on white head and face, and intensely black throats and W blazoned thickly upon the breasts. In the winter the head and breast of a turnstone are of a uniform olive-brown with his back: in striking sobriety to the glorious tortoiseshell, white, and black of his breeding plumage. Strangely plumaged, he demands a second glance at each encounter, if only for the pleasure of seeing how bright a pink on brown rocks are his sturdy shanks, and how delightfully the black tongue at the base of his tail contrasts with snowy lower back, by his habit of carrying his tail somewhat depressed to the ground.

His manner of feeding is an abiding joy, and different to that of any other species of bird with which I am acquainted: for, prying energetically in black mussel-beds or in great heaps of brown and orange oarweed, he goes head-first into his potential hunting ground, pushing away and upward from him, with short, conical, up-pointed bill and head, weed, mussels, and pebbles: surprising the small game lurking beneath; whereas other birds scratch backwards with bill and feet. The attractiveness of his method is increased by the vigorous nature of his operations, for often he pushes his head right through the weed, shoveling it to either side with a little run, not unlike that of the greenshank plowing through his oozy pool. Feeding with such energy, turnstones are pugnacious *inter se,* and maintain a continual redpoll-like, musical chatter, which breaks out at each fresh quarrel or alarm into the whirring rattle of a fisherman's reel (melodious enough), merging sometimes into a kind of chirrup. This is also their flight call, and is often the first sign that they are about, for against dark mussel-beds, rocks, or heaps of weed they are difficult to pick up; it is a call most like the dunlin's, but drawn out more musically. Less often, I hear a clear *pew-pewt:* his nesting cry; and in May male and female trill excitedly at one another, with sharp mandibles apparently touching, open point to point, with a musical, grating *wood-yer-woodyer-widge.*

Seven miles out to sea is a bare reef, with rock pools and quantities of oarweed when the surging tide ebbs. I do not know any other place so favored of turnstone and purple sandpiper. Here in the late summer and autumn I have seen as many as two thousand turnstone in a single flight, and with them two hundred pipers. It is difficult to pick up the chocolate pipers against the dark-brown rocks, although there is much white on their throats at this season and their shanks are very brightly yellow.

And so to the three commonest small waders, often in the company of turnstones: dunlin, ringed plover, and sanderling. The dunlin is a delightful little bird: my favorite wader; and for all the year but a week or two at midsummer he is everywhere in creeks and on saltings. I cannot accustom myself to regarding him as a resident British bird, nesting sparsely in southwestern counties and from Derbyshire and the Peak northward. I tend to think of all waders as sub-Arctic and Artic breeding birds, despite the fact that so many ringed plover, redshank, and curlew nest in the British Isles.

Whether probing busily in the ooze with one-and-a-half-inch sharp black bills, or standing one-legged on mud bank rising from swirling tidewater, with heads tucked back, little dunlin are ever conscious of alien intruder into the customary pattern of their element; even so, they are almost indifferent to Man, and go about their business within a few feet of me watching, and, like most birds, tend to ignore me walking. The unrhythmical movement of human legs is disturbing to birds.[1] When I am waist-high in a creek, or smoothly drifting in a boat, they pay little attention to me. But more disturbing still is the human eye. I have often walked up to a dunlin hidden against a little mud cliff, unaware of his presence until he flitted up at my feet; but, deliberately watching one, twelve feet is the nearest I can approach. The quaint habit of standing upon one leg only is common to many waders, par-

[1] By this I mean that, while most birds take no offense at my walking past them, abrupt stopping and starting inevitably puts them to flight.

The tiny dunlin with a pair
of ringed plover

ticularly the smaller; a little flight of sanderling will hop
one-legged all along the tide-line if I disturb them at rest,
and break into flight without putting down the other, so that
I am often asked why many small waders have but one leg.

When a full gale is blowing it is amusing to come upon
dunlin sheltering beneath the tiny fretted eaves of a mud
bank grotto, ranked along a ledge, as I might shelter in the
lee of a protecting cliff. On a September day of tempest I
chanced upon two dunlin and a bored and anxious ringed
plover feeding in a tiny Hebridean bay. Disapproving of my
close proximity, the ringed plover was diffident of feeding. A
bird of the year, he was no doubt oppressed by the full gale
nearly blowing him away, which later hurled me off my feet
when I left the shelter of the cliffs. For fifteen minutes I
watched the two dunlin probing with sturdy black beaks betwixt the pebbles of a freshwater trickle cutting its narrow
channel to the sea. One was warmly marbled in terra cotta
on back and blackly smudged on lower breast; the other pure

white under, and pepper-and-salt mottled on back, with only a faint chestnut tinge on head and shoulders remaining from the splendor of his breeding plumage—when his mantle is brilliant chestnut, and gray rays irradiate from throat to intensely black belly. As with the golden plover, so with the dunlin there is no comparison between Northern and British nesting birds in the intensity of the black patch on the belly and in the brightness of the chestnut.

Diminutive dark knots, dunlin, only on an average seven and a half inches in length, are most perfectly proportioned, with the neatest figures imaginable: shaggy bellies, black in breeding plumage, pale silver in the winter. Their spread wings unexpectedly disclose a black rump, when they *tizzee* up and away in simultaneous flight, many hundred swarming up and down the creek in intricate evolutions with an impressive rushing of wings beating in perfect time. They dwell upon their whispered notes, caressing them to a twittering song: beautiful when its melody is lost and heard in their swiftly changing flight. Trivial in the telling, its intangible, unusual beauty haunts me. After many preparatory stoops, they alight with an inexpressibly graceful, butterfly gesture, common to many small waders before and after flight, arching slender, tapering wings vertically above their backs, revealing the soft white silk of their undersurface: a lovely movement suggestive of an infinite luxury of physical contentment.

Yet see how the inspiration of courtship crowns perfection! For, over their nesting territory on a Cumberland marsh, a pair of dunlins arch their wings in flight long before they alight, and float to earth thus, with the thistledown buoyancy of a little tern. So, too, the courting snipe. Circling round and round with his mate, the male dunlin glides like a joy-flighting redshank, with vibrant interludes, but straightly, with only a suspicion of the upward swoop. Coincidental with the vibration of his wings is his pleasant, purring trill, the diminutive of a common tern's cry when he chases another with a fish, or the drumming of a tiny bullfrog: a resonant, trilling *doo-doo-doo-doo*. Joy-flighting alone, the male twists to a little height and vibrates: trilling his elusive purr that carries so far over the spacious saltings. Then mounting in effortless circles to a couple of hundred feet, he hovers like a skylark, but with motionless wings, so that he seems to be treading the air: an astonishing feat!

Where seashore and creek-cut saltings are adjacent, I have few records of dunlin on the shore, and a spring tide may drive them right up to the sea-wall, beyond which, to the fresh-marshes, they do not often venture—although I *have* found them probing in the ooze of a fresh-marsh some four hundred yards from the shore—and the saltings of estuaries know them well. Their place on the shore is taken by the sanderling, so like them, and these I have only seen once or twice on salting or fresh-marshes. Turnstone are often with sanderling on the shore, but the perfect link between dunlin and sanderling, between fresh-marsh and salting and shore, is the ringed plover, who is impartial in his choice of habitat and equally at home on the grassy verge of some Norfolk mere. His plumage must be familiar to the most casual visitor to breckland or seashore. The black banding about his face and head make him seem puzzled, like a shore lark; he stands as watchful and aggressive as a bulldog. His shanks are normally some shade of orange-red, and those of the young, olive, but in birds of the year I have noted the strange effect of shanks olive on one side and bister on the other. Seeming little smaller than a turnstone, a ringed plover is, on an average, but a quarter of an inch longer than a dunlin, and is actually a quarter of an inch shorter than a sanderling. Yet both on the ground and in flight he seems far bigger than either of these, because of his exceedingly long wings which are nearly three-quarters of an inch longer than a dunlin's and just over half an inch longer than a sanderling's. Hotly pursued by predatory merlin, he cuts faster downwind than most British birds.

Ringed plover usually feed farther up the beach, where the sand is still wet from an ebbing tide, and aswarm with sand hoppers, whereas ashy-white sanderling (pearl-gray of back and black at the shoulders), though no less eager in their pursuit of the hoppers, run along the very edge of the waves, and often into the foam, retrieving stranded molluscs before they are sucked back by the undersurge. They twinkle along the tide-line on short black legs quicker than I can walk: covertly, but indifferently, observing my coming, for they are as confident as dunlin. It is most comical to see them scurrying ahead of me hundreds of yards along the beach, until, pushed too far west or east, they skim out on black-bordered wings over the waves, with sharp *sweet,* in a half-circle back to their original feeding grounds—white kingfishers: whitest waders on the shore.

VII

SIMULTANEOUS FLIGHT-MOVEMENT

I cannot watch little waders for long—nor godwit, nor knot for that matter—without being aware that they are past masters in the art of simultaneous flight-movement. The swift, complex evolutions of five hundred dunlins are executed simultaneously, with sharply angled turns and stoops, at fifty or sixty miles an hour, with the exactitude of a Guards regiment on parade—a still more wonderful evolution when it is performed by two thousand godwit. At one second they shine separately silver (the which has a more than aesthetic significance), and at the next appear as a black cloud, as first pale undersides and then dark backs are turned to the sun. No bird is left behind nor loses his exact place in the ranks.

How are these waders able to perform their evolutions with such perfect simultaneity? Am I to consider the flight a well-drilled company, moving in line or column at command? If so, what bird gives the command? I do not find it possible to believe that any one bird can possess enough "intelligence" or magnetic force to convey his commands to several hundred other birds with such speed that on a hypothetical order, "wheel to the right," the outer ranks change direction at the same instant as the inner. Can every bird decide spontaneously to execute the same movement at the same moment? It is clear that such a simultaneous thought can never occur in a flight of birds, unless stimulated by some immediate danger apparent to all at the same instant. Yet this coordination of movement is the invariable practice of some species: its motive purely one of pleasure.

This perfect synchronism of mass movement has many parallels in the animal creation. A swarm of many thousand bees weaving aerial figures-of-eight with such collective exactitude that no individual breaks the fluid outline of the swaying mass; a shoal of minnows darting suddenly at an angle, with swift caudal flickerings, when my shadow falls athwart the waving weeds of a sunlit stream; a bunch of rabbits skeltering, at a single impulse, to the shelter of their burrows; a herd of red deer away with one accord when my danger-scent reaches them on a down-breeze; and a thousand other instances, all show, with varying degrees of spontaneous unanimity, this synchronism of movement. But none are as impressive as the synchronous flight-movements of birds, even if some others, such as a swarming of bees or a darting of minnows, are executed with an equal and more rapid precision of unity. No doubt that the same sixth sense, almost forgotten of Man, is the instrument making possible the concurrence of action in every case, though the special make-up of a bird is particularly suited to such movements.

Broadly speaking, the higher I look in the scale of evolution, the less efficient do I find the unanimity and spontaneity of these composite maneuvers, in proportion as the slower-working processes of certain powers of reasoning replace the unthinking celerity of instinct. Some of the many instances of simultaneous movement among birds must be familiar to everyone—the sudden flutter of a little party of starlings feeding on the lawn; the precise flight-movements of a flock of homing pigeons circling above the house; or, again, the regular ranks of the great flights of starlings swooping down in their thousands upon their communal roost on winter evenings; and the flight-movements of plover. Less familiar are those of the small waders, in whom these flight exercises reach their acme of spontaneous unanimity.

I can approach the problem from the standpoint of, partly, a form of telepathy (physical as much as mental), and, partly, a sensitive visual alertness of one bird to the actions of another: interpreted with a celerity beyond human emulation, but in keeping with what I know of the hypersensitive nervous and physical organism of a bird. I have only to watch a bird for a few moments, more expecially one of the smaller species, to be greatly impressed by his vivacity, mobility, and swift reactions to external stimuli. I am not then surprised to learn that the normal temperature of his body varies, according to his species, between 100° F. and 112° F., and that his bloodstream is maintained at this human fever-point by a respiration more intense than that of any other organized body. I can thus appreciate that a bird is an entity whose whole life is governed by nervous reactions of an acuteness and a rapidity that are perhaps beyond my true conception.

The animal creation possesses certain "senses" that Man has lost in the process of evolution. The most obvious is the hyper-accurate power of orientation of most animals: supreme in the migrating bird. This is not the only sixth sense that Man does not possess or understand. Experiments by Spallanzani with bats, whose organs of sight, smell, and hearing he removed, proved that they were able to thread their way at full speed in and out of an intricate mesh of wires in a room without coming into contact with them: guided apparently by the sensitive whiskers around their muzzles and by the delicate membranes constituting the wings and the external ears. A different power is found among the *lepidoptera*. When a female butterfly is emerging from pupation, several males of her kind make their appearance at the barken crevice where she has lain as a chrysalis, though none have previously been seen in the vicinity. Fabre arrived at the conclusion that the males are attracted by what he ingeniously terms "X-rays of odour." But in a bird's synchronous flight-movements—his reactions being so quick of response—it is conceivable that an unusual rapidity of visual perception enables the members of a flight to respond so swiftly to each other's alterations in direction, that the maneuver appears simultaneous to my eye.

I may expect that in a flock of, say, fifty birds it will often happen that more than one bird will change direction, oppositely, at the same instant. When the green plover indulges in aerial exercises, the flock quite frequently splits into two or more sections. In the swifter, more complex evolutions of tiny waders, such division is unusual. The reactions of small birds are so rapid, their immediate response to one another's actions so unquestioningly faithful, and their perception of time so acute, that conflicting directional changes by individual members of a flight are almost impossible. To a bird perhaps a second, as I know it, may represent sixty well-marked divisions of time, so that, to all intents and purposes, one individual's change in direction must always precede another's by some margin of time.

That a bird should always follow the lead of another with implicit regularity I can understand, for a wild creature pays strict heed to the actions of his fellows. If a bird observes, or senses, that another is changing direction, instinct bids him do the same. Generations of mutual reliance have bred in him the instinct to imitate his fellows without hesitation. On such unthinking obedience depends the safety both of the individual and of the species. Nature does not permit second thoughts. A bird is almost, or completely, governed by instinct from the time that he develops from the yoke into his component parts and chips his way through the shell with his egg-tooth, until his extinction.

The green plover is a wary bird. Observe him when he takes off into flight. Before mounting into the air, he runs a few feet with great wings outspread. Those nearest to him do the same, and the movement spreads outwards very rapidly, so that the actual take-off of the flock impresses me as being simultaneous. Yet so swift is the adoption of the first bird's action that, when the flock takes the air, those birds farthest away from me when on the ground are still farthest away when in flight—for the birds naturally move away from me —but now form the van.

It is on these principles, I think, that perfect coordination of flight-movement is attained; but since the flying-speed is at least twenty-five miles an hour in the case of the slowest species under consideration, the starling, the slight difference in the timing of individuals is imperceptible to my comparatively slow-registering eye. Thus, in these united evolutions on the wing, a bird turns, and the movement is *anticipated* by those birds nearest to him. It is not uncommon for me to anticipate the movement of my adversary, or colleague, in some ballgame, though it is not anticipation in the literal meaning of the word. In a first-class ballgame player this anticipation is so spontaneous and accurate that I am led to believe that it must be partly telepathic intuition, and not solely a rational, positional anticipation by the brain. The particular evolution is adopted by the rest of the flock, who *sense*, rather than follow, the direction of the turn with a swiftness that deludes my eye into interpreting the whole movement as one coincident action, which indeed it is, according to my measurement of time. It is, above all, this quick, part visual, part telepathic sensing of another bird's slightest alteration in direction that is responsible for the apparent spontaneity of a turn. Nor do I forget that the pale undersides of the supreme exponents of simultaneous flight-movement are particularly arresting to the eye, and that a bird's angle of vision is lateral rather than forward.

In these synchronous turns, then, there may be a telepathic message from one bird to a hundred others, though without the slightest consciousness on the part of the originator of the particular movement that the remainder of the flock will be influenced by his change of direction. But when I consider the "stoop" of a flight of waders rather than the "turn," I find that the mechanics are different. In the really large flocks of homing starlings, containing a thousand or more birds, I can see how the perfection of this sensing may have originated.

*The starling,
a gregarious bird in its
feeding and roosting habits,
and an excellent mimic*

As the first hundred or so approach the roost, they swoop down upon the trees, followed in their turn by the remaining sections of the flock, when they reach that position where the first section had gone down, so that there is one continuous swooping onto the trees that, for the moment, deludes me into thinking that all the birds swooped at the same time.

It is this large-scale performance of the starling that holds the secret, I think, of those perfectly executed steep stoops of the twenty, fifty, or five hundred dunlin, whose swifter flight and more skillful maneuvers tend to be too rapid and precise for my eye to follow the evolving of the figure, as it can with the larger flocks of starlings. But if I choose to concentrate on the mechanics of a stoop, and do not allow my aesthetic appreciation to distract my attention to detail, I note, when a flight of dunlin dip down to the water and up again, that all the birds do not dip at the same instant, as my eye for beauty bids me believe. In precisely the same manner of the flight of starlings stooping down on the roost, there is that same pouring down and swooping up of the dunlin. If it were possible to "fix" a flight of stooping waders when those in the van had reached the culminating point of their upward movement, I should find that the rear units of the flight were about to begin their downward movement. The column of birds would represent a concave flight, with individuals stationed at all points of the arc. There is a drug that accelerates the perceptive powers of the mind, which would not need to be speeded up very greatly to enable it to follow the individual movements of a flight of knots. A slow-motion film of an actual evolution should show the slightly different positions of the units of a flight.

Watching knots, pre-eminent at synchronous flight, I can see how this type of flight as a movement of pleasure may have originated—for, being shy birds when in flocks, though confident enough as individuals, they are continually rising from the mud as a flight, with, thus, a continual invitation to move to another spot, or to circle about their immediate feeding ground, in synchronous flight. In the very doing of this, the breaking into flight may, from being a necessary corollary to alarm, become a simultaneous movement of pleasure. In these flight-movements the knots continually skim the mud, spreading out and seeming about to alight, without doing so, time and time again: to alight finally, uneasy, watchful, upright: perhaps to take off, once more, in a second or two, with but a single impulse.

This mass sensitiveness, found in various animals, is responsible, no doubt, for the superior intelligence ascribed to many of them in their possession of leaders. Certain of the larger and warier birds, such as geese, may seem to appoint definite watch-birds at their feeding grounds, but close observation shows me that outlying birds are merely so by accident. Far from rising in a pack at the instigation of a leader,

Graylag geese

gray geese, when disturbed, tend to move off in great and small detached gaggles, with much disintegration during flight. Many observers claim that older and wiser ganders form the spearheads of their flight-chevrons; but it is obvious in actuality that the wild goose, like many other birds, reacts to the easier flight conditions to the leeward of a companion; where there is less wind resistance, so that naturally the stronger flyers tend to get pushed forward into the van of the flight. My observations of the flying formations of geese, ducks, and swans, plover, gulls, starlings, and a host of waders, show the spearhead of chevron and flight to be in a constant state of flux, as first one leader and then another drops back into the shelter of the flock, isolating another bird in the van; nor is chevron formation very much commoner than any other.

The conception of organized leaders can be ruled out so far as birds are concerned. Their incredibly swift flight-movements are controlled by a mass sensitiveness of visual perception and drilled into a remarkable cohesion of flight-order by ages of immediate obedience to flock laws, with some element of physical or mental telepathy—probably of a sensitized physical nature, as yet not understood.

VIII

FRAGMENTS FROM SUMMER SALTINGS

WILD WINGS

In the very first days of February, when winter is perhaps at its most intense, I am aware of new life stirring on the saltings and on the green fresh-marshes beyond the grassy-banked sea-wall: a summer's tale is already beginning. From many thousands of green plover, who winter on these marshes, one or two break away on a sunny morning. With lazy flaps of broad wings these solitaries run off into brief tumbling flight, and swoop to earth in a corner away from their fellows, before rejoining the flock.

Three weeks pass before I watch the male plover rise from a territory that is now his alone, often in company with his more sharply-winged mate, to perform his reckless spring flight. His splay-tipped wings of great breadth and strength, he banks this way and that with alternating, soughing wing-beats: now swift, now leasurely; tumbles two hundred feet, and when about to strike the ground soars with buoyant swoop: only to fly upon his back, swerving this way and that a few inches above the ground, turning in the sun, a lustrous metallic green; or somersaulting twice with wings beating at double speed, falls a hundred feet in a corkscrew-spin, crying the while his wild, throaty whistle: *wulloch-wooee/zoowee-zoowee/zoooowee.* On a day of hot sun and blue skies it is a joyous cry, but when a sea-mist shrouds the marshes I hear the wailing of ghostly *peeweeps:* sad as the mournful *oo-ooyee/oo-ooyee* of lone curlew when the winter moon is pale over Northumbrian slakes.

He drops lightly to earth and stands a minute closing his great wings. Suddenly his two-pronged crest curves up over his head, and he runs to his mate and bows to her. Then, in a vivid instant, he crowns the swelling prologue of the courtship with the consummation of the mating and its promise of the future. For this wild flight is born only of the exuberant vitality of the mating season. It is kin to the joy-flights of curlew and redshank and snipe, to the song of the blackbird, and to the drumming of the spotted woodpecker. The courtship with which he wins him a mate is terrestrial, when, long-crested, he runs and dips before her, dazzling her with the golden-copper links of his green and purple back-armor and the brilliant chestnut under-coverts of his banded tail. He is ten times brighter and whiter than she. (But see footnote on page 100.)

Shaggy Galloway cattle, led by a white Shorthorn bull, graze the green marshes year in, year out. Coincident with the first joy-flight comes the finding of their dung patches everywhere scratched thin, laying bare yellow-green grass. In the ecstasy of their courtship, growing nidificatory instincts incite both male and female plover to fall forward on their breasts and scratch a little with their pink shanks. Through March, April, and May, the cocks continue to scratch their little round hollows, a third smaller than the nesting hollows, in dung patches and tufts of grass: their excess of nidificatory zeal unbounded. Bowing forward on his chin, with a flash of those wonderful chestnut under-coverts, the male scratches very quickly and delicately, often taking a little leap or two forward, in which he resembles nothing so much as a fly polishing its wing-cases with its hind legs. He may follow his scratchings with the significant pecking and throwing back of grasses to either side of him when he walks away.

All through March the plover are taking over their adjacent territories, stooping at my head with plaintive cries and musically lapping wings when I trespass upon their domain —continually I catch the glint of chestnut; tirelessly harrying squawking crows and rooks, kestrels and screaming herons that cross their territories—not without reason in respect of the *corvidae;* constantly interrupting their courtship to go up in pursuit. And in April the first eggs are laid in big hollows of bents, dung-cupped in tufts of grass. The female stands watching me at a little distance, while the male banks in wide circles overhead, ceaselessly crying his wearisome *peeerwit/peeerwit,* his crest rising and falling with his cries. But as the eggs set harder, so the female's attachment to them grows stronger from the association of long sitting, and she beats low around my head with piteous plaint. She may even respond to the life within the shell.

All night long through April and May the male plover call through the darkness, and especially through the radiance of those glorious nights at the full moon: their musical cries and soughing wings sharing the night silence with the drumming of snipe and the throbbing notes of a nightingale from a spinney at a corner of the marshes. But in June when their mates are pattering away, at my approach, from the chicks of second or third clutches, the male plover fall silent and lap the skies no more. Chipping the shells with their egg-teeth in the morning, the chicks are running through the forest grass by evening.

Robbed by man and crow alike, the unhappy plover are still mobbing either from their territories in August; and only then may I pray silence from the ceaseless crying of the females, when once more they gather in silent packs.

STONE-RUNNERS

In the first days of February, too, pairs and threes and fours of ringed plover are chasing one another in ecstatic courtship everywhere about the island, with the airy flight of hawking swallows: banking like the lapwing, first right then left with alternating, slow wing-beats. At one bank silky undersides are turned to the sun, at the next tawny backs, as they twist and turn, minute after minute, with ceaseless, melodious *cadooee-cadooee-cadooee* that runs away to an indeterminate and momentary conclusion.

It is March before the first courting scrapes are scratched, in a sudden frenzy, and in the first days of April there are dozens of scrapes on shingly beaches, in the marram grass, and in the *sueda;* but it is the third week before the eggs are laid. Inevitably year after year these first clutches are washed out by the spring tides, but still the "stone-runners" continue to lay in equally vulnerable places. Thus it is that courtship becomes more intense than ever: a pair running along side by side in curiously humped, disheveled manner with fanned, depressed tails—like all plovers, they are exceedingly plump at any time; rival males running at each other, with raised "hackles," comically aggressive. With passions rising, the ceaseless calling of the lovely joy-flight grows more intense: *doee-woodawooee-woodawooee-woodawooee,* shortening, in the excitement of the pursuit, to a dying *woodyer-woodyer-woodyer.* At such moments I hear an echo, as it were, to each mellow two-note: a little pebble-grating purring or a rubbing of damp cloth on glass. Indeed, in May and June on the saltings I sigh for a little quietness, for from dawn till midnight the crying of anxious redshanks, oyster-catchers, terns, and ringed plover is ceaseless, and hardly less so the uneasy whistling of sheldrake; and from midnight to dawn the harsh screaming of terns makes the night hideous with a rude clangor.

It is May before second clutches are laid, cunningly hidden in marram tufts or exposed on shingle-beaches. Exquisitely pear-shaped, the gray-fawn eggs, speckled with violet dust, are hardly to be detected against their dun background. And by the middle of the month feinting ringed plover are everywhere, leading me away from their eggs long before I am anywhere near them. Their feinting differs hardly at all from the display antics of their courtship, for they go running over the shingle with shuffling wings and spread, depressed tails pressing against the ground—displaying, incidentally, the bright white edges. With the hatching of the chicks, the feinting grows more intense, and both parents tumble over the ground, one wing tilted and flapping slowly (as in the joy-flight), the other trailing brokenly along the ground (exaggerated only slightly from the courting antics)—but to this interesting habit I refer more fully at the end of the chapter.

Nesting in such suicidal places, eggs are even washed out by the tides of May; but by the beginning of June there are many chicks just out of the egg, uttering melodious pipings and little trills. Quickly leaving the nest, these tiny atoms in green and gray down, black head-banding already in evidence, stumble feebly on colossal feet and inordinately long pink stilts over the wide, open spaces of shingle and sand. They are shepherded by the female with mellow, piping *pheep-pheep-pheep,* and she broods them anywhere and confidently within six feet of me. Roaming far and wide and swimming in the pools, it is a miracle that any such fragile Lilliputians survive, although it is their salvation that they are desperately hard to pick up against the multi-colored shingle.

ARIEL

When March is in, the redshank's summer call, *plleeder-plleeder-plleeder,* infrequently heard throughout autumn and winter, takes on a more passionate note: a liquid trippling

lovely to hear—for he has now won him a mate, with perhaps the most daintily beautiful of all courtships. A-tiptoe before her on dancing stilts cerise, he draws himself up like a
game-cock, with half-open wings fanning slowly: their silky
undersides catching my eye at one hundred yards, when his
body is lost against the dun of the tidal mud. Softly sounding
his *plleeder-plleeder,* he is soon a mist of swiftly fanning
wings: as if he would compel her with his vibrant passion to
submit to the ardor of his courtship—a beautiful thing to see
of this most fairylike of all wading birds! [1]

How swiftly his summer's tale develops! Three days after
that first trippling, there sounds from every corner of the
marsh a ceaselessly monotonous, plaintive *plew/plew/plew.*

[1] I am beginning to think that these most perfect patterns of display
of ground-nesting birds (and perhaps of *passeres* too) are common only
to *mated* pairs. They serve the purpose of exciting the nidificatory, or,
rather, the egg-laying machinery of the female. Deluded by the superficially convincing arguments of the mighty; by the peculiar but, I think,
false examples of displaying ruff and blackcock; by the "territory" theories about warblers; I have all this time been looking for display from
unmated birds, instead of from mated. I believe now that, given the opportunity, I am going to discover that the pairing of two birds is dependent upon some quite other phenomenon than display. If this should
prove to be so, there falls the last of my mentors, Edmund Selous.
Throughout the text the reader will have to permit me an elastic use of
the terms *courtship* and *display,* for in the present state of my knowledge I do not find it possible to draw any hard and fast distinctions between the *courtship* that leads to the pairing of two birds for a new
nesting season, and the *display* stimulating ovulation that occurs after
the initial acts of coition. Possibly no distinction should be drawn, and
pre- and post-mating antics regarded as integral parts of the whole nesting drama. Have we not all been barking up the wrong tree? Has anyone ever witnessed an act of courtship leading directly to the pairing of
two birds for a new season? Three or more males displaying about one
female, but is there any good reason why one of these males should not
be paired up with the female, and the other males (probably young and
unpaired) stimulated to display by her presence? The more I think
about it, in the light of my observations in the field, the more I am con-
vinced that the display of male and female has no bearing on the pairing. The perennial coming together of male and female is governed by
some subtle factor that at present eludes me. Subsequent references to
courtship and *display* must be read with this qualification in mind.

This belongs, properly, to his joy-flight, which does not begin until three days later, when he planes with convex wings in figures-of-eight. At regular intervals he breaks his gliding motion with a rapid vibration of his wings (similar to that of a swift scratching itself in flight), then his beating wings are stilled for a few seconds while he glides earthwards: only to shoot upwards again with the impetus of his previous drop and a new vibration, which begins just before he arrives at the lowest point of his descent and ends just before the highest point of his ascent.

Another two days only, and I begin to hear soft greenshank cries, *tewk / tew-tewk,* which signify that the taking over of territories on marsh, water-meadow, and sheep-cropped salting is in full swing. The next day the male redshanks are running at each other, aggressively, with lifted wings and spurring of wonderful shanks: as daintily perfect in their motions as ever. With the acquisition of a territory, the male's joy-flight tends to suffer an aerial change. He dances in the air above it, with bright pink shanks hanging free, what time he yodels a trilling *tooee / tooee / tooee;* hovering in one spot, with his wings curved above his back, he rises and falls with the buoyancy of a Ping-Pong ball on the fluctuant jet of a fountain, ceaselessly yodeling.

At mid-April are born the first scrapings of their dual passion—those so-called "cock" nests; and a few days later polished brown eggs, red-zoned, are cunningly hidden in young marram, whose tips are bent in to form the concealing framework of a wigwam. From every territory floats over the salting the lazy *tewk / tewk* of watchful males.

When the chicks hatch in the middle of May, the male circles above my head in his joy-flight, with ceaseless, anxious *plew / plew / plew.* Jealousy and fear react upon him, organically, as do the emotions of courtship: resulting in a similar physical display. The black-billed chicks in their rich velvet-brown plumage, black-striped like young snipe, scuttle on pink legs all ways into the marram, while the lovely brown-shaded female perches, tangerine-shanked, on a *sueda* bush.

It is at this season, at the end of May, that I hear most often the liquid trippling of the male. There is often a dead calm over the saltings at ten or eleven o'clock at night, with a pink flush on the sea, and the marshes sweet smelling, as in the early morning, with an incomparable freshness. Over the lush water-meadows falls the ethereal twittering of larks, which really belongs to that mystical half-hour before dawn. Standing on the sea-wall, there comes to me from a mile over the pink and gray saltings—gray with tangled *obione* pink-flushed at its tips, pink with thrift—the soft *tweedle-eedle-eedle-eedle-eedle* of curvetting ringed plover and the clear *plleeder-plleeder-plleeder* of dashing redshank. The beauty of such hours haunts me. There is a physical spirit abroad charming all creatures, for calves go mad on the marshes, and dogs race in crazy circles.

At the end of June, when unlucky mates are sitting on second clutches—and some sit so closely that I may lift them from their eggs, not that there is any pleasure in treating a wild bird so—the males stand for hours at a time on the *sueda* bushes of the ternery: preening their smooth brown feathers, and working their tweezer mandibles with inward calling. Overhead, in packs of twenty together, scream the paler plumaged birds of earlier clutches, bright orange shanks streaming out beneath black-barred white tails.

PIPING QUADRILLES

The stage is set, this time, on the banks of a salmon river that runs down to and skirts the salt-marsh of a northern estuary. The season of the year is mid-January, when, after weeks of gales, there has been a change in the weather to frost and sun and blessed calm. Just this side of the sea-wall an oyster-catcher is standing in a pool on top of the broad river bank, asleep—very fast asleep. At six feet from him I can see his third eyelid occasionally flickering over his vermilion eye; yet for a minute and more his uncovered eye flashes no warning of my coming to his consciousness; then he suddenly unpacks his tangerine beak buried in his scapulars and sweeps away in a hurry, brilliantly echeloned in black and white: to alight by the river, and calls *perwee*—which I believe to be the cry of the male bird; but, since the sexes are alike in the field, I am not yet certain that this is so. I have heard it said that the white slotting at the shoulder of the male oyster-catcher is bigger than that of the female: but this is incorrect; true, there are occasional variations in the size of the slotting, but this appears to be a distinction not of sex, but of age. I have watched hundreds of pairs of oyster-catchers and have found very few displaying any sexual distinction.

Nothing very startling, you will say, in encountering a lone oyster-catcher in January! But wait! In autumn and winter as we have seen, most oyster-catchers feed far out on the mud flats. Although they nest for seventy-two miles up the river, there have been none about this particular marsh since the previous September. This is the first oyster-catcher to respond to the call of the nesting territory; but it is nearly a month later before a pair fly downstream past my window, and by the end of February there are pairs all the way up and down the river. Once again I settle down to watch their remarkable display, which is already widespread and continuous. I should like to have given, here, my notes taken down in the field, but as they amount to several thousand words, this is not possible, and would in any case leave the reader in some confusion of mind, for the intricate movements of the display are not easy to unravel. To watch so swiftly moving, so complex, and so apparently contradictory a display as these quadrilles of the oyster-catcher, and to make comprehensive, but accurate, notes on the spot, has often been a matter of frantic difficulty. Like the bizarre dances of the spur-winged lapwing of the La Plata, these piping quadrilles of our own red-billed sea-pies are generally held to be a form of social enjoyment, originating out of what was once direct courtship but now meaningless. If there is truth in this theory, it is a forced half-truth.

I have never seen more than nine oyster-catchers setting to a quadrille, though seven frequently, and seventy-five per cent of those I have watched have included three performers only; indeed, three oyster-catchers are far more commonly seen together in February, March, and April, than a pair. This seeing of three birds of a kind, who, by their actions, are clearly a pair and an intruder, is a regular feature of the spring domesticity of many species of birds. I think especially of green and gold finches, of skylarks, of green and ringed plover, of redshank and of wild duck, and, notably, shelduck and oyster-catchers. Rarely are there signs of animosity among the three, although there is often a recognized pattern of agressive display. Up to the very day of incubation these trios of oyster-catchers are constantly in evidence, not only on river and marsh, but flying over the village and fields inland, with shrill, ringing *kervee/kervee/kervee*. But once incubation has begun the threes are seen no more. With the sexes similarly plumaged, it is not easy to determine what role is played by the third bird. Oyster-catchers do not mate in their second year when they associate, during the nesting season, in packs of fifty and a hundred—and more, for all I know—and are distinguished from mature birds by their dull plumage and by white slots across their cheeks and throats. I believe that the intruders are third-year males in search of mates, although, remembering how often I have seen two ducks flying with a drake, some may be females.

However that may be, the pattern of the famous display is this: With heads stiffly down-stretched and hackles raised, with half-open, vibrant mandibles straightly pointing the ground like scarlet clothespegs (John Donne's "twin compasses"), and broad tails depressed, two birds run side by side at a third bird, piping hard the while: their motion like nothing so much as two old rams charging, hell for leather. Beginning with plangent *peek* or *pic,* the cheery piping swiftly gathers way into a prolonged diminuendo: *kervee-kervee-kervee-kervee-kervee,* etc., etc., which dies away and crescends into a beautiful rippling. The precision with which the piping pair charge and turn together with lightning swiftness is as astounding as that of small waders in simultaneous flight. They do not attempt to drive away the "pipee" by physical force, but persist only with this automatous running and turning together when short of, or alongside, the intruder: to and fro, to and fro. I am strongly reminded of the haphazard rushes of the displaying ruff, who is as likely to bow to a clod of turf as to a reeve. But this "ram-piping" of the oyster-catcher serves its purpose, and, ninety-nine times out of one hundred, the "pipee" soon takes to flight, although I have known a pair to pipe at a third bird for fifteen minutes without a break before achieving the desired end. The intruder seems to be inherently aware that the piping means "Get out! We don't want *you* here!" What is more, he shows physical signs of such an awareness, and an invariable factor in the pattern of the display is the obvious chagrin of the "pipee," who continually sidles away from the pipers with an uneasy motion suggesting that he is most uncomfortably conscious of their attentions. Those who have read Edmund Selous will appreciate how what was once physical aggression may have passed into this mere display of aggression: which serves the purpose of ejection equally well, without there being any dissipation of valuable energy in actual fighting.

The oyster-catchers do not nest anywhere near the river-marge on which they display; therefore in this piping of two birds at a third no direct territorial values are at stake. But with the perennial regrowth of the reproductive organs there is a concomitant welling up of sexual emotions, bringing in their train multiple inherent and familiar associations of courtship, mating, and nesting. Undoubtedly both male and female experience an acute sensation of jealousy at the presence of an intruder of their kind: jealousy, not only of mate, but of the immediate territory in which they chance to be feeding or resting—a nervous reaction automatically stimulating the appropriate, inherent pattern of display. That oyster-catchers are in a state of extreme nervous sensibility at this season, like every other species in the spring, is almost a truism. A thousand times, the slightest untoward incident is immediately productive of a spontaneous outbreak of "ram-piping." Any oyster-catcher alighting near others, any oyster-catcher merely passing overhead, is sufficient to cause an outbreak of piping, even from a bird sitting on an imaginary nest. Four oyster-catchers at the edge of the river, for instance, are joined by three others; the four "residents" are immediately provoked to an outburst of piping, which as quickly dies away, and all seven preen and bathe and rest peacefully together. Again, another seven oyster-catchers are resting at the sandy edge of a creek: four standing one-legged with fiery bills tucked back into scapulars, three "at ease" in that curious attitude peculiar to the oyster-catcher, with one leg bent at the knee so that the heel of the web is raised off the ground (after the fashion of a tired horse). Suddenly one bird flies away, inciting the remaining six to a prolonged muttering of nervous *pic/pic/pic*, which is the prelude to an outbreak of "ram-piping" among four. The parallel with the *passeres* provoked to song by the slightest jarring of his nervous sensibilities is obvious.

Not only is the "ram-piping" an instrument of aggression against intruders and an automatic nervous reaction, but it is also part and parcel of the oyster-catcher's organism at the spring season. It is very rare to see a male oyster-catcher actually courting a female; when he does so, his attitude is, significantly, that of the "ram-piping." She, too, responds to its pattern. For example, on top of the river bank are a pair of oyster-catchers some yards apart. The male (by what goes after) bobs around and around what looks like a stick and a clod of dead grass. At one point he tugs at it, but, for the most part, he appears to be picking up things and placing them on the clod—though this may be in theory only—nor does the female go near him: she is "ram-piping" all by her-self, while the male *kervees* persistently. In the end he flies to her and alights on her back, but is up and away as lightly and quickly as a gull brushing the tree-tops, and nothing comes of it. Although this episode took place on March 1, he was already reacting to both nidificatory and mating sensa-tions.

The incitement to pipe, indeed, colors every part of their daily lives at this season. By the third week in March it is a common sight to see three or four or five oyster-catchers flying over village and fields and marsh, with quick-beating, feeble wing-strokes, maintaining, for the duration of their long fly round, the rippling *kervee-kervee* of the "ram-piping" —which, after all, is only an ecstatic prolongation of the spring call-note, *kervee*.

Thus far, it has been fairly plain sailing. The "ram-piping" is seen to be as germane to the spring season as song to a pied wagtail: an automatous nervous reaction to almost any stimulus, and an adaptation from direct courtship for the pur-pose of keeping intact the mating tie. But now, alas, I must put on record some of those twenty-five per cent of excep-tions to the rule of a pair piping against what is probably an unmated young male.

Here, for instance, are two oyster-catchers "ram-piping" at the usual third; but, on this occasion, the two pipers are dis-tinctly ill-disposed towards one another, and, in the end, when the intruder flies away, it is joined by one of the pip-ers. This looks as if old and young cocks have been piping at a female. Again, a third bird flies up to a pair, who pipe at him; but, woe is me, one of the pair flies away, leaving the in-truder with the other piper! What am I to make of this, if it be not that the male of the pair has flown up and driven away an intruder male? And yet it is strange that he did not pipe.

Single pairs (not necessarily in the mating sense) are con-stantly flying in great circles over the extensive nesting terri-

tories of the oyster-catchers on the marsh for many minutes at
a time. A bird of one of these pairs glides and circles with
gentle sinuation of supple wing-tips. This, I imagine, is a
male in joy-flight with his mate, but she lands and he is
joined by a bird from a pair on the ground—no doubt because he is passing over the latter's nesting territory. However, the owner returns at once to its territory, and is piped
at by its mate and another pair—which points to her being a
female.

Again, out of a gathering of six at the edge of a creek, three
"ram-pipe" at once: presumably three males piping at a female, their respective mates standing by. The "pipee" sidles
away, *peek*ing, as uncomfortably as ever, while they pipe
after her in single file. All six then fly away, at the instigation
of one bird, and are joined by another bird flying up. The
seven alight in scattered twos and threes. Alas, I cannot turn
a blind eye upon the continual interchanging of the units of
pairs and threes of oyster-catchers prior to the beginning of
incubation. However permanent their pairings may be, they
are not proof against temporary reshufflings. Yet these take
place on the marsh, where, in a great circle around me, are
some fifteen pairs of oyster-catchers, who, despite their frequent reshufflings, occupy approximately the same sites on
the marsh from the latter half of March onwards

As April draws on, and the marsh is alive with scores of
potentially nesting pairs of oyster-catchers, the fun becomes
fast and furious, my notes legion, and confusion chaos. Although four birds out of a set of seven actually mate while I
am watching their intricate evolutions (would that I had
space enough to give the details in full), the interchanging of
the units of different pairs is so swift, that never once am I
able to follow the movements of any two birds of a pair from
beginning to end, and I find it difficult to draw any logical
inference from what I see. The only grain I can winnow from
the chaff is that it appears to be the constant aim of one
piper to keep between the "pipee" and the other piper: which

Oyster-catchers

supports the theory of the male of the pair piping aggressively against an intruder male. I have watched one of a pair of pipers pertinaciously hedging off the other piper from the "pipee" for minutes together, continually turning on the inside berth. And this is also true of two birds piping at two others, for, after gradually splitting up *C* and *D*, *A* and *B* "ram-pipe" with extraordinary persistence at *C* only, for fifteen minutes, driving him away to a considerable distance before turning their attentions to *D*—I smell territorial jealousy.

Whether it is invariably so I do not know, but all display appears to end directly the first eggs are laid at the beginning of May; only to break out again at the beginning of July, when some pairs have finished with nesting duties and before they go out to the mud flats for the autumn and winter. In this there is, again, a close parallel to the seasonal song pattern of a pied wagtail: a bird whose simple cluster of notes is provoked in the spring and again in July by the slightest incitement to his nervous system. Thus I can well understand that the oyster-catcher is similarly incited to display in any circumstances, in any company. It is a social form of display only in so far as the gathering together of four or five oyster-catchers is, in itself, an incitation to display, because of the mutual jarring of nervous sensibilities. To conclude that they gather together with intent to display is to approach the "ram-piping" from a false angle. Oyster-catchers, from the very nature of their habits, will always tend to feed and rest together in creek or on mud bank, whatever briefs they may hold for the conservation of actual nesting territories. It is not so much the display of the oyster-catcher that puzzles me, but the roles played by the various participants in the continual splitting up and re-forming of the various threes and sets. In the display of the shelduck I may, perhaps, be able to find the key to this inconstancy of the oyster-catcher.

RED-BILLED SEA-PIES

It is wonderfully interesting to watch the oyster-catcher's nesting drama develop. Would to God that I could live seven months on an uninhabited island of nesting sea birds! What an epic tale is there!

Mid-January saw the return of the first oyster-catcher to the vicinity of his nesting territory; nearly a month later the first pair; and by the end of February there were pairs all the way up and down the river, and "ram-piping" was widespread.

At the end of the first week of March one of a pair of oys-

ter-catchers is *sitting* on the grass of the river bank: a sight
not to be seen out of the nesting season. And a very pleasant
and restful sight it is to see an oyster-catcher sitting on the
grass, so beautifully compact: that fiery bill projecting
straightly forwards. Her recumbence is all a part of her shy
and apologetic scuttling away at my approach, and her continual looking round to note my progress: a most un-birdlike
pattering gait of a shambling cow! So will she sit, and so will
she run from her eggs two months later: delightfully self-con-
scious! Far from sitting in a potential nesting territory, she
may sit all by herself out on the wide, wide sands: a very solitary little being!

At the end of March far-nesting pairs of oyster-catchers
begin to feed in fields as much as a mile inland from the
marsh; and by the middle of the month the well-cropped
sward at its base is dotted with pairs all along its two-mile
length, and for half a mile in depth: many of the birds, both
male and female, sitting, though not on nests of course.

In the first days of April there are large "cock" hollows out
on the shingle-beaches, wastefully strewn with broken cockle
shells and splintered violet mussels. Towards the end of the
month territorial and nesting instincts grow more intense,
aggressive display becomes physical aggression, and one of a
pair of oyster-catchers on the marsh catches an intruder by
the tail, whereupon the latter returns to his mate. Both pairs
then join up, and all four proceed to pluck and throw grasses
backwards and to either side of them, after the fashion of
nesting and potentially nesting birds—a significant habit con-
sidered more closely in later chapters.

At this season, the male (presumably) begins to indulge in
a more complex joy-flight of the exact pattern of a ringed
plover's, when he hawks like a swallow, with tapering wings
arching over his back. Only, in so big a bird as an oyster-
catcher, this becomes the incomparably buoyant motion of a
short-eared owl: a slow, flapping flight, high and low, revealing the astonishing length of his silky wings.

It is the end of April before the nest is finally decided upon, and the familiar, telltale figure of glossy black and silver oyster-catcher stands on a shingle knoll one morning, very watchful, of carmine-ringed, ruby eye. Rarely have I surprised an oyster-catcher on her nest. While I am yet seventy yards distant, she begins to patter away on salmon-pink shanks, in little uneasy spurts. Bowed forward in her secretive get-away, her straight, carmine bill almost points the shingle. Her mate is one hundred yards away at the edge of a creek, pretending to be probing in the ooze with his orange-red bill, but constantly looking up in my direction. Quite near him is a pack of fifty non-breeding oyster-catchers. She has scuttled away well wide of her nest, and it is extraordinary the difficulty I have in picking up the colossal olive-brown eggs blotched with purple and terra cotta, lying anyhow on the broken shells of their shingle-hollow: contrary to the neat habits of most waders.

At the beginning of June when the young hatch, blacker and bigger than tern chickens, to scatter from their splintered nest as soon as dry, the parents fly around them all day with ceaseless, clamorous piping, and come trotting up past me, feinting with half-arched wings and depressed tails. By the end of the month the chicks are gray, with lengthening bills, and swim well. An adult oyster-catcher swimming is an odd spectacle: he has the style of a phalarope. By August, when they are black with very pale pink shanks, I can hardly differentiate the young from their fading parents. A year's tale is ended.

RESTLESS DRAKES

Both in pattern and seasonal limitations the display and nesting sequence of the magnificent shelduck affords an obvious parallel to the oyster-catcher's. Some are paired and are beginning to spread all over island and creeks and marshes up to the sea-wall in the first days of February. By the middle of that month there are pairs all the way up the estuary and river, and display is in full swing. Through March and April it is incessant, at all hours of the day and night, but especially in bright moonlight and at dawn.

As with the oyster-catcher, so any number from two to nine shelduck may display together. Odd numbers of the latter are no less common than they are of oyster-catchers: three again, especially: a duck and two drakes. All the familiar combinations of "ram-piping" oyster-catchers are in evidence: a pair and a drake consorting and separating, three drakes displaying before one duck, two pairs displaying, three drakes and two ducks "smothering." Curiously enough, as in the case of the oyster-catcher, I have not seen more than nine shelduck displaying, although forty or fifty may be dibbling together on the tide-wet sands. Display is provoked most often when four or five happen to come together in the river territories to which they repair in February every year on their return from the flats: one pair to approximately every seventy-five yards. These, as with the oyster-catchers, seem to be set up as pre-nesting territories, for, of course, their nesting burrows are at a great distance from the river. The mere passing of another pair of shelduck at a considerable height is sufficient to provoke display from any pairs having adjacent territories below, or an. uneasy *seep*ing from a head-"snaking" drake. On the other hand, three or four pairs will feed together in the territory of one pair for a considerable period in perfect amity. And then, for perhaps no visible reason, there is a sudden outbreak of display. It is as spontaneous in its immediate origins and as spasmodic as the oyster-catcher's piping; but I am not left in any doubt as to the meaning of the shelduck's display. "Display," indeed, is a misleading epithet: seven-tenths is actual physical aggression, colored by three-tenths of display pattern originating from direct courtship. It is ninety per cent sexual jealousy. With sexual distinctions in plumage to guide me this time, it is obvious that its constituents are, firstly, a seasonal state of acute nervous sensibility;

secondly, the attentions of mated and unmated drakes to mated ducks; thirdly, the jealousy of both drakes and ducks for their respective mates (I had suspected this jealousy to exist among female oyster-catchers, but had little proof of it); fourthly, an element of direct courtship; and fifthly, jealousy for imaginary territory. Actually, there appears to be very little attempted in the way of ejecting intruders from territory: rather does the mere collision of neighboring pairs result automatically in friction and fighting, which may take place on land or water. The latter is, clearly, its ideal medium, and the drakes take the major parts in the action, though the ducks are by no means shy.

On land, with characteristic and comical aggressiveness, the drakes run suddenly at each other, with stiffly downstretched beaks, humped chestnut shoulders, and spread, depressed tails—which is, of course, their attitude when courting their ducks. It is interesting to see how a drake will run at another drake once, with obviously aggressive intentions, and immediately afterwards run again, but not directly at any drake or duck. The which reminds me of that harmless turning short of, or alongside, the third bird of two oyster-catchers. The instinct to attack is still present, the objective forgotten. And in this way, no doubt, direct actions pass, in time, into display patterns.

The ducks run at other ducks and at intruder ducks, and in company with their own drakes. Their shoulders are similarly humped but their outstretched necks are flattened horizontally to the ground, which they sweep with chins and uppointed bills, and "snake" supplely up and down. What a colorful picture they make, dredging the illimitable sungolden sands under the bright blue skies, with tide-wet, cerise bills and legs glistening and for the rest, wonderfully sharp-cut in chestnut and white and black!

In the water they bob up and down like rubber ducks, revealing bright chestnut bellies. When five or six are excited together, the ducks stretch out their necks along the surface of the water (like courting black-headed gulls and so many other female waterfowl, especially when inviting the male to court). In this attitude they spin about their drakes, with up-pointing bills and heads weaving from side to side and continual *urr-r-r-r*, in an absolute ecstasy of jealous and sexual excitement. The drakes advance on one another with swift *gar-gar-gar* and whistling *tsew-tsew-tsew*, their heads "snaking" up and down and gracefully backwards and forwards. . . . Passions rise higher; the intensity of sound and action heightens. . . . Both drakes and ducks, poker-necked, go leaping and shooting through the air, with wonderful flashes of color from humped chestnut shoulders, at rival drakes and ducks, who neatly avoid their attacks by quick dives and, excited themselves, retaliate in kind. . . . The drakes plopping up a few feet and plopping down upon one another, until all the combatants are churning the water in a threshing smother. . . . As quickly as it began, it ends with that excited wing-flapping and bathing so common to all waterfowl stimulated to any nervous excitement, whether it be after mating or fighting, or from territorial jealousy or fear. Once more they return to their feeding and preening—only to break out again in sudden orgasm.

Again, the prime instigator of nearly every "display" is, I think, the unmated young drake; and again, though obviously not promiscuous, the mating ties of sheldrake during the pre-nesting season are as loose as those of oyster-catchers. Both ducks and drakes desert their mates for considerable periods: the drakes to pay attention to ducks of other pairs (there appear to be no unmated ducks) often hundreds of yards distant; the ducks to fly off short distances and settle alone. The parallel between oyster-catcher and shelduck is obvious.

BURROW-DUCKS

The display of the shelduck, like the oyster-catcher's, is coincidental with the preliminaries of the nesting. By the begin-

ning of April the packs have left the remote mud flats, and in
the early morning I come upon ducks scratching at rabbit
burrows on dunes and saltings, fresh-marsh and common:
often as far as two miles inland and several hundred feet
above sea level, with the drakes, ever watchful of danger,
standing on observation tumps at a little distance from the
burrows. About ten o'clock in the morning they hurry down
to the salting again, after their house-hunting. Seven may
come down together, and unmated drakes continue to cause
excitement in their feeding territories until the ducks are sitting in May.

At this season the diamond tracks in the sand of the latter
lead to every rabbit burrow; but later, when they have decided upon a suitable nesting hole, a stray soft white feather,
chestnut-tipped, entangled in the marram roots laid bare at
the sides of the burrow, is the only evidence of a duck sitting
on eggs in its dark interior. For now she enters and leaves the
burrow with spread, depressed tail, obliterating her webprints and smoothing the sand. Observing that this is her attitude in courtship, I surmise that, stimulated by the presence
of the drake who usually accompanies her to and from the
burrow, the duck goes to and comes from her eggs with
courting gait, unwittingly destroying traces of her occupation
—Nature, once again, fulfilling two vital purposes concomi-
tantly.

With conversational *seep*ing and warning *garr-garr*, solitary drakes circle widely over the dunes, where the ducks are
sitting hidden an arm's length and more around the first turning of the burrow; or stand about in small packs in the center
of the nesting area: five or six rising at a time, with guttural
arrk, to mob the coasting harrier; or chasing recalcitrant
ducks back to their burrows, or away from other amorous
drakes.

In May I have known there to be nineteen eggs around the
first bend: no doubt the produce of two or even three ducks;
but when, as early as the first of June, I see the top of an old

sheldrake's head snaking along in the lee of a creek bank, and then the duck running along with crouching gait, also in a great hurry, it is usually six or seven little chocolate-striped, gray and white ducklings who are scuttling to the safety of the water in single file on very black legs. Sometimes I confuse their swift, thin *peep-peep-peep* with the plaintive notes of titlarks. At this season the duck flies in low, wide circles about them, with anxious *urrk:* a guttural call almost identical to the angry *arrk* of two old drakes jealous of either's proximity to the other's family—for at the first hatching the drakes are jealous of their young, running at each other fiercely.

The families of shelducklings spread, not only over marsh and creeks, but onto the shore: a parent at either end of the file. The hardiness and precocity of the ducklings is remarkable. They dive like corks for as long as eight seconds, swim strongly, and run over the surface of the water and faster over the flats than I can run them down. Sometimes a shelduckling loses its parents on the way down to the sea and is unfortunate enough to trespass upon the nesting preserves of a mute swan, who kicks up more of a commotion than any bird I have seen—threshing the nine inches of water with colossal wings, spearing down with beak, stamping with huge webs . . . yet the innocent little duckling diving repeatedly, gets away safely: a miracle in such shallow water!

By the end of June, when the mature shelduck begin to pack about the marshes or go out to sea, the various families of shelducklings are becoming hopelessly mixed up. Here will be one family without any parents; here sixty-two ducklings of varying sizes with a single pair of adults; there two pairs with a single family; and here one pair with a single duckling, for whose safety they betray the greatest anxiety. What governs this faithfulness of some parents and unfaithfulness of others? Certainly not the moult, for I have seen shelduck parents with twenty flappers at the end of July, when nearly all other mature shelduck had gone out to sea and mud flat for the winter; and they are still feinting with water-threshing wings, for the flappers, some of whom—perhaps all—are not of their hatching.

I have seen a pair of shelduck with their own family of six quarter-grown young on August 10, so terribly in the moult that the duck—who seems to moult first, at the beginning of July, with that characteristic discoloring of beak and legs and baldness of head—was almost colorless, and only the exquisite oxidized-green on the wings of the drake showed no white abrading. Some mated ducks, the young birds (?), appear to retain white patches on brow and cheeks throughout the year.

I have seen a large flapper with almost colorless parents on August 23 in the nesting area, when other flappers were about in little packs of their own in the creeks and at sea—I infer, therefore, that so long as a pair of shelduck have any ducklings to tend they stay by them, but as soon as their hatch gets lost or mixed up with other families, they tend to go off on their own, with the natural waning of the parental instinct at this season. The losing of their ducklings is no difficult matter, for often, when a duck and a drake fly up to lead me away from their brood, they eventually come down half a mile away. They may stay away for half an hour or an hour, during which absence it is quite possible, and indeed likely, for their brood to join up with another family.

"broken wings"

The most seemingly intelligent act of a bird—almost universal among ground and water nesters—is the apparently simulated distress of parent birds to detract attention from their young. On first seeing the "broken-wing" fluttering of trailing partridge or ringed plover, cleverly leading me away from the vicinity of eggs or young birds, the ruse seems rational and deliberately thought out. When an oyster-catcher is first brooding her eggs, she runs silently off the nest to a distance long before I approach: to return as furtively when I have gone. As yet her attachment to her eggs is not strong. She has not sat long enough for physical association with them to stimulate an emotion of jealous anxiety for the eggs stronger than the normally dominant emotion of self-preservation. The longer she sits, the stronger becomes her attachment to the nest and its eggs. When they are hard set, she flies around my head, piping plaintively. The emotion of jealous anxiety is ousting that of self-preservation. Nothing may freely approach her eggs at this stage in their incubation, and male and female mob, fearlessly, robber gull, hawk, or rat, or even passing boat. When the chicks hatch she swoops down upon my head, fear for herself forgotten, where before her jealousy had emboldened her only to circle around at a distance.[2] Now, too, she runs slowly away from the chicks with drooping wings and depressed tail (almost her courting antic): attracting my attention, against my will perhaps, because of her unusual action; or, when the chicks can swim, lies stretched out on the water with feebly beating wings.

But the oyster-catcher's simulation is not so complete as a ringed plover's or a partridge's, who trail a broken wing so convincingly. And in all these feintings, and those of lapwing, redshank, and a host of other ground nesters, I am continually reminded of the antics of courtship.

When the chicks hatch, the parent birds' attachment to the nesting site and its contents is at its strongest, after perhaps three weeks of almost unbroken attendance at the nest. As day succeeds day, the incessant labor of brooding and feeding the nestlings drains the parents' vitality, and with it their half parentally-instinctive, half physically-associative attach-

[2] Considering the birds that swoop to my head most often in this manner—terns, gulls, owls—it seems probable that, once again, I have one action drawing its inspirations from another quite different: the stooping for fish or vole in hunger replaced by the stooping at my head in jealous fear. And just as the emotion of fear reacts upon gull or gannet, causing them to disgorge, so the tern's or gull's emotion of jealous fear causes it to excrete in swooping.

ment to the chicks. The parental instinct may be exhausted for the season, or stimulated afresh, for later broods, by the male bird's new courtship. It is, I think, true to say that, when more than one brood is reared and the male's plumage is distinct from the female's, the latter does all the incubating and takes the major share in the care of the young in the nest, so that, freed from such arduous duties, the male black-bird or chaffinch retains a reserve of vitality with which to incite the female to a second laying by a fresh courtship. Such male birds are often to be seen feeding the fledged young, their mates already incubating second broods.

Thus it so happens that when the young are helpless, that complex emotion, part parental instinct, part physical asso-ciation, is at its most dominant: strong enough to eliminate, to greater or lesser degree, the normal emotion of self-preser-vation. When an old sheldrake and sometimes his duck as well come flying up from their brood of ducklings on the water at my approach, their first emotion is jealousy at my proximity to the young; often the duck, whose attachment to the young after long weeks of incubation is instinctively and naturally stronger than the drake's, stays with the young when the latter flies up. When he draws near to me the emo-tion of fear becomes dominant, and he turns away to seek safety for himself. It is probable that the sudden change of emotions affects his physical and nervous organism, as in courtship, so that the antics of his feeble water-threshing flight are involuntary, provoked by sudden fear: just as his antics of courtship are mechanical, provoked by sexual im-pulses. But in this involuntary gesture of simulation, the par-ent bird, being much larger than the young birds, tends to at-tract the attention of any natural enemy. Thus, following normal channels of evolution, this physical distress is intensi-fied and perhaps made unconsciously deliberate at the ap-pearance of any animal threatening the safety of the young. The so-called death-feigning instinct common to almost every type of animal seems to me analogous. Associated always with sudden shock or fear, there is no feigning of death; the animal at my feet or in my hand is temporarily "dead" and has no reactions to pain. So long as I remain in the vicinity this state of suspended activity continues, but, in many cases, so soon as I release my hold or walk away, the full vigor of life is recovered with such suddenness that the immediately previous "death" seems hardly credible. . . .

At some distance from the place of the young, the parent bird abandons this simulation when the perfect balance of its emotional organism is restored, as parental instincts become less dominant at increasing distance from the chicks, and flies back to the vicinity of the nest, mate, or young: its emotional lodestone at this season of the year. If the dog, say, follows it back, the same procedure is gone through again: for the bird's physical entity is organically and emotionally affected by the shuttle-movement of jealous and fearful reactions between dog, self, and chicks. As the chicks grow older, and as it happens, better able to fend for themselves, the parental instincts of the adults wane with the seasonal decline of sexual emotions, and two parent shelduck tend rather to fly up and away, leaving the ducklings to their own devices, than jealously out at me. And a pair of oyster-catchers, with a three-parts grown chick, are indifferent to my approach. That this simulated distress is a mechanical impulse provoked by a special combination of circumstances, working on their organic condition at a certain season of the year, I can infer to a certain degree from the behavior of shelduck. Almost as soon as the ducklings are hatched, they follow the parent birds to the water, and in a very short time, as I have related, the different broods of all ages and sizes are inextricably mixed. Despite the fact that one pair of shelduck may be in attendance on thirty or forty ducklings and another pair have but a single chick—and that perhaps not their own—their parental emotions are still aroused by my presence in that area where they have been accustomed to bring their brood, with the usual simulatory reactions.

IX

SEA SWALLOWS

Sea swallows! Blessed the shores that know the nesting tern and the consummate grace of his slow-beating, inconsequent flight! On a day in the latter half of April the first little tern of the year hawks over a creek. Hovering over the shallows, supremely buoyant, he draws his tiny body up in flight against a half-gale, quite leisurely, with long slender pinions arching above his back like the folded wings of a butterfly, and then drops perpendicularly and falls and dives into and under the water, with miniature crash, after his shrimp. A charming little bird, pearl-gray back and silver breast are strikingly set off by the unexpected white triangle on his black forehead and by his bright yellow legs and black-tipped bill. All the while he fishes he calls a ceaseless *whuit/ whuit,* which I hear alike from fresh-marsh dyke, salting creek, and shore lagoon.

At dawn on another morning a common tern flies high over the sand banks, with familiar harsh screaming. There is a fish in his bill which once he drops and stoops to catch again. Later in the day two are falling and playing at a great height, with occasional *squewt-squewt*. High up in strong sun they are exceedingly difficult to pick up. Their pale breasts are momentarily visible as flashes of silver, but when they fall headlong, turning their backs, they fade out like shooting stars, though I still hear their harsh cries.

It is a misty day in May before the giant Sandwich terns, in from their sea fishing, are gray phantoms in the harbor,[1] and I begin to number the common terns in hundreds. . . . A morning in mid-May, when the saltings are palely carpeted with tide-washed sea-pink, and a score of common terns are screaming in pursuing flight over the ternery—the stage is set!

After all, what is this perennial nesting of birds but a five-act play? The egg is the catastrophe of the five acts of a bird's life-drama. The swelling prologue of the courtship, the mating, and the building of a nest, culminate in the egg containing new life:[2] the outward and visible sign of the perpetuation of the species. Thenceforward, the drama resolves into its dénouement: the breaking of the imprisoning shells with their egg-teeth by the chicks in the fifth act, the brooding of the young birds, and the gradual cessation of nesting duties; to swell to lesser climaxes, perhaps, with the raising of second or third broods. But with the laying of its full quota of eggs the bird has fulfilled its natural destiny. Whether the young hatch off successfully or not is a matter of accident, dependent upon favorable weather, a plentiful food supply, and good fortune in evading predatory enemies. And before the purpose of courtship can attain consummation in the laying of an egg there must be, each year, a complete revolution of a bird's organism: even if the parents are last year's mates.

The first scene in this opening act of a bird's life is concerned with the seasonal growth of its generative organs, and, consequent upon this organic change, a reawakening of the

---

[1] They have been fishing out at sea in the vicinity since the end of March.

[2] But see footnote to courtship of redshank in previous chapter.

sexual impulse, and an ever-growing physically-associative awareness of the place where it has courted, mated, and nested in previous years. This is faithfully retained in its subconscious—and the stimulus of subconscious place-memory is one of the governing forces of a bird's actions. How can I question its power, when there is a wealth of evidence to show that the migrant returns in successive seasons many thousand miles to the same nesting territory? It may even make use of the nest of a previous year. The young bird, too, tends to return to the territory in which it was born. While this is occupied by its parents it is not able to nest there. But, as the old adults die off, those in direct line of succession take their place: so that a permanent nesting site tradition is established. Obvious enough of colony-nesters, such as rooks or gulls, or of swallows and house martins who build conspicuously, I have scores of instances in my notebooks showing this to be generally true of all British birds. Small birds do not live very long, and their nests do not endure; the undergrowth and hedgerows in which they nest are periodically cut down or cleared, so that it is often difficult to establish their perennial return to the same nesting territory. But all over the British Isles are place-names reminding me of immemorial nesting sites of long-lived and conspicuous birds, such as eagles, hawks, or ravens: hardly less enduring than badger "sets," old when the Romans came. Nor is this faithfulness to place any less true of winter feeding grounds or even of passage resting-places *en route*, of which I have hardly credible firsthand data—some of which I shall quote hereafter.

With the stage set, then, there are by mid-May more terns to be seen than at any previous date: several hundred in fact, including sixty pairs of Sandwich, a lovely tern, who comes near to being the loveliest British bird. If the black tern is supreme in flight, the Sandwich is in beauty. Rising in a swarm from nesting colony into blue skies, the dazzling virgin-white plumage of Sandwich terns, their silver wings sun-transparent, is crowned with the classically perfect harmony of rich black hoods and bills pale-yellow-tipped: a vision of hardly earthly loveliness—comparable, as a creation of beauty, to the black and silver lacing of a gray plover in the full glory of his breeding plumage, the scintillating turquoise and pale scarlet of a kingfisher speeding through a rainbow, or the fiery golden-red of godwit turning in the sun. . . .

More like black-headed gulls than terns in flight, there is yet that inconsequent, slow flickering of finely tapering wings peculiar to all terns. But they circle, plane, and hurtle downwards like gulls, with harsh querulous screams, shyer than other terns. A colony of Sandwich dip and hover over their eggs, seeming to alight, but only to brush the ground as gulls do tree-tops, and away up again, creating the wonderfully beautiful illusion of a host of restless spirits housed in perpetually volatile silver bodies. To complete this ethereal illusion there is a rosy flush at the breast of the sitting bird, whose black cap, extending far down the nape, is raised in a crest when she alights.

At mid-May, too, the first eggs are laid: two of common terns and seven of Sandwich, who here nest away from the other terns, three hundred yards out at the end of a spring tide-banked shingle ridge, on a little bluff of sand and marram tufts—seeming so few in numbers after the colonies of thousands I have seen elsewhere. And the first little terns are scratching their shingle-hollows in raised beaches on the saltings and below the spring tide mark on the shore. For centuries the fishermen have known the low tides at this season as the bird tides, for they are likely to fall high just before the terns begin to lay and after the chicks are well fledged—not, however, favoring the unfortunate ringed plover in this manner.

Towards the end of May, when there are twenty-six Sandwich nests out on the little nod, more than seven hundred of the common tern, and some seventy little, the ternery is a very pleasing picture. Observation at a large ternery is a curious experience. There is an inexpressible atmosphere of

Little tern male
offering a small fish
to his nesting mate

freedom, light, color, and space, and a sense of vivid life in
the perpetual unrest of three or four thousand silver hovering
birds. Sometimes the ternery becomes almost silent—all the
old males are fishing out at sea or standing about in groups,
preening, in sand deltas where there are no nests. And then,
for no obvious reason that I can locate, a spirit of unrest
spreads through the company, and all with one accord rise in
a silent cloud seawards, only to wheel back and alight beside
their nests again. But, normally, day and night, particularly

when the moon is bright, the ternery is babel: hen-birds "bickering" with harsh pleasure when male birds heave in sight with fish, uttering a continual, triumphant *squee-oo/ squee-oo;* other males quarreling in swift, slanting flight with quickly repeated *qua-qua-qua-qua-qua;* and others, again, hovering above their nests with uneasy and typical common tern call: a harsh, grating *squee-arr,* long drawn out.

Many of the eggs are beginning to set hard, and the terns sit very tight. If familiarity breed contempt of the beauty of the common tern, there are occasions that bring me to a proper appreciation of her splendor. To lie upon the shingle but seven feet from so volatile a bird as a nesting tern is a notable experience, reminding me again of that splendid heritage of beauty my forbears have sacrificed by destroying the confidence of wild creatures. After swift stoops to my head, with threatening *zitta-zitta-zitta-zarch,* and sharp blows with beak hard enough to make me desire no more, a common tern, brushing the pebbles once or twice with uncertain hover, alights into the wind with a swoop of incomparable grace, and after a moment's uneasiness shuffles onto her eggs. When the chicks first hatch she stoops even more fiercely.

Uneasily brooding, she maintains a ceaseless, "bickering," *ca-ca-ca-ca-ca* of protest, stressing this complaint at intervals with a grating *quee-aa:* her mandibles ceaselessly vibrating. At such close range I am suddenly aware of how vividly scarlet are her shanks, dainty webs, and slender black-tipped bill, and how brightly painted its scarlet interior. She is not a white bird, for her pearl-gray breast deepens to a sooty dove-gray on her belly, sootier still on her back, a deep gray-black on her wing shafts, and hawking over the sea she seems in certain lights as dusky as a black tern. Her black eye is just within the black hood margining the white cheeks. My abiding impression is of the unique volatility and vivacity of the bird.

On the wing there is little physical distinction between common and Arctic terns, though the tail-streamers of the latter are considerably longer. At rest his breast is very dusky, and his black cap is thicker and shaggier and extends farther down his nape. The new-painted scarlet beaks vary from one Arctic to another, from coral to dark-red and even puce; and many have black tips. But in the various cries there is no resemblance at all: those of the Arctic all being pitched in a much higher key, including the scolding *kreech* which is softer than the common tern's and less excruciatingly jarring. *Duk-duk*, he calls, and *pee-wee*, not at all unlike a green plover, and a thin, squeaky trilling peculiar to his kind alone. The young Arctics chitter, with wide-open beaks, a note so piercingly monotonous that, after a long bout of it, I find that the screeching hurts my ears, as does the demonic chugging of a nightingale a few feet from me; and on the wing they pipe like sandpipers.

At an Arctic ternery alone have I seen in early summer one or two immature second-year birds with white heads and colorless beaks. If then terns, like gulls, do not breed until their third year, what happens normally to these second-year birds during the summer, so few at an Arctic ternery and absent from other terneries? Nor have I chanced upon them at sea.

With a colony of several hundred or thousand terns all courting and nesting at different dates, I see more courtship in June, when the banks are bright yellow with tall ragwort and its legions of black and golden cinnabars, than at any other season. A pair of common terns, screaming and playing in wild, exuberant flight over the ternery, stoop to alight on low sand dunes. . . . The female postures, the male circles about her: but all to no purpose. How many scores of times have I noted down how seldom it is that both male and female are in the mood to perform what Chaucer describes, with unwonted delicacy, as a "Spring observance" at the same moment! The male treads around and around, like a cat on hot bricks; the female, with characteristic sexual coldness, unwilling to humor him. For every occasion that the mating is consummated, there are a hundred unsuccessful attempts by the male. In most birds the mating is the fulfillment of the tremendous stimulus of prolonged courtship, for, clearly, if coition is effected when the male first begins to display, the too-early young must often perish for lack of a nest yet unconstructed. Thus the female is physically unable to respond to the male's early invitation to mate. Moreover, I learn from Mr. Eliot Howard that "sexual posturing in birds has a definite physiological significance in that it exercises a stimulating influence upon the anterior lobe of the pituitary body, thereby causing it to secrete in greater quantity and so bring about those ovarian processes which result in egg-laying." [3] But once the building of a nest has begun, and even after eggs have been laid, all is changed, and it is the female who plagues the male for satisfaction, until he exhibits every trace of unwillingness to humor her. And none more notorious in this respect than terns and shags.

At some later date the male common tern circles again about his mate, with head stretched high, wings half open, pushed out and forward at the shoulders, and tail spiked in the air, while she bows forward on the ground in similar attitude, all set for the mating. Some such coitional pattern of courtship is common to every British bird, modified according to the primitive or complex nature of the display of a particular species, or adapted to suit the nature of its habitat— eider ducks, for instance, courting on the sea. The male is repeating to the female the generic mating actions: significant both to him and to her, either of previous matings or, in the case of young birds, of the mating formula they inherit. Courtship is the logically-evolved invitation to coition: its actions born of primitive matings, and sometimes elaborated

[3] Mr. Howard's actual text in *The Nature of a Bird's World* reads: "In view of these facts (researches on rabbits by C. W. Bellerby), Marshall (F.H.A., *Physiology of Reproduction*) says, there is a strong presumption that . . ."—In this case there really does seem to be good proof of the pudding in the eating.

from their original crudity by natural selection, operating through successive generations.

After an interval of desire and coyness, my terns mate . . . another interval . . . then, side by side, both, of a sudden, bow forward on their breasts, pivoting violently with drooping wings and "spiked" tails. They scratch backwards in the sand, in an ecstasy of passion. When they rise, calm once more, there are two hollows in the white sand. One later day, the female comes again to the mating site and pivots, rounding a sand cup with bowed breast. Another day, and in this cup she lays her first egg on the bare ground. Thus the mating spot develops through the medium of blindly instinctive, coitional gestures of pure courtship, into a simple nest, in which, as it happens, the eggs are more effectively brooded and less conspicuous than if deposited upon a flat surface.

The roseate tern has not progressed beyond the stage of laying her egg on a flat, bare surface—even when on sand in marram—though during the incubation any grasses about the nest are likely to be rounded into a rude shell by the performance of her settling onto the egg. But common terns, you will say, almost invariably fashion some kind of lining to their nest hollows. True, but not until an egg has been laid. What follows then suggests to me the next evolutionary step in nidificatory architecture. When she moves off her egg the female common tern, or the male if he has been relieving her for a short space, picks delicately with her bill at any small bents that may be lying about her nest hollow and jerks them backwards either side of her. She may continue to do this until three or four feet away from the nest, but some, at any rate, fall about the egg: to be fashioned into a rough lining by her pivoting breast at each successive brooding. By the time the young hatch, a quantity of stray grasses, pebbles, or shells have been rounded into a fair-sized nest. If she nest on the beach, shells take the place of grasses. If she nest on rock there may be no lining, though she may still persist with the jerking throw back; for not always does she pick up material in her instinctive action. Nesting on the sand, away from marram grass or shells, her cup remains unlined. She will not go to a distance to fetch lining material deliberately.

But there are exceptions to this as to every other law of Nature. Among two thousand nests of common terns I find two on the shingle-beach with rims of cockle shells fashioned about them. Amid her splintered, violet mussel shells an oyster-catcher drops a tiny, shining crystal pebble. In my mind is a gay picture of her probing carmine mandibles delicately seizing in triumph this bright, unusual pebble. These, and many more exotic instances of birds placing peacock feathers, bright wools, or bus tickets in the structure of their nests, seem to me analogous to the sparrow snipping off the petals of crocuses, the magpie taking silver spoons, or the hawk singling out the brightly plumaged small bird for his prey. The quick vision of a bird is always attracted to singular objects; some birds of a species will tend to react more than others of their kind to such stimuli. If placing rings of cockle shells about their breast-hollows proved especially advantageous to the species, no doubt natural selection would operate to ensure that, in time, such a habit became a part of the nest-building of all common terns. . . .

There is much courtship during the weeks when the female is actually brooding eggs or young. Most cock-birds feed their sitting mates and share in the feeding of the nestlings. They take the opportunity to do a little courting at the same time. A perennial feature of the courtship of Montagu's harrier is the passing of prey in mid-air by the tercel to the falcon, who stoops to retrieve it in her talons before it drops to the ground. When she is sitting on her eggs, dependent upon her mate for her food, she leaves the nest at his piercing cries, and receives the offering from him in the manner of the ritual of their earlier courtship. The male common tern dips buoyantly in from sea screaming triumphantly, a silver whitebait drooping from his scarlet bill. His mate, brooding three multi-colored eggs in the marram grass, cocks black eye aloft at

his cry, and "bickers" harshly. When he alights, she runs a little way from the nest to him and takes a hold of an end of
the fish he proffers. For some seconds they tug at either end
with many discordant ejaculations of pleasure and antics of
courtship before he finally releases it to her.

At mid-June, after several of the earlier clutches have been
deserted—a yearly inevitability—and the first chicks hatch
and mostly die, the terns begin to moult: the black abrading
from the nape and forehead of the common tern, and a triangular white patch, reminding me of the little tern, appearing
on the black brow of the Sandwich. The toll of nests mounts
swiftly to more than thirteen hundred common tern, ninety-
seven Sandwich who by this time are colonizing a new area
at the far end of the shingle-spit, and one hundred and
twenty little.

Terns make little fuss about getting onto their eggs, and sit
head to wind with perfect grace. They brood in a strikingly
upright position, with heads well up, smart and alert: sickle
wings, upwards curving, crossing swallowlike over their
backs, "sliced" black hoods giving them a very *chic* appearance. Old males beating slowly in with fish for their sitting
mates stand beside them for some minutes, surveying the ani-
mated scene curiously, or chase back their mates to their eggs
with sly pecks at tail-shafts—at least, that is what it looks
like to me. When chicks are hatched, babel increases, for they
leave the nest after the few hours necessary for the drying off,
and the parent birds have difficulty in locating the precise
chick they wish to feed, and still more difficulty in transfer-
ring fish to chick: other terns swooping in to seize the prize,
especially when whitebait are scarce and they are hungry. I
have seen an old bird hovering at intervals for three hours
over her squeaking chicks, unable to deliver her catch safely.
Clearly, colonial nesting has disadvantages. From the beginning the chicks have to survive a rough time, and those wandering to nests other than their own are severely pecked,
even killed. A pecked chick at once lies doggo, coming to life

again after thirty seconds or so, when the vicious adults are less heedful of its presence. When whitebait are scarce the infant mortality is as high as eighty per cent, for when the chicks hatch, the adults normally abandon their fishing for sand eels in favor of the smaller whitebait. It is a common sight to see a chick with a sand eel hanging half out of its bill for minutes at a time in a vain attempt at swallowing. Many chicks, weakened by an indigestible diet of sand eels, are overlayed by the old birds settling down too hard when there are eggs as well as young in the nest, and many more, panting with the heat, are suffocated by sand storms, which also bury a proportion of the eggs. But in a good year some seventy per cent of the young birds leave on their autumn migration. . . .

Little bands of Sandwich chicks, which have wandered down the shingle ridge from their own nesting bluff, are followed by various parent birds answering their ceaseless "bicker-hiss" with anxious *pewt-pewt/pewt-pewt-pewt*. With white quills just showing, the chicks remind me of young hoatzins. Sandwich males, beating in from deeper waters, for they fish farther out to sea than other terns, fly high over the main ternery, with harsh *putch-putch* calls, announcing that they bring fish; while the shoals are a-boil with common terns diving in hundreds for whitebait, and a continual stream of fishers dips to and fro the ternery.

Common terns lay three, sometimes four, eggs; Arctic, three or two; roseate, one; [4] little terns, two or three; and Sandwich, two or one. Very rarely have I seen dead chicks of the two latter species, who leave the vicinity of the nest sooner

[4] In Ireland, where there are big colonies of roseate terns, two eggs is, I believe, a normal clutch—taken in conjunction with Dr. Fraser Darling's theory that the ability to lay eggs depends upon the getting together of a sufficient number of breeding pairs, the single-egg clutches of these scattered East Coast roseates are not without significance. The immediate presence of thousands of common terns stimulates the roseate to one egg, but it takes hundreds or thousands of its own kind . . . to produce two eggs—?

than common terns, swim more strongly, and run faster. It is as if the larger clutch of a common tern weakens the resistance of the chicks, for I have yet to see three chicks of one nest alive after the lapse of a few days; but they remain much the commonest species. The vigor of little tern chicks, who hatch no bigger than a crownpiece, is astonishing. Though the puncture in the shell of the white egg-tooth, which is retained for a day or two, be hardly noticeable, the chick may be out in five minutes—the female removing the shell to a distance while the male watches with interest—and active when it has dried in a few hours, staggering out to meet the male bird coming in with a shrimp, often much too large for it to swallow.

It is unbelievably difficult to pick up sitting little terns on a shingle-beach. Even if I know the exact whereabouts of every nest, I can guarantee that, watching a few yards distant, I shall not be able to distinguish the full complement of nesters. With scolding *whitta-whitta-whitta whit,* male or female little tern is constantly hovering, like a hummingbird, over the pebble-nest; but once at rest upon the yellow shingle and the bird has vanished. Would that I could recapture their nesting image, for there is not, I think, any more beautiful little bird to be seen at a nest. *Chic* epitomizes the smart appearance of the sitting little tern: white pyramid blazoned on the brow of erect black head, forked tail crossed high to the heavens.

At mid-July the sand dunes are beautiful with the wonderfully pale green of sea holly, whose mauve cornflowers are lost in the green leaves delicately veined and barbed in mauve, so that the banks are sunlit with an indeterminate violet mist. At this season the first three-quarter-grown terns are laboring in flight on rounded, brown-blotched wings, their wing-beats swift and feeble. There are still a few pairs courting—the Arctic continue to do so into August—though already many are packing on the hot sands in preparation for migration, like martins on the warm roof of a church, and more than five hundred Sandwich terns have collected here from other colonies. I note the signs of the season when at this time Sandwich terns begin to dive in creeks where before the sea has been their fishing ground. A fine sight it is to see a Sandwich tern drawing himself up into the wind with the loveliest motion, to dive, almost with the velocity of a gannet, with an angular, corkscrew plunge. The young Sandwich take good care not to submerge in their dives.

At the beginning of August, when the marshes are very lovely with the purple of the giant sea lavender, there are still chicks of all three species hatching, although some young and old Sandwich terns are beginning to migrate. It is significant that they migrate *inland*, screaming over the village and several miles of hinterland at sunrise and sunset, for due south from this particular nesting island lies inland. Half the tern population has gone by the middle of the month, though there are still common terns unable to fly. At the end of August, when the purple lavender gives way to the yellow-centered blue aster, there are little packs of common terns, twenty-five or so in a bundle, scattered all along the shore. And day and night Sandwich terns scream over the island and village. . . . Their phantom bodies are lost to me in a dense sea-mist that wraps us about in heavy silence for days at a time, but at all hours I hear their strong calls: *krooeech/ krooeech:* eerie in the mists, when they stoop through the clouds in their screaming pursuit.[5] When I go out with the fishing fleet in September I still see them at sea, and in October and even in November, but after that, while I shiver for six months on northern saltings with the wild geese, their tenuous silver bodies, coral and black and yellow, are renewing the fire of life in the warm blue seas of the Tropics.

[5] Spring, summer, or autumn, fog *invariably* brings the terns inland to harbor, flats, and islands, from their pelagic fishing grounds, screaming all day and night—which suggests very strongly that they are unable to see the shoals of fish at such times, although it is affirmed that the bird's eye is as penetrative as the infrared camera.

X

MÉSALLIANCE

The nesting habits of the various species of terns about our shores are unusually irregular. Their patronage of different colonies appears to vary from year to year according to weather conditions and the movements of the whitebait and sand eels. Generally speaking, Arctic and roseate terns are not English-nesting species; but every year odd pairs and birds of both species appear at southern nesting colonies of other terns. Do the accidents of migration prove too hazardous for some young birds? For in the first place, no doubt, this isolated nesting of, say, roseate terns on English coasts came about when a pair were caught up in the migratory company of common terns, to return north with them. Although it is difficult to produce infallible data, I have little doubt but that migrating pelagic species are paired up long before they arrive at their breeding territories. How often have I not seen divers and grebes and other seafowl courting in bays and estuaries hundreds of miles south of their nesting grounds!

However that may be, on May 27, when there are two

hundred pairs of common terns nesting in the marram on the sand dunes and a thousand others, not yet nesting, creating babel, I hear distinctly, though I do not see her, the drawn out *caa* of a female roseate tern. My interest is quickened by the acquaintanceship of a previous year. The roseate tern is sometimes described as a small Sandwich, for she is much whiter and slenderer than a common tern, and her head and bill are black. But her tail is long shafted, two or three inches longer than the common tern's, and her legs are a bright coral-red. With respect to the color of her beak, all bird artists depict a red base, whereas the mandibles of the roseates I have watched have been black from tip to base, although, like the Sandwich tern, the white of the cheeks runs far into the base of the bill in white slots. The delusion of a scarlet base arises no doubt from the brilliant scarlet of the gape, which, as in the case of the kittiwake, may overlap the outer bill in certain specimens in the breeding season.

On June 6, when I am, as usual, lying behind a sand bank among some three thousand common terns, of whom one thousand are incubating, I am suddenly aware that a roseate female sits on that ridge of sand where she sat the previous year, when a solitary Arctic nested just beneath her. Like all terns, she sits smartly upright; when she turns towards me, I can see the rosy flush of the sunlit down at her lower breast. She lays her egg on the bare sand of the previous year's exact site. Its color and markings are the same as before; a uniform gray speckled with varnished brown: brighter, slenderer, and more pointed than those of a common tern. As yet there is no sign of her mate, but no doubt he is fishing out at sea.

She is already *in situ* when I arrive on the 9th. How lovely is the contrast of black bill and hood with sun-silvered plumage! Suddenly a common tern alights by her side. This, in itself, is not unduly disturbing, for she nests cheek by jowl, as it were, with several hundred common terns. But, without any preliminary blandishments, my roseate sidles off her egg after a minute or two for the common stranger to take her place leisurely, but gladly, as if by prescribed right. After the customary pretense or actual pecking of grasses and throwing them to either side of her, backwards towards her egg— which may now be termed to lie in a nest, for her constant incubating has rounded stray grasses in her breast-hollow in the sand—she hies her straight out to sea to feed. This common stranger sits for twenty-five minutes, with much turning and settling comfortably on the egg. He casts a quick eye aloft from time to time, as is the way of nesting terns, when a company of screaming males, chasing one of their number with a whitebait, swoops close above him. At the end of this time the roseate, unheralded, alights on bright coral webs beside him and stands looking at him, as if hoping that it will not be necessary for her to make a broad hint that she is anxious to resume her incubating. However, he goes off leisurely, as if not quite certain of the orthodox procedure in such matters, and after standing about for a little while, with an air of being left out in the cold, flies off.

This has all been very strange: no male roseate yet having appeared. But there is at present no case of immoral proceedings made out, for I remember that on June 8 the previous year when this same roseate, then safely mated, deserted, a common tern, who had had her own eggs taken from an adjacent nest, obligingly incubated for her until she returned to her trust the following day. In their favor, too, was the fact that I had seen no evidence of courtship or affection. A brooding common tern always welcomes her incoming mate with noisy chittering, long before I can pick him out from the throng above, and there is usually some byplay of tugging at either end of the newly-brought fish, some caressing of bills or titillating of the neck-feathers—which, in serious mood, I interpret as fundamental incitements to revive any flagging ardor there may be in the business of incubating. But the most noticeable feature of this unusual exchange of duties has been the apparent indifference of one bird to the other, particularly on the part of the roseate.

At two o'clock on the morning of the 11th there is a wonderful moon, and I lie all night among the terns, soaked by a drenching dew. All night long they play over the ternery with devilish crying and harsh screaming, seeming in the silence of the night to be noisier even than in the day; and from their far nod the Sandwich continually rise in a swarm, with a beelike screeching hum. What vital flame burns in these tenuous bodies that they may fly and fish, incubate and court, and never rest? Conserving energy under African suns through the winter, they are yet constantly on the wing.

The night is without incident, and in the gray dawn at a quarter to four o'clock the roseate is sitting on her ledge. There is a curious quality in the air at dawn on the saltings. I hear strange sounds that I do not hear at other times: dull, hollow thuds of ringed plover and oyster-catchers breaking into flight, and queer "popping" cries of ringed plover, inaudible later in the day.

The next day, when the first common terns hatch, another roseate arrives. She, too, seems to be without a mate. And on the 15th this bird lays an egg some forty yards distant from her compatriot: a brown-varnished egg, thickly speckled with darker brown upon violet. Three days later her egg is trodden upon by some visitor to the ternery; but she will lay again, for her incubation has not gone nine days.

It is fine the next day, though half a gale blows from the southeast. My roseate is absent for more than two hours, the common tern sitting for an hour. While she is away a male roseate dashes in from sea several times, but he circles buoyantly above the nesting site of the other roseate, with ringing *chu-vee chu-vee:* the peculiar tern "grating" bestowing a pleasantly melodious emphasis upon the clear cry. Twice he utters the whirring *ca-aa* of my female, but she never appears while I am at the ternery from half-past nine o'clock to four o'clock in the afternoon—surely these are strange birds! He passes his time poaching whitebait from male common terns.

By now it seems probable that the common tern is the mate

of my roseate. In two species so distinct in plumage, call, and nesting habits—for the roseates that I have watched lay but a single egg—this is an extraordinary phenomenon. But it is still possible that she has mated truly before her arrival at the ternery and that the common tern is a foster brooder. I must wait for the hatching of the chick.

In the days that follow it is the usual practice of the roseate to go out to sea from approximately half-past nine o'clock until half-past twelve o'clock every morning and sit for most of the rest of the day and night. The common is usually on for an hour or so during her absence, but I never see him bring her fish while she is sitting, in direct contradiction to all my observations of terns. What strange bond unites these two? Can it be that after all this common tern is a female? On June 23 the roseate goes out to sea at half-past eleven o'clock; her aide comes in shortly afterwards, and sits until three o'clock in the afternoon when she returns. Again there is not a suspicion of courtship or of affection between the two. This is the common tern's longest bout to date. The egg must be getting hard set.

Every day tercel or falcon merlin or golden-dusted, short-eared owl languid in slow-quartering flight, take a sitting tern, but providence preserves this strange pair; preserves, too, the egg from heedless feet, from voles, rats, and stoats; a pair of carrion crows enjoy a brief but profitable harvest. But on the 24th the egg is still *in situ* and warm, and in the morning the male roseate comes in with my female. Is this something more than the natural affinity of two of a kind among so many aliens? His own mate has not yet laid a second egg.

Turning in the sun, the bright rose on the snowy belly of the male is beautiful to see, his tail-streamers inordinately long. Today, for the first time, I hear my roseate utter a fainter likeness of his ringing *chu-vee/chu-vee*, and today, when frightened from the egg, she rises with a querulous *peep*. It is the nineteenth day of incubation: life must be stirring within the shell. She is on most of the morning, and

The short-eared owl

the common tern for a little while. Merlins and owl still work
havoc in the early morning among the sitting terns. I find a
headless body here, a head without a body there; and little
black beetles strive to bury the shells of sucked eggs. How
small are the chances of a successful hatching!

Another week goes by of rainstorms and unseasonable
weather. Many eggs are deserted, and the mortality among
chicks is very great. The roseate is surrounded by some sixteen hundred nests of common terns, many of whose chicks
will be essaying their first flights in a day or two. She has
been sitting all day lately: the common tern hardly in evi-

dence. On June 30 her egg is chipped: on the twenty-fifth day of incubation. Thunderstorms and torrential rains intervene, and I forbear to examine the chick until July 3, for it wanders from the nest into the surrounding marram. On this day, too, the other roseate lays again, one hundred yards away from her first site; but this discovery is nothing compared to that of finding that my roseate's chick has the plumage of a nestling common tern, rather lighter in color than the normal, but the call of a roseate nestling! In such diversely marked birds, patterning alone might not be convincing, but (fortunately) whereas the chick of a common tern has a soft down lying smoothly to the body, that of a roseate stands up in a multitude of pointed tufts, in the manner of a Sandwich chick.

On the 17th, when a third pair of roseates pass along the coast, the chick is still safe on the sand banks, but straying amid the thick marram it is hard to find, and I see it no more. In its first flight plumage it will in any case be difficult or impossible to differentiate between it and its fellow common terns. It is enough.

On July 13 I find a common tern sitting on the second roseate's egg, but on the 26th, the twenty-fourth day of incubation, this chick hatches, and proves to be a normal roseate. It is clear that a common tern, bereft of her eggs, will sit on a neighbor's egg: an event obvious only when her neighbor happens to be of a different species to herself. There is nothing unusual in this, for individuals of almost any species of bird will sit on eggs or brood young of another species, under certain conditions; but that a roseate tern should mate with a common tern is analogous to a great titmouse mating with a blue titmouse, or a stockdove with a ringdove. The closest analogy is to be found in those occasional instances of wild mallard mating with pintail or widgeon. But, logically or not, this mating of two distinct species of tern seems to me much more extraordinary.

The mate of this roseate must have met with some accident in the winter. During her migration north her organism is undergoing fundamental changes demanding that she mate and lay eggs. Isolated among thousands of alien terns, and no male of her own kind arriving when she is ripe for ovulation, she mates with a young common male returning to his birthplace and as yet unmated, and brings him to *her* nesting territory. If their chick survives it may prove a mute, but it seems more likely that, following the usual law of Mendelian inheritance of closely related species, it will be fertile: its young reverting back to full roseate or full common—for in this way Nature obviates the possibility of a continual succession of new species.

For four years, if she be the same bird, this female nested with a roseate male; in the fifth she took a common tern— what next?

XI

THE SIGNIFICANCE OF COLOR

The diverse coloring of birds' eggs is usually attributed to "protective" influences. Observing the exceedingly efficient camouflage of the eggs, and particularly the young, of ground-nesting birds, especially terns and waders who leave the nest a few hours after hatching, it is clear that selective forces have been operating on eggs and young devoid of the protection of an efficient nest. Little terns, who lay their eggs in almost negligible breast-hollows on the tiny shingle splinters of raised beaches covered only at spring tides, are consummate protectionists. It is possible for me to stare fixedly down at their fawn or pale olive-yellow eggs, water-washed in mauve and brown, not quite twice the size of a blackbird's, and still not see them. More remarkable are the gray-fawn chicks stippled with black, who, leaving their hollow almost as soon as their down has dried from the egg, are hardly to be seen against the shingle-sand, even when running, which they do very nimbly.

Such protective devices are essential to species whose only defense against the wonderful eyes of gulls and crows is the

perfect camouflage of their plumage. And if in some colonies
the eggs of common or Sandwich terns seem conspicuous to
my practiced eye against the plain fawn of the sand among
the marram, it is apparent that where they lay on shingle,
their true nesting ground, they are hardly more obvious than
the tiny eggs of the little tern. Against this theory of protective coloration must, however, be set the fact that from pale-
shelled Sandwich eggs hatch silver chicks, and from dark-
shelled, black chicks: both variations lightly striped, which
phenomenon suggest that there may be some chemical synchronism between egg marking and the chick's down. In this
respect I note, too, that enforced second clutches of eggs, particularly of waders, are usually paler in color and often of a
different patterning to the first clutch. Where green plover
are still mercilessly harried, it is no uncommon thing to find
pale-blue eggs with almost colorless scrawls: both in clutches
of normal eggs and dropped on the ground. I am acquainted
with a ringed plover whose first clutch has been washed out
by a high tide in successive years. Both years the coloring of
the second clutch has differed from that of the first; and in
both years, remarkable to relate, this second clutch has differed identically: four ashy-white, mauve-and-black speckled
eggs being replaced by two of the same, a third of brown,
and a fourth of gray! Thus the extraordinary position arises of
a normally one-clutch bird preserving the sequence of a
changing color rhythm under abnormal conditions in successive years!

It is interesting to find that in a wet season the infant mortality of common terns is very much less on the exposed, but
well-drained, shingle-beaches than on the damp sand among
the rotting marram. Very seldom do I pick up the gray chick
of the Sandwich tern, with its white and black stippling,
against its shingle background: to which it wanders from the
sand and marram as soon as, or a few hours after, it has
dried. And again, if the fluffy white breast of the yellow-
legged common chick is comparatively obvious to me, a crow

quartering fifty feet above will have no easy task picking out
the tawny-olive back with its black stripes.

The eggs of all terns, and indeed of most sea birds and
waders, display a remarkable diversity of coloring. The very
lovely eggs of Sandwich terns, as large and slender as pul-
lets', are shaded with mauve and black blotchings on back-
grounds of white or fawn; sometimes a rich brown egg is
stained with a darker brown, and oil-washed with overlapping moons of mauve and black. The eggs of common terns
are even more varied in their coloring: ranging from chocolate or rich red-brown, gray or olive-fawn, through every
shade of green to blue, the majority heavily scrawled and
blotched with brown and black. Nor is the variegation restricted to different birds. One common tern that I watched
had two slightly different dark-olive eggs and a third a pale
blue, unblemished but for a single black blotching and a few
faint stipplings. It is, I think, true to say that it is not possible
to find a clutch of common tern's eggs uniform in color and
marking.[1] If most of the beautiful pear-drop eggs of the little
ringed plover are ashy-white, with that same lavender-mauve
underlying the black speckling, I have known clutches an exquisite dusted red, others as boldly brown-blotched as a redshank's, and others again light brown, with dark brown stippling; and if the huge eggs of oyster-catchers are usually
olive-dun, some are a rich olive-brown, chocolate-stained.

This irregular patterning of the eggs of waders and sea
birds can, I think, be attributed to the natural influence of evolutionary forces on the plain color of eggs laid on the broken
background of shingle-beaches, for it is the variegated marking of the shells that makes it so difficult to pick up the eggs
from their background. Since the color pattern of chameleons,
lizards, and fishes reacts spontaneously to that of their immediate environment, it seems not unreasonable to conclude
that the color pattern of the eggs of birds has reacted, in the

[1] Since writing this, a photograph has appeared in the *Field* of a
clutch of three pure pale-blue eggs of a common tern.

course of millenniums, to that of the ground upon which they are laid. In either case protective purposes are well served. Another evolutionary factor contributing to this irregular patterning may well be the habit of sea and aquatic birds of soiling and staining their eggs, which, as it happens, tends to break up their background, rendering them less conspicuous.

But when I turn to a consideration of the eggs of arboreal-nesting species, a theory of protective coloration has certain objections to surmount. It is reasonable to conjecture that plain white was the original hue of birds' eggs, and that the diverse colorings and multifarious blotchings and stipplings have been evolved by natural selection, to the end of blending eggs with background for purposes of concealment, as surely as the size of a bird's egg depends not only upon the size of the bird that lays it but upon the condition of the nestling that hatches from it: wherefore the eggs of oyster-catcher and tern are huge out of all proportion to the size of the parent bird, because the young hatch in full down, ready to leave the nest, which offers them no concealment, directly they have dried. So that when such birds as sand martins, kingfishers, and woodpeckers, nesting in deep holes, lay the generic white egg—a protective color pattern being superfluous—all is well with the "protective" theory. But then I find that the ringdove, nesting in dark coverts, lays white eggs in open nests so frail that they are visible, not only from above, but from below through the openwork structure of twigs, whereas colored eggs would be inconspicuous in the dim light of the woods.

Am I to assume that, at an earlier epoch a nester in caves and holes like his relatives, rockdoves and stockdoves, the ringdove has not yet reached that stage of nidificatory evolution at which his eggs react to the influence of their background? But then the ringdove is very plainly a species in no need of protection at the present era. His two white eggs must surely be among the most obvious of any to such thieves as jays, magpies, crows, jackdaws, and squirrels, commonly frequenting his nesting haunts. It is difficult to understand how any eggs or squabs escape the sharp eyes of so many filchers—yet he multiplies exceedingly. His success must be attributed to his adaptability. The female lays in many months of the year, and rears two or three broods: though even three are only the equivalent of a single full blackbird's clutch, or half that of a long-tailed titmouse's. But, a hardy bird, in a severe winter when perhaps only one blackbird of the year survives and no long-tailed titmice, a majority of the squabs may win through, battening on acorns and beechmast: to breed, themselves, the next spring.

I have previously referred to the color synchronism between shell and chick of the Sandwich tern. This is a matter to which I have not as yet been able to devote any study; but, remembering the white eggs and downs of such as owls and pigeons, it may be worthy of more detailed examination.

There then arises in my mind the question of why dunnocks nesting in open nests and redstarts in concealing holes both lay bright blue eggs, for against the dark background of her nest the April-blue of a dunnock's eggs renders them particularly obvious. Clearly, protective coloration, as instanced in the eggs and young of modern ground-nesting birds, must have been more general and more essential to the well-being of the species in past ages when nests were rudimentary or nonexistent. Thus, like so many obscure surviving habits, what was once protective coloring has outlived its original purposes. Nor do I forget that a color conspicuous to my eyes is not necessarily so to the mammalian and avian egg thieves responsible for protective measures. Blue is, in any case, a natural color for a bird's egg, because of the chalky texture of the shell, and often washes through a white, as in the instance of a starling's egg. Though the bright eggs of the dunnock are obvious in their open nest, it has to be remembered that normally the latter is well hidden in bush or hedge. Indeed, I might be extreme and argue that the conspicuous color of the eggs ensures that in a backward spring, when concealing foliage is sparse and food for the nestlings insufficient, the first clutch of eggs is more likely to be despoiled: resulting in later clutches when foliage is denser and food more plentiful. But this is perhaps far-fetched and reversing the normal processes of evolution: for a continued failure of first clutches would tend to result in a later nesting date or less conspicuous eggs.

Curlew with eggs nesting upon
the moor in a hollow lined with grass

In estimating the part played by "protective" measures in the lives of birds it is true to say that in temperate zones, where natural colors tend to be comparatively dull, birds with tropically-bright plumages—kingfishers, green woodpeckers, redstarts—nest in holes, concealing their obvious colors, and have white eggs (the pale blue of the redstart's egg may be ascribed, like the starling's, to the texture of the shell), because there have been no external color or protective influences at work upon their patterning. Thus, according to the usual inter-reactions of natural selection, bright plumages are efficiently offset, where such obvious hues are likely to be inimical to the rearing of young and the perpetuation of the species.

Although a bird's way with its eggs and young is supremely interesting, there are often drawbacks associated with its study. One argument against the taking of eggs, perhaps the most important, appears to be overlooked by both bird protectionists and oölogists. Regrettably, it also applies, in a manner, to bird-photographers and bird-watchers. Man, it is too true, is often a menace to the well-being of birds, but their natural enemies are predatory beasts and birds. No matter how careful the ornithologist who habitually examines birds' nests *in situ,* he leaves traces of his handiwork, obvious to these enemies. A broken twig, a bent nettle, disturbed grasses, invisible or without significance to my eye, all arouse the curiosity of sharp-eyed jay or crow, with inevitable results. The honest naturalist admits that the nest he has examined has, more often than not, been quickly despoiled by natural enemies. The certain knowledge that misfortune is likely to overtake closely-watched nests either deters me from such practices or detracts from the pleasure of any interesting discovery made by such observation. I am content to judge the course of events from the actions of the parent birds and the calls of the young. But from such open-nesting, colonial birds as terns or gulls or divers I can garner a full and satisfying harvest of valuable notes, with easy conscience.

XII

ORIGINS OF MIGRATION

Reading of the autumn and spring comings and goings of ducks and geese, and waders and terns, there may be some readers who are asking themselves what is all this to-do about birds flying north in the spring and south in the autumn, and who are not conversant with the generally accepted theory of migration. It is an intensely fascinating study, but it is also the least tangible of all avian phenomena. I can watch almost every detail of a bird's courtship for weeks on end, but I cannot take flight with knots, even with the aid of an airplane. Because the migratory movements of birds cover the world and their flights are so vast, because my ignorance of their origin and practice is so complete and the biennial precision of these movements of incalculable millions in both hemispheres is so exact, I am more intrigued by them than by any other aspect of avian existence. Perhaps, too, my interest is quickened by the soft, clear calls of unseen flyers in the night sky; stirring my blood in the small hours by their mysterious freedom . . . whence? . . . whither?

There is one fundamental applicable to all mature birds. In

spring and summer their lodestone is the nesting territory: in autumn and winter the feeding territory. From April to October I am aware that there are swallows, cuckoos, nightingales, and many other species in this country, which are not here in the winter. At that season they are to be found in southern Europe, Africa especially, and perhaps India: so I am told. The solution is obvious. They are species too delicate to live through a northern winter and must therefore retreat south, to return to their nesting places in the spring. Alas, while climatic influences are present, they are far from being the sole arbiters of migration, for:

1. A percentage of the members of those species that I am accustomed to regard as residents in this country throughout the year emigrates south in the autumn, and also immigrates from countries farther north: *e.g.*, blackbirds, robins, chaffinches.

2. Many species, as well-suited to wintering in the British Isles as close relatives who do so successfully, go south as a species: *e.g.*, ring ousels (blackbirds), tree pipits (meadow pipits), whinchats (stonechats).

3. Certain species of birds wintering in the British Isles survive with difficulty: *e.g.*, long-tailed titmice and Dartford warblers. The eleven other British-breeding warblers go south in winter, though an occasional odd bird winters in Devon or Cornwall.

4. In certain species birds from the same nest are both resident and migratory: *e.g.*, blackbirds, green plover, pied wagtails.

5. Certain species come to winter in the British Isles from northern countries, for whom English winter still proves too severe: *e.g.*, redwings.

6. Immigrating species arrive in this country in spring when the weather is still unsuitable for them, or linger too long in autumn, in either case to perish: *e.g.*, chiff-chaffs.

7. Certain migratory species leave the British Isles immediately after the nesting, while their special food is still plentiful: *e.g.*, cuckoos and swifts.

8. There are some east-to-west lines of migration and local climatic movements, but the vast majority are markedly north

and south—although in any attempt to explain the mechanics of a bird's power of orientation, I have to remember the
proved ability of such species as terns and shearwaters to return
to their nesting territories, over terrain uninhabited by their
kind, from any point of the compass, from any distance: a power
possessed, no doubt, by every species of bird.

9. There is a marked restlessness in migratory species at the
appropriate seasons.

10. There is no immediate climatic or dietetic reason why
these southern-wintering species should fly north in spring from
their tropical or sub-tropical winter homes.

Clearly then, the phenomenon of migration has a deeper
underlying stimulus than one purely of climatical necessities,
especially when I recall the precision with which many species come and go year after year, almost to the day, regard-
less of weather conditions. Any hypothesis of the origins of
migration must show some connection with climatic factors,
and, at the same time, account for that inner force that appears to control the migrating bird. Some ornithologists ad-
vocate a sudden territorial expansion: a radiation from the
hub of long-occupied breeding grounds to regions that are
climatically fit for habitation only in the summer; the innate
instinct of most birds to flock together bringing about the return of such foreign-nesters in the autumn to their original
homes. But such a theory assumes certain species to originate
in parts of the world where they no longer breed.

Another supposition is that migration springs into being as
an irruption from overcrowded territories into empty regions.
But these spasmodic movements of such as crossbills and
sand grouse show me that if new colonies are established, the
founders and their progeny become residents, while if colonizing attempts are unsuccessful the pioneers perish. Thus
there is no returning to their original haunts to establish the
necessary shuttle-movement north and south, or east and
west, of seasonal migration. There is no regular migration
east and west across the Atlantic because, on those rare occa-

sions when plover and woodcock cross to North America, none return to perpetuate such a migratory tradition in their young.

There remains the story of an Arctic dispersal, which seems to me, at present, to account most satisfactorily for many of the irrelevancies of migration as I see it today. The most notable feature of the geographical distribution of birds is that only one order, the penguins, cannot definitely be assigned an original birthplace north of the equator. In explanation of this sole exception I can reasonably suggest that, being pelagic birds, fossilized remains of penguins will be rare. Nor do I deem it impossible that such an order of birds might evolve from a species that had previously penetrated the Southern Hemisphere from the Northern. Such species as trogons and parrots, essentially southern-breeding birds today, have been found fossilized in France. Nor do I forget that our earliest feathered bird, the archaeopteryx, was located in Bavaria, and that all other traces of birds still retaining their reptilian teeth have been found in North America and England. I conclude that the earliest birds inhabited the Northern Hemisphere.

When their numbers increased, the various species of these early birds tended to spread north, south, east, and west in search of suitable feeding and breeding grounds; I know that the groupings of certain species of birds and beasts over the world are complementary to the suggested outline of landmasses once joined but now separated by oceans. Northern Europe and the Arctic regions were the limit of their northerly advance. Summer in the Arctic endures less than three months, yet the Siberian tundras are still the breeding grounds of countless millions of birds from both hemispheres. What is the nature of their especial attraction for nesting birds?

There is no spring in the Arctic. The southwest wind blows, a thaw sets in, ice and snow melt, and a luxuriant foliage, nine months buried under several feet of snow, grows rapidly everywhere. When the snow melts, these tundras become a land of dwarf trees and bushes, still bearing last year's fruit, preserved by the snow: cranberries, cloudberries, creeping willows, and low lichens and mosses. Pools, swamps, and large lakes dotted with islands, abound. In such areas, of almost incalculable extent, there is food for all: gnats and larvae in the pools, insects in myriads over the swamps, and an abundance of berries. But to a nesting bird the short Arctic summer offers something of greater value than all these advantages together: the stimulus to its reproductive system of long weeks of perpetual daylight.[1]

When in August the sun starts to set for an hour or so every day, after many weeks of continuous daylight, the migrants begin to leave the tundras and northern forests for the south, and soon the tundras are entirely deserted. About scattered villages, or Samoyed and Astiask *chooms,* and in the forests, a few resident species remain: magpies, northern jays, woodpeckers and nutcrackers, the scarlet bullfinch and the hooded crow; but in comparison with the numbers of those that go south they are as nothing.

I see no reason to suppose that in past ages, glacial eras excepted, the Arctic proved to be any less attractive. As the limit of northerly dispersal, it would tend to be the rallying ground and final nesting territory of a vast number of species. Today, migratory streamers from the Arctic tundras stretch out to every corner of the world. That amazing species the sanderling, for instance, breeding as far north in the Arctic Circle as any bird but the Arctic tern, winters as far south as the Antarctic, at such widely divergent points as Australia and Patagonia. Such an astounding range between winter and summer quarters may have been built up by southern-

---

[1] The endocrine glands and reproductive organs of birds subjected to light from the ultraviolet end of the spectrum are excessively stimulated and their breeding seasons accelerated. Moreover, when liberated at the wrong season, birds so subjected have emigrated in the direction of their hereditary breeding grounds.

moving sanderling "o'er-leaping" others of their species already in occupation of wintering places nearest to their
breeding quarters, successive waves "o'er-leaping" ever farther south in search of empty country. So that I arrive at
what is said to be an observed fact that, generally speaking,
the farther north a bird breeds the farther south he migrates
in the winter.

In some past age, then, there was a huge resident avian
population on the Arctic tundras. Then the first of the Ice
Ages set in. At the outset there was a slight lengthening of
the polar cap only in winter: sufficient to drive those birds
breeding farthest north, south in winter, though they were
able to return to their breeding grounds in the summer, with
the melting of the southern fringes of the icecap. In course of
time the polar glaciers steadily lengthened. There came an
era when the whole of the Arctic was uninhabitable in the
winter, though the birds were still able to return for a short
breeding season at midsummer. The habit of north-and-south
migration was already becoming ingrained in successive generations of birds. But when the glacial epoch was at its most
intense a vast area of land, extending right across the Northern Hemisphere and as far south as central France, was too
cold for the birds throughout the year. I can see for myself,
today, how strong is a bird's inclination to return to its nesting place or feeding ground. Thus these ousted birds flew as
far north as the icecap permitted every spring, so that the
north-and-south seasonal shuttle-movement continued, and
was gradually strengthened to become an essential part of
their life-cycle.

Then the glaciers of the first Ice Age began to melt north-
wards, so that the birds were able to breed ever farther north
again, and ever nearer to their true homes. But they still flew
south at the approach of winter, as they had been accustomed to do, and perhaps farther south than the severity of
the climate demanded, to those lands where they had win-
tered when the polar cap was at its most southerly point. In

spring, mating and nesting ground was the dominant attraction. When, after the nesting, sexual emotions waned, there filtered into the bird's organism the cumulative, inherited instinct to fly south to winter feeding grounds: an instinct associated with the post-sexual season. It is generally held that there were three or four distinct Ice Ages, with considerably milder climatic eras between them. Thus, over many thousands of years, this north-and-south seasonal migration became so powerfully ingrained that there came a time when in some species many of its provisions seemed to have outlived their original use—like so many other instincts of birds. So that, today, the migrating bird responds rather to an instinctive call than to a climatic demand: the which accounts for the many irrelevancies of migration in the field.

XIII

MIGRATION IN THE FIELD

Late in March, or in the first days of April, a new spirit quickens on winter saltings. A spirit of unrest has spread from southern lands, where millions of wintering birds have felt the urge to return to northern nesting territories in Europe and the Arctic. Observation of their migratory movements proves especially favorable when, as in the two localities with which I am most intimately acquainted, a small island is cut off from the East Coast by a mile or two of tidal flats and saltings. In such a locality I can differentiate between British birds moving into immediate nesting territories and other migrants on passage to countries farther north and east. Last land this side the North Sea, these two islands—one off the north Norfolk coast, the other off Northumberland—afford striking similarities and dissimilarities of migratory movements.

My most satisfactory approach to the study of migration would be to recount and annotate the movements of the migrants day by day, as I have noted them down in my field diaries; but this, I am told, would prove too tedious a compilation for the reader. Instead, I give in this chapter my deductions drawn from firsthand observations in the field, which in every case are based on a day to day study embracing the whole period of the spring and autumn migrations of various years.

Any essay on migration must open with the truism that such a phenomenon is primarily the returning of birds to their nesting territories. The shelduck moving up from mud flat to sandy common, the curlew from estuary to moor, the oyster-catcher from mussel-bank to shingle-beach seventy miles up the river, are migrating as truly as wheatear or chiff-chaff; and it is in February that such movements begin. In February, too, the lesser black-backed gull returns to East Coast waters after a three months' absence, and the first woodcocks and short-eared owls are both departing from and arriving on our East Coast sand dunes. This understood, I can go on to consider the more familiar movements of what are usually termed summer migrants.

The laws governing East Coast migration are, on a general principle, simple and regular. In the last days of March come British wheatears, and with them a few of the Continental wheatears—of whom I shall have more to say later. In the first days of April, Continental birds nesting in temperate zones, such as black redstarts, siskins, fieldfares, and robins are returning from wintering in the British Isles. These are more likely to be observed on the Northeast Coast than the East Coast. For the remainder of April typical British summer birds are returning from southern Europe and Africa to nest in this country: wheatears and chiff-chaffs, swallows, cuckoos, and warblers. Normal migration—that is to say, that of migrants coming in to breed in the British Isles, rather than birds on passage to countries farther north—reaches its peak in the last days of April. But then for three weeks the character of the migration changes, and it is birds on a curve of passage from west Africa to northern Europe and the Arctic that pass through. If this migration of north European-breeding birds happens to coincide with abnormal weather conditions, observation is likely to prove fruitful. But there is little or no packing of spring migrants, nor autumn either, for that matter—they must be sought for diligently.

This new migratory movement is heralded by Greenland and Continental wheatears and redstarts and followed by various Continental buntings, bluethroats, and flycatchers, gilding the mass of familiar species, and reaching its peak about May 14, to be followed by a glorious fortnight of northern waders. And this is not the schedule of odd years, but, with favorable weather, invariable; within a day or two I can mark down the bird I wish to see and the locality where it should be seen in any year.

It is not possible to draw an arbitrary division between spring and autumn migration generally: of *passeres*, always excepting swallows, sand martins, and swifts, yes; Greenland wheatears, warblers, and whitethroats are passing through up to the middle of June, but after that no more *passeres* until the first young of the year are drifting south in the middle, or more usually the end, of July. And of certain other species, yes; for there is a marked absence on mud flats and marshes from four to six weeks in June and July of gray plover, purple sandpiper, sanderling, golden plover, whimbrel, green sandpiper, greenshank, and common sandpiper. And the July return of the last four species is as regular to the day every autumn as the spring coming of wheatear and chiff-chaff. But there are non-breeding green plover passing west over Norfolk marshes from the end of May onwards; there are swifts speeding south in the last days of June, fifty or a hundred in a scattered flight; when immature herring, greater black-backed and common gulls are packing on the sand banks. And to curlew, dunlin, turnstone, knot, and godwit, it is not possible to assign any definite limitations: curlew are on the saltings every day of the year, and there are still dunlin and turnstone in full breeding plumage on the shore in the first days of July. But, generally speaking, the tide turns in mid-July.

Oyster-catchers flying

Spring migration, then, on the East Coast, shows three distinct phases. There is first that passage east and northeast of Continental species wintering in the British Isles; then the northerly progression of British-nesting birds from southern Europe and Africa; and finally Arctic and sub-Arctic species passing over the British Isles on a great northeasterly curve of flight from West Africa, although concurrently with these come a few species, such as Greenland wheatears, whose orientation is north and northwest to Greenland and the North American islands. The directional nature of these migrating Arctic and Continental species I can only infer from the situation of their nesting territories, and from such movements as I observe at sea; but of British wheatears and swallows I can watch both migration in being and its finis: for all day long single twittering swallows and pairs of swallows, tens of sand martins, and occasional house martins are skimming up low over the sea and island and saltings, deliberately unhurried, but never loitering, on a direct line of flight south and north.

They bring with them resident swallows who chitter about the houses and farms. And some of the newly arrived wheat-ears immediately set about the examination of nesting holes in walls and rabbit burries. Thus I can visualize a tenuous, straggling line of migrants, hundreds of miles long, with individuals continually branching off the main stream to settle in their nesting territories.

But if the migration of swallows, martins, and swifts is correctly south and north of Northumberland, it is due east and west over that Norfolk island, where the coastline lies east and west. Moreover the westward migration of swallows is of almost daily occurrence up to the end of June, and, beginning again in the last days of July, continues through the autumn. Similarly, there is a westward spring migration of swifts in April and May, taken up again late in June, to continue throughout July and August. This westward passage is carried on in October and November by the gray crows. This latter line of flight is intelligible, for the crows are on their way southwest from their breeding territories in northern and western Europe. But it is perplexing to find swifts and swallows migrating west spring, summer, and autumn, and it is difficult to understand why their line of flight should be so directly west. There are two possible solutions: one, that swifts and swallows invariably follow a coastline on migration; and two, that these are East African- or Indian-wintering birds migrating west-northwest. In autumn, when their numbers are greater, they are, like the hoodies, Scandinavian- and north European-breeding birds on a southwesterly passage to West Africa, for those regions lie some twenty degrees west of the East Coast of the British Isles. Thus these species, at least, do not return by the same route that they have come, and this seems to be true, generally, of all migrating birds.

This brings me to the question of perennially constant migratory routes. My own observations confirm those of Geoffrey Watson and Abel Chapman that it is almost unique to record godwit, knot, or gray plover in full breeding plumage on the Northeast Coast; whereas, three hundred miles farther south in East Anglia, quite a fair proportion of passage birds are red and silver, although the numbers of their kind passing through are infinitely less on that part of the coast. Whatever way I look at it only two things are certain: one, that breeding godwit, knot, and gray plover (and other waders? and all other species?) tend to follow different migratory paths to those of the non-breeding and first-year birds of their kind; and two, that these migratory paths are constant year after year. Hitherto, I have not favored the theory of migrating birds following specific, perennially constant flight-lines, let alone different ages and sexes of the same species doing so; but I begin to think that I shall have to alter my views. There are so many field observations militating against haphazardly directional migration. Elsewhere in this book I have noted that one of the strongest forces governing a bird's existence is the pull of place. Day after day, year after year, and century after century a majority of birds and their descendants return to the same nesting, feeding, roosting, and wintering territories, and call at the same places on passage. I have literally hundreds of such instances of conservatism in my notebooks. The most striking, though you may call it coincidence if you will, concerns a wood sandpiper, rather a rare passage bird on the Northeast Coast. Abel Chapman records that in 1877 a wood sandpiper was shot at a certain headland on an island off the Northumbrian coast, and this was the only wood sandpiper that particular gunner ever obtained. In 1922 the only wood sandpiper Abel Chapman ever observed in the British Isles he saw at this same headland. Fifteen years later, the only wood sandpiper that I saw on the island was also at this headland. The point is not that this rare species should be observed three times in sixty years at the identical spot, but how many times it has passed there on its autumnal passage without being observed. However, I do not suggest that you should base any argument on so unique (?) an instance of conservatism; but you will agree that your own experience confirms the remarkable conservatism of solitary birds and flocks of birds to favored places. If, then, birds have so strong an affection for place, it seems to me more than probable that they will have no less an inherent affection for especial lines of flight between wintering and nesting territories, as gulls and starlings and cormorants between feeding and roosting grounds, although the distance to be covered is so much greater. By taking different species to migrate on their respective curves, I can see how certain types of migrants are perennially observed on one part of the coast and not on another. Thus, too, immature waders, rather than flying more or less nonstop on their curve, will be drifting north at the seasonal urge, keeping pace, perhaps, with the apparent northern passage of the sun, and *feeling* their way towards those territories to which they will repair to nest another year, and from which they have drifted the previous autumn.

A second point is this restriction of some passage migrants to one part of the coast and not to another. Red-breasted flycatchers,[1] Continental wheatears, Continental robins, thrushes and blackbirds, in my experience, are regular spring migrants in Northumberland, but not in Norfolk; red-spotted bluethroats [2] and black terns in Norfolk, but not in Northumberland; just as I observe fully plumaged waders in one place and not in the other. I remember, too, how, inland, I look for my migrating wheatears each spring at certain well-known spots; and how each autumn I meet families of young whinchats and red-backed shrikes following the same old autumnal routes; and many other such instances.

It is not, I suppose, generally realized that typically British birds, whom I am accustomed to regard, rather, as strictly resident, feature in a trans-North Sea migration: yellow, common, and reed buntings; chaffinches; kingfishers; meadow pipits, who perch in trees when on migration (as do garden warblers); song thrushes, including the small, dark Continen-

[1] See End Note A.
[2] See End Note B.

tal (?) species: their vivid spots almost black; and blackbirds, very extensively—indeed the blackbird is probably the commonest migrant on the Northeast Coast, especially during the autumn and winter—and robins, who appear to me slenderer than our British robins, and tend to migrate in pairs. Other robins, incidentally, return to winter on the island at the end of August but no longer stay to nest as they used to do; but these are robins from the mainland. All these common species, and others, immigrate and emigrate.

Nor is it realized, I think, that three varieties of wheatear pass through the British Isles on migration, all clearly distinct to me in their plumage—and let no museum ornithologist inform me that all these wheatears are indistinguishable: in the life and death of birds there is no comparison of plumages. The British wheatear is a fine bird, with his powdered-silver brow and chocolate slashings, but he is eclipsed by his Continental representative, who seems to me bigger, with the splendidly broad, dark-chocolate (almost black) folded wing-slashing of the Greenland wheatear; and whose breast and belly are pale yellow, superbly ivory-white in strong sun; with broad silver superciliary stripe, and intensely black lores. But whereas the throat of the Greenland wheatear is orange-buff, that of the Continental is pinkish-fawn, very pink in certain lights. His tawny-pink female, like the Greenland's, is very much brighter, and her contrasting buffs and fawns are more sharply demarcated, than the British female's. These tawny females stand up in the new corn like song thrushes.

The giant Greenland wheatear, seeming almost a third bigger than the British bird, I rank in magnificence with silver plover and red godwit, kingfisher and Continental redstart. On seeing the first male each spring, he seems always the loveliest bird I have ever seen. Intensely dark gray on back, and almost black of lores and wing margins, his brilliantly shining belly is often exquisitely tinted with rosy pink; at other times it is a flaming dark salmon or a varnished chestnut, according to the play of the light; his great eye-stripe is silver; when spreading his square tail in flight, the revelation of white is astounding, and the black margining to it broader than in other wheatears. As is customary with all Arctic-breeding species, he is not normally to be observed in this country until the first days of May, the females following some days later.

*Wheatear
on its typical perch
of low rocks*

Thus I begin to appreciate that most, perhaps all northern-breeding species, *passeres* and wader alike, are much more brightly plumaged than their British congeners, redstarts and golden plover in particular. The bright flicker of a British redstart's flaming tail, when he flits behind an elder bush, never fails to thrill me every spring. But the breasts of Continental redstarts are superbly flame-black: burningly vivid against their powdered-silver brows; for once, the breast seems more astoundingly fiery than the tail. Most elusively shy on migration, their *tack-tack* notes and burnished tails may alone betray them. I notice, incidentally, that female redstarts are much more numerous than males on migration, the reverse being the case with wheatears.

The northern and the British golden plover are almost to be thought two different species, for never does the British plover attain to the splendid purity of that S-shaped silver margining to neck and breast of his northern relative. The northern bullfinch is immeasurably brighter, and bigger, than our British bird. The curlew is not a bright-plumaged bird, but there is an especially bright chestnut tinting in the plumage of northern-moving birds. And so I could continue.

How am I to account for this undoubtedly deeper intensity of coloring of northern-breeding birds over their British-breeding representatives? Has it in it the inherent stimulus of those long hours of daylight during the short northern summer, which enable a nesting bird to fulfill its nesting duties in a much shorter period than that required by British-breeding species? Light, not necessarily sunlight, but just daylight, is the dominant force in the life of a bird, who is always traveling thousands of miles in search of it, or welcoming it at dawn, at sunset, and at moonrise. With light I can make a bird breed out of his season and out of his hemisphere; with light I can make him change his plumage out of season; with light I can increase the intensity of his coloring.

Returning to the theme of migrants following perennially constant lines of flight, I have to consider the occurrences on migration of rare birds. I have instanced the remarkable conservatism of a wood sandpiper, but I expect to be no less certain of observing, at their appointed dates and localities, little buntings both in Northumberland and Norfolk; dotterels in Northumberland; ortolan buntings in Norfolk; and red-breasted flycatchers in Northumberland—providing that abnormal weather conditions induce them to land in these localities (a matter to which I return farther on in this chapter). These species are accounted rare migrants, but considering that they are migrating to similar localities as wheatears and redstarts, to almost the Arctic limits of Scandinavia, I see no good reason why they should not be met with in this country. Rather is it more remarkable that these scattered birds of passage should be noted as often as they are. Those able to watch birds at all seasons are few in number. The chances of such observers being in the right place at the right hour to snap up a rare migrant are small. I think it more probable that such rare migrants are passing through or over the British Isles every year.

For some evidence on the mechanics of migration, I can turn to the curlew. Immature non-breeding curlew are about at all seasons—indeed I should be surprised to learn that any waders breed in their second year—but migratory curlew associate in packs and, when put up, tend to slant off to a distance before dropping down to resume their feeding, whereas resident curlew, seldom more than four or five in a bundle, alight again a short way down the creek. Redshank behave in like manner. There are further distinctions between English and Continental curlew: English curlew begin to return to nesting moors in the very first days of March,[3] streaming up to the moors in thousands at dawn every morning to take up their nesting territories, flighting back to the flats again at the darkening; until at length they stay on the moors day and night. In April and May, when there are even more thousands of curlew passing along our coasts, British nesting territories are full. The rear guard of these northern-moving curlew does not go north until well on in June, when the chicks of many of our own curlew have hatched. It will be understood that the short northern summer necessitates a late nesting season. There is yet a third distinction, to which I have already referred: the brighter plumage of northern-nesting curlew.

In the first days of April, about the time that the shadows are lengthening in the evening, little packs of curlew, never more than two score, and sometimes even solitary birds, begin to go out due east to sea from the sand banks, with the familiar *cu-curree*. As the days pass, their migration intensifies until these little bundles are going out east about every ten minutes, day and night, with a great calling of *phwee-*

[3] In any numbers, that is to say; the first curlew return to the moors early in February.

phwee/phwee-phwee-phwee-phwee and sometimes a mighty "bubbling." It is vastly interesting to see how they come down the Northumbrian slakes in small packs to mass on the sand banks, until several thousand are gathered together. From the gathering shoot off these tiny straggling bundles, with perhaps a solitary bird in the rear hurrying to catch up with those that have gone off before him. Only their calls and direct, mounting flight out to sea show me that this casual, unimpressive flighting is that of curlew on migration. There is no orderly method about it. It seems a matter of complete chance when and with what companions a bird sets out on migration.

Much has been written about mass migration. From the earliest times it has been assumed that millions of birds band together and migrate in great armies. Admittedly I see little of migration, but what I do see is wholly against mass movement. So far as migration over the British Isles goes, the greatest number of birds I have seen actually in migratory flight in normal weather is about one thousand widgeon. Thousands of martins gathering in the summer on some sloping church-roof, thousands of waders carpeting the mud flats: but do I see martins or waders actually in migratory flight in such numbers! Thousands of non-breeding waders pack on a winter salting, but do I ever observe them putting out to sea thus! In my experience the nearest approach to mass migration is a continual streaming in and out of little packs. Just as the curlew put out to sea, so the gray geese drop down in little gaggles, at leisurely intervals, to their winter saltings, averaging twenty-five or so in a gaggle. Only in times of fog or tempest do migrants appear in large numbers together, when bad weather brings a bunching of separate flights. I read of enormous migrations of such birds as storks and quails in other parts of the world, but as I have not been able to observe for myself the factors influencing such movements, I cannot include them as typical of normal migration.

Autumn migration is usually written of as an ornithologist's paradise, but, on the contrary, it is far more diffused than spring migration, and weeks pass with hardly a sign of a migrant. At the end of May the restless spirit of autumn migration is already abroad, about the time that young brown starlings are first packing on the fresh-marshes, when small flights of stranger plover, with many flight-feathers missing from their wings, are already flickering westwards low across the marshes day after day, often skimming the ground in leisurely flight, but always making steadily west. A dozen such small flights go over in a day, some of only eight or nine birds, others of seventeen or twenty-five, but never more than thirty, although these movements are of almost daily occurrence up to the end of August. Nor have I watched any migratory passage so extraordinary as this in the unwavering accuracy of its flight-line, which hardly alters by a yard from day to day for three months and, to the end, is composed only of birds in the moult. Unlike most passage movements it is to be observed every year, whatever the weather conditions.

And after May there are birds migrating west and south from the last week in June right through into January of the next year. It may be argued that these later movements are solely climatic in their origins, but I cannot leave them out of the picture of autumn migration as a whole, because they are part and parcel of it. Nor is there any autumn parallel, abnormal weather conditions excepted, to that five-week rush of migrants in the spring. The autumn movements of birds are spread more or less evenly over the six months covering the period from August to December, with the stragglers in July and January. Late in July there straggle by young British willow warblers and chiff-chaffs; but the bulk of these early southing young birds come in the last two weeks of August and the first two of September: whinchats, whitethroats, pied and spotted flycatchers, willow warblers and garden warblers, yellow wagtails, Greenland wheatears, and perhaps a barred warbler [4] to lend majesty to the procession: one and all im-

[4] See End Note C.

mature. It will be the end of September, and especially October and November, before the adult birds are passing south, and the vast majority of these, not summer birds going south, but northern and eastern species coming in to winter in the British Isles. At the end of September British redstarts and wheatears and red-breasted flycatchers are going south, and perhaps the first snow buntings and blackbirds are coming in to winter. In October come more blackbirds, and black-spotted song thrushes and redwings, stonechats and goldcrests, woodcock, gray crows, green plover, and the first fieldfares. In November come still more of the same species and perhaps chaffinches with them.

The character of these movements differs from those of the spring, and the vast majority of observable southing summer migrants are birds of the year. To my mind, a paramount problem of migratory movements in the field concerns this nonobservance in the autumn of the breeding adults I saw in the spring. This can be accounted for only by presuming, as I have already suggested, that they return south by routes different to those they came by in the spring. In which case why do the birds of the year travel by this route? But, if this is generally the case over northern Europe, why do not we in the British Isles see something of European birds in the autumn returning by different routes to those they came by in the spring? Perhaps we do, and I have the key to the mystery here? It is a baffling problem.

Assuredly my observations of spring passage show that some species of migrants are to be seen at certain places on the coast, and not at others, year after year; but, equally certainly, the numbers of migrants I observe are in no way proportionate to the numbers that must be passing over the British Isles to nesting territories farther north; moreover a large percentage of this small proportion I observe only because they are weather-bound by abnormal conditions of fog or tempest: with certain exceptions of such as swallows and lapwings who pass through every year, whatever the weather.

Nor can migration by night explain this phenomenon, for, in the first place, where are the migrants, then, during the day? And, in the second place, why do I hear their night calls so seldom, or not see them more often on moonlit nights? My own records and those of lighthouses and ships prove conclusively that there is much migration by night, but it must continue through the day too; and if all these migrants fly below three thousand feet, as is generally affirmed, then why do I not see them during the day? Moreover, the best time to pick up the rare migrants of misty weather is in the early morning and in the evening when they are obviously very anxious to go to roost. In the early morning they are on the move, and it is at such hours that I have seen most *passeres* at sea. Curlew and common gulls, on the other hand, most commonly set out on their migration in the evening—but, truth to tell, all sorts of migrants are on the move at all hours of the day.

I am left with only two possible answers: one, that there is not that vast migration to Arctic and sub-Arctic regions along British coasts there is always said to be; or, two, that the majority of migrating birds fly at least as high as five thousand feet, so that only the lower-flying migrants are forced down by terrestrial storms.

Weather conditions, with one exception, have little effect upon the movements of migrating birds, though a percentage are gale-blown and storm-bound; and fog is all-important. As a factor in bird migration sea-fog or mist is liable to be misinterpreted. If fogs are rare during the migratory season, it proves a poor year for observing migrants or migratory movements. I can go further than this and state that ninety-nine per cent of the big migratory movements and rare migrants I observe in spring are intimately connected with the presence of fog—as I note in my field diaries time after time.[5] But its presence or absence makes little difference to spring observations of northern waders or autumn observations of young

[5] The extraordinarily fine spring of 1938 offered pleasant confirmation of this: nothing resembling a rare migrant appearing.

passeres. Fog, by influencing these Continental *passeres* to alight on these outposts of the East and Northeast Coast in spring, rather than continuing on a nonstop passage across the North Sea, affords me an abnormal glimpse of migratory movements. Every year I patiently note down odd representatives of these rare species reacting in an abnormal manner to weather influences; but how many hundreds or thousands of their kind are flying through or above the fog or tempest? —and do so every year, and have done for milleniums! In the British Isles I see nothing of Arctic-nesting birds in the spring but stragglers: *passeres* and waders alike—for how few are the fully-plumaged waders I observe in this country! Nearly all the latter are immature birds, thousands and thousands of them wandering slowly north, alighting and feeding where they will: the call of the north and the nesting and the mating as yet but feeble. On the autumn return, identification is made harder by the moult, but, quite certainly, of distinguishable species the vast majority of *passeres* I meet are birds of the year. What, then, happens to southing adults? Having made the trip, haphazardly directional as an immature bird, once or a number of times, according to his species, it looks remarkably as if the mature bird, urged on by the call of nesting or wintering ground, tends to cover his now familiar migratory flight nonstop—or as nearly so as his specific powers of flight permit. And though it may amount to several thousand miles, this is not unduly extraordinary, for the male swift flies at least six hundred miles every day of his existence, perhaps as much as a thousand miles.

Fog also throws some light on the mechanics of migration. Often we fish off some islands at sea, where nest many thousands of divers: guillemots, puffins, and razorbills. When feeding the young, their favorite fishing grounds lie several miles from the islands, so that a continual stream of divers pass all day in a direct line between feeding grounds and nesting cliffs. On days of dense fog, when sharp-eyed gulls do not come down to feast on offal from the smack and visibility

Puffin coming in for
a landing, its tailfeathers spread
and feet extended for braking

is only a few yards, the divers are still flying on a direct compass-bearing between fishing grounds and islands. I learn that it is now proved that the emission of strong wireless waves confuses the directional powers of homing pigeons and that an emitting station between the homer and its loft causes it to lose a sense of direction, until a wide circling brings it outside the local field of intense electromagnetism. I recall in this respect the preliminary circling of swifts, cormorants, gulls, owls, and other species, before setting out on migration. It is probable that the organs of orientation are the semicircular canals in the ears, for these are peculiarly sensitive to electrical impressions. Their removal in certain animals has resulted in an inability to steer themselves. I see so absurdly little of migratory movements that I find it reasonable to suppose that the migrants fly high, in regions where magnetic currents are subject to little disturbance from terrestrial forces. Their migratory lines of flight being predominantly north and south to Polar regions of intense magnetic activity, I conclude that a bird orientates partly by visual and inherent memory—particularly when nearing nesting or wintering territory—partly by attunement of the magnetic forces of his body to those of the Polar Stream, but primarily by some at present obscure power on a par with an insect's "X-rays of odour."

End Note A. It may be of interest to append some description of the red-breasted flycatcher, a bird that I associate with both migrations in Northumberland, although I have seen only females passing through. No bigger than a chiff-chaff, this flycatcher seems a tiny, perfectly proportioned robin, with staccato *tchick/tchick.* With wings sharply drooping, she jerks her longish tail up and down between them, after the manner of a blackbird. Her head and back are a uniform olive-fawn, and her round black eye is ringed in pale yellow. Her breast and belly are most distinctively white. Her legs are an oiled greenish-black, and her longish, slightly curved thin bill is a typical flycatcher's. Her wings and tail are much darker than her fawn upper parts, and, an unusual distinction, her undertail-coverts and the undersides of her tailfeathers are snowy-white. But the most striking feature of her plumage is revealed to me only when she spreads her tail in quick, darting flight from bush to bush; then a wheatear-like patterning in dark brown and white arrests my eye: white slottings running down either side of a dark brown central shaft to the dark brown base of her tail. In October she is tinted on breast and belly with a wheatear yellow-buff, the throat paler, with a suspicion of a dun line encircling it— or is this the young male?

End Note B. The red-spotted, or Norwegian, bluethroat is, I imagine, a fairly familiar migrant, but a note on the white-spotted bluethroat observed in April on the Solway may be of value: a copper flicker of spread tail constantly jerking up and down, and brightest of blue breasts; a brilliant dark ultramarine breast, deepening at the edges, shading and lighting wonderfully brightly in the evening sun; and a continual glimpsing of sparkling white, crinkly, silky crease inserted amid blue throat and breast—a lovely touch!—hidden in the blue, when the bird was bowed forward in its typically secretive bluethroat elusiveness: diving into piles of brushwood at the edge of the tidal river, desperately anxious to roost, and flitting a hundred yards and more along the bottom of a narrow runnel, often popping up to perch on the marsh. The blue breast is bordered by a three-quarter-of-an-inch shaggy band of dark chestnut, or copper, channeled on either side by the pale fawn of the belly—which is very lightly striped in darker fawn—running up to the blue breast. A typical robin with those same yellowish uppertail-coverts, slightly darker back, pale superciliary stripe, and pink legs.

End Note C. The barred warbler is a fine big bird, appearing as large as a yellow bunting in the field, which is correct to one-tenth of an inch in the hand. Slinks about bushes and hedgerow with typical warbler secretiveness. At some yards distance a very pale, uniformly colored bird, with gray-white breast, pale fawn back, and high-crowned warbler head. Closer, it is browner, with tawny barrings on wing-coverts.

XIV

SAINT CUTHBERT'S DUCK

Over the wide mud flats between the island and the green and gray country of the border sweeps a cold, fresh wind, clean-cutting beyond belief after long night hours in a filthy train. I am conscious of a splendid sense of space about this island of vast slakes, sand banks, tree-less gray-stonewalled pastures, and rocky shore; with its red-turreted fort built on the naked cliff and its far horizon of castles and lighthouses on sea-girt islands, and red and white beacons, from whose triangular points there sounds across the harbor to me the shrill *kee-lee-lee* of a kestrel and the chattering of starlings. A tiny harbor, with the green heugh of the coastguard lookout on one side and the fort cliff on the other, backed by a red-roofed gray and white fishing village and the magnificent weathered red ruins of an Abbey arching the whalebone ridge of the Cheviots. Ten fishing-cobles pitch and toss in the bay, whose half-moon beach is ringed by tarred boathouses: each a herring boat sawn in half, keel uppermost.

To every place its characteristic bird. To antiquarian, islander, and naturalist alike, living witness of the island saints is the most beautiful of all ducks, the eider, who deserts it not the year through. Officially he is Saint Cuthbert's duck, but the islanders have shortened his saintly patronymic to the Culvert duck—not that either name is used much these days.

At high water a circular reef of brown rock is cut off from the island's cliffs. Here the bones of the saint were interred a second time, because in his first resting-place in the Abbey he had been disturbed by the bad language of the fishermen passing to and from their boats—their language is still bad. Nor did the saint enjoy peace in his new haven, for the wailing of the gulls jarred his sepulchral nerves, so that he was borne across the wide sands to Chester-le-Street. But there the Danes threatened his sanctity, and only in his fourth burial site at Durham is he deemed to have found a thousand years of tranquillity—that is one legend; there are others.

A cross marks his empty tomb amid the pink thrift on the tiny reef, and his spirit clings to it in the guise of the eider: who lives only over a rocky floor. Excepting for a little island thirty miles to the south, this gale-swept Border island is the most southerly home of the eider in the British Isles.

There is a rocky bay on that side of the island facing Norway, backed by a wall of hundred-foot cliffs, and flanked by long black and bistre reefs. Piping rock pipits flit about the boulders or parachute lightly from crannies in the cliffs, with strong musical trills. Looking down one hundred feet from the cliffs and seventy yards out, it is a gladsome sight to see the scarlet-billed oyster-catchers, immaculately silver-white at breast and slotted shoulders and so glossy black-backed in the sun, probing at the limpets studding the brown flagstones. Their pink legs are hardly to be picked up against the brown weed of the rocks, whereas the redshank's surpassingly bright rose stilts arrest my wandering eye everywhere. One stands on the black-brown seaweed of a rock pinnacle weathered an orange-brown, the color of his body. Standing high, with the sun behind him, his shanks are sunset-pink against a background of blue-gray sea and white breakers. Little black-tailed turnstones also ferret among the reefs, twinkling about on brilliant orange-pink shanks, pushing the oarweed away from them vigorously with short, conical bills.

Turnstone

From the waters of the bay, where ride occasional coal-black scoter, parti-colored long-tails, and crested merganser, gray seals rear their anvil heads from the breakers, moaning like calves and crying like little children: saddest sounds of the sea. Since the bottom is rock, this bay is the eider's especial hunting ground about the island, for it is only in the early spring, when the giant dog-crabs emerge from their hibernacula on the mud flats that there are more eiders on the wide slakes than about the reefs and bays. On the wave-pitted reefs knobbly with limpets I have sat hours marveling at the exquisite hues of drake eiders, when the sun lit the rosy flush at their breasts. Roseate and Sandwich terns have a lovely rose-red flush at the lower breast, but that of the eider is quite different; I almost sense rather than see, so ethereal is its nature, that there is rose—or is it buff, or pale mauve?—arching from the intense black of their bellies into the silver-white of their breasts. It is a color-effect that I never study without emotion. To have a little pack of eider crooning and *cok-cok*ing a few feet from me is an experience of beauty hardly to be equaled. Then I can see that an even fainter rose suffuses their glistening white backs and the white moons slotting their black flanks, just as the pastel green at the nape tinges their white necks and crowns with the palest of greens, and a primrose tinting washes the white of their wings— though, like all the beauty of birds, this tinting is lost in death. The green, almost olive, of their heads is superbly vivid. It dominates the silver and black and rose and yellow, so that I forget them. To come suddenly upon some old drakes asleep on the rocks, with their heads half tucked back into their scapulars and the sun upon their green napes, makes me catch my breath. As perfect foil, the shapely black crown is split into half moons by a narrow white channel. A tract of feathered skin brings into one straight line conical head and well-oiled, olive-yellow beak. This is grooved and toothed on the outer side of the lower mandible and the inner side of the upper so that the two may intermesh.

In flight the drake seems almost wholly silver-white, with black either side his undertail-coverts; his quick-beating, broad, black-shafted wings set very far back, his head and tail depressed, he is unlike any other duck that I know. It is a great sight to see two hundred drakes in full plumage moving off the sand into flight from some island bank where they have been at blissful ease in the sun. Where they have rested are hundreds of little pyramids of blue mussel shells.

To have a wild eider drake alive in the hand should be an exquisite experience; but as with a gray goose so with an eider duck. On a fine, warm March morning, the very first day of spring, though deep snow on the mainland, I came upon an eider drake sitting out on a reef of the bay. At my distant approach he began to waddle off to the sea, but soon sank down into the seaweed. He never moved, even when I stooped to pick him up, marveling that the eyes hidden in the black cap were dark blue. The while I held him, his fine head gradually fell forward, as if he were dead; and when I put him in a rock pool he lay stretched out along the water. . . . He recovered slowly, paddling feebly away at first, and then more strongly as the paralysis of fear began to wear off. When I stood up to watch his progress, he showed signs of alarm, as if aware, again, of my inherently dangerous presence. Hopping out of the pool, he waddled over the slippery seaweed of the creviced rocks, falling occasionally in his hurry, and almost flew into the sea, where, paddling strongly, he dived through the surf and flapped his short wings three times: in full health once more.

In a dull light the heavy duck seems a sober brown, but in full plumage she proves to be beautifully mottled with a darker shade of brown, and her flanks penciled with blackish stripes; in bright sun she gleams unexpectedly ruddy: her head almost red when the strong light plays on the chestnut edges to its feathers. More confident than the drakes, five or six ducks will squat upon the rocks a few feet from me or upon heaps of seaweed, as though upon their nests: eventually slipping off into the sea, heavy of crop, with characteristic sidling motion, after hopping, both feet together, from rock to rock. Eiders, especially the ducks and young males, are intensely inquisitive ducks. To stand out on a reef with a couple of dogs is sufficient to bring every eider swimming up from as much as a quarter of a mile out to sea; and in those fishing villages where they are fed they quickly lose any shyness.

They swim superbly: riding the breakers, diving through surf, aswirl over curling crests, with complete nonchalance, weathering a whole gale on the open sea with heads tucked back into scapulars. For such heavy ducks they dive well, remaining below for as long as half a minute, for they feed mainly on small, green shore-crabs ("Swinners" we call them in Norfolk), the big dog-crabs, mussels—especially the half-inch young ones—and some small marine game cast up at high water, which also provides a feast for gulls and every

kind of wader. So minute is it that I have not been able to as-
certain its precise nature, but its attraction to all is manifest.
How often have I not watched the eider battling, with the
greatest determination, against the swift undersurge on a
steeply sloping shore, and imbibing quantities of this obscure
minutiae, for which those intermeshing mandibles (dull blue
in the case of the duck) are no doubt an efficient sieve.[1]

Their crab-eating operations are amusing to watch, for the
dog-crabs may measure two inches and more across the shell.
Bringing her crab to the surface, the duck literally shakes its
claws off, often holding it by a claw and beating the body on
the water, in between efforts to swallow the crab as a whole,
with much jerking of head and throat. This is a matter of considerable difficulty even without the claws, and the crab is
often dropped, but retrieved before it sinks far—although
sometimes the duck finally drops it after repeated attempts at
swallowing and gives up the struggle.

A single eider or a pack of eider at sea is almost invariably
attended by a herring gull or a greater black-backed gull
swimming alongside. All gulls are inveterate filchers, especially the great gull, who subsists almost entirely on carrion
and on what he filches from smaller gulls: too slow and lazy
even to catch the guts flung from our fishing-smack, prefer-
ring to chase a herring gull until he disgorges. Watch a gull
playing gooseberry to a pair of eiders: continually flapping
up from the water, to plop down upon one or another emerging from a dive. Nine times out of ten his banditry is unsuccessful, his victim promptly submerging, to pop up elsewhere,
when the comedy is re-enacted. Occasionally the gull has a
good day and harries an eider into dropping three or four
crabs in succession. In his efforts to gulp down the inflexible
body he may drop one himself, but, rising from the water,
dives neatly and vertically, submerging *in toto,* and successfully retrieves it.

[1] But, after all, I believe that their prey is nothing more distinguished
than what, in my ignorance, I call "sand-hoppers" or "sandy-lopers."

It is on the first fine day in February, when the shallow waters inside the bar are mirror-calm under the castle on its steep cliff, that I hear again the soft love-notes of the eider drake. True it is that in October the eider, just come to the full glory of his strength after long months of moulting, is inspired to unseasonable courtship. I remember rare autumn mornings of crisp sunshine in the Hebrides, with snow capping the jagged peaks of the sloe-blue Cuillins, when a deep blue sea was shivered by only the gentlest of ripples and the calm was so absolute that I could hear, a mile away, the threshing wings of eider drakes rising in the water and vigorously flapping, as is their way, while spinning around sun-red ducks in ecstatic circles of courtship.[2] In the pitchy blackness of moonless nights their lovely crooning betrayed their presence in the quieter Kyles, when colossal seas were running in outer waters.

As winter hardens and one gale follows another for weeks on end, the eider's exuberance wanes, until the year is once more on the turn: with all the corresponding organic changes in a bird that that implies. Days of courtship in February are few, depending to some extent on weather conditions, but as the days go by the pairs increase until in March there are whole packs of pairs about—for the eider is intensely social at all seasons—while in April courtship reaches its noisiest. There are often more than a hundred birds in a single gathering: diving and flapping, spinning and crooning with a continual "snaking" backwards of heads and bills pointing at an angle of forty-five degrees to the heavens. Lovely cries, these courting notes of the drakes: soft, lingering *awoo . . . oooo* and *owoo . . . oooo*, and a powerful, indignant *goo-oooooo:* modulation and timing synchronizing with the convolutions

[2] Dry cold, with sun, is undoubtedly another stimulus to a bird's nervous and glandular system. Every observer of birds will have noticed the sudden outburst from many singing birds on a frosty day of crisp sunshine—though this only holds good so long as the frost has not cut off their food supplies.

of head and neck, which are often employed by the ducks in their conversational *cok-cok-cok* and *gog-gog-gog*.

There may be as many as five drakes shooting through a calm sea with venomous acceleration at each other about a single duck. Moreover, at the end of May, little flotillas of drakes, whose mates are sitting, are to be seen forcing their attentions upon an as yet non-sitting duck, with much *coo-hoo*ing: greatly to the jealous annoyance of her mate, who is kept busy shooting vindictively at one after another with sudden swirls of water. She may shoot at an overbold drake herself, but more often she dives, to emerge elsewhere.

At all seasons ducks and drakes of varying ages have a habit of rearing in the water, with, or without, the flapping of wings habitual to the *Anatidae*. And I see how closely the display of the drake adheres to that natural exercise of wing flapping common to all waterfowl, for in their courtship the drakes are continually standing in the water: thereby revealing the intense blackness of their bellies, which contrast so startlingly with the rose and silver of breast and back. Whether or not they flap their wings is comparatively unimportant, although such an action may well serve to attract the attention of the ducks: either way their display purposes are served, when they swim backwards and forwards high in the water on either side of her, showing off their black flanks. The intensely black bellies of the drakes are replaced in the duck by a darker shade of her prevailing brown.[3]

By the middle of May most of the ducks are sitting: in fields hundreds of yards from the sea, matching in color the dried hummocks of dung; on turfy islands pitted with rabbit holes, fifty or more over a few square yards; in nettle-beds; in odd corners of ruined chapels; on the naked rock under a heap of wreckage; on the bare pebbles and shriveled oarweed at the foot of the cliffs; the five or six huge but beautifully shaped, pale-green eggs laid in the exquisitely soft dark gray and white down plucked from the duck's body: a great circu-

[3] See Appendix A on eclipse plumage.

lar ramp of it, deeply hollowed in the center. The palish, Norman forehead, with eyes so very near the crown, bestows upon the sitting eider the queer, but characteristic, cross-eyed profile of a flatfish. Many of them are so confident that they continue sitting with heads tucked back when I squat beside them. Those who do get off at my too-near approach stain the eggs as they leave: a natural fear reaction, which may, however, serve the purpose of making them obnoxious to marauders such as foxes, who prowl about the cliffs and fields. This does not apply in the case of sharp-eyed carrion crow, summering hoodie, or gull, who nip in on those rare occasions when the eider, a very conscientious sitter, deserts her eggs for a short space. This she does in the evening, and just before the darkening—or, rather, the setting of the sun behind the mountains, for in these northern latitudes there is a pale light all night at this season; one hundred or more eider

*Common eider duck male
in breeding plumage, unique
for its black underside*

ducks come flying up, one after another, from the tide-wet slakes to their nests in the "banks."

I have never seen a drake eider at the nest, although the duck sometimes flies down to her mate at the water's edge. At the beginning of June, when the first young are hatching, fleets of one hundred or one hundred and fifty drakes cruise about the lagoons, or sunbathe on the brown reefs, with one or two second-year ducks and drakes in attendance. Some of the mature drakes are already in the first stages of their eclipse plumage (referred to more fully in Appendix A), with the silver abrading from their heads and necks.

With the hatching of the young eiders, who are taken straight down to the sea, there is an extraordinary mix-up in the bays and lagoons: drake eiders cheek by jowl with sheldrakes (a blaze of color, this!), young shelducks surrounded by curious drake eiders, and packs of mature eider higgledy-piggledy with second-year drakes and ducks and ducklings straight from the nest, for the eider knows no family jealousies: different families of ducks and ducklings mingling amicably. Dark balls of fluff these eider ducklings, with paler heads and breasts.

From the end of June onwards through the summer the packs of drakes display every conceivable stage of ugliness of eclipse plumage. On the same day I have seen one jet-black with a white saddle, another a smoky-gray with a patch or two of white on his back, another with a greenish scalp-lock down the back of his black-abraded neck, and another that has reverted to almost the full plumage of the duck. Losing, at this time, the central tract of feathers running from forehead down onto back, the characteristic Norman profile of the head is also lost, and the drake eider appears as a fine, upstanding, black-headed mallard. Such oddities drift by, idly circling with the tide, their heads resting on their backs. Such a posture, together with the jet-black of the flanks slotting into white wings, creates the perfect illusion of a bird floating on its back, with its paddles in the air, as if its carcase had been blown up by a fisherman for use as a float!

In the first days of July all the ducks are off their nests, cruising in fleets of their own or with the eclipsing drakes, and seldom has one lot of ducklings fewer than two ducks in attendance. By the middle of the month not more than three drakes in every hundred show more white than black, and their resemblance to the ducks is striking. They pass long hours resting on the rocks and are loath to go afloat on stormy seas, which are nearly as frequent in July on this gale-bound coast as in any other month. From the very beginning the eider ducklings are seaworthy: equally skilled at diving in the quiet waters of the lagoons (the baby drakes more brightly yellow-striped on their heads than the ducklings), or bobbing like corks on the breaking surf of a high tide, feeding with gusto on that *minutiae* beloved of their parents.

At the beginning of August there are three or four hundred eiders packed about the reefs of the north shore, the wretchedly moulting drakes having by now only little stumps of wings; yet still they achieve flight at urgent moments, which is not so strange considering that the eider normally begins his flight by paddle-plashing over the surface of the sea for some distance before flying fast and straight a foot or two above the water. Indeed I do not recall seeing eider flying at any greater height than a couple of hundred feet, and that is exceptional. In short, to get under way in flight, the eider relies mainly on the impetus gained from his preliminary paddle-plashing, after the manner of small divers. Even when in full plumage he has considerable difficulty in rising from a rocky surface which gives no opportunity for a preliminary run. If harried during eclipse and cut off from the shore, the eider, after much diving and shooting through the sea, and seventy or one hundred yards or so of paddle-plashing and bouncing off the waves like a puffin, whirs away: unfeathered quills white-shafting his wing-stumps. At the beginning of September the first drakes are coming out of their eclipse and showing a little more white, but it is the middle of October, after the normal full moult, before all are in their full plumage again.

There is a little mystery for me about the growing up of the young eider—at any rate on this coast. In September the ducklings, now nearly full-grown, though still in duck plumage, are in little packs of their own. Before the end of that month they vanish, to reappear towards the end of November in their second-year plumage, which varies considerably from one to another: the ducks grizzled about their heads and faintly latticed in white about their breasts; the drakes white-ringed about their necks with a whitish patchwork showing through the brownish-black mottling on their backs. As the winter draws on into spring and early summer, the black and white percolates more and more through the gray and brown, until it is evident that the young eiders will attain to their full plumage in their second autumn. Thus in the late summer and autumn none of these white-ringed varieties are to be seen. But where do these young eiders go for their moult in September, October, and November? They are not about the island and the slakes, nor the reefs and islands out to sea, nor *at* sea where I am often with the fishing fleet and where in any case they would starve. The solution is no doubt a simple one that I have overlooked, but for the moment the tempestuous beauty of the eider is heightened a little by this riddle of his growing up.

XV

THE PRIMITIVE FULMAR

The fulmar petrel nests on the cliffs of the bay of eiders. It is only a decade since the first fulmar's egg was taken from the ledges of these cliffs—taken, incidentally, by perhaps the biggest collector of birds' eggs in the British Isles. But what is interesting—indeed, it is one of the most interesting facts of bird lore I have stumbled upon—is that for many years before this first nesting, fulmars were to be observed on these cliffs in spring, only to vanish as the nesting season drew on. Now this is an ornithological fact of supreme importance. Most birds are smitten with the periodic impulse to display in autumn and winter, and spasmodic courtship takes place at communal winter feeding grounds, or among sea birds *en route* to nesting territories in the spring. This instance of the fulmar affords remarkable evidence of how such a temporary resting-place can become in time—the impulse to return to it becoming stronger with each successive spring—an inherently remembered spot, whose association with occasional courtship is strong enough to lead eventually to its establishment as an actual nesting site. Especially is this likely to happen if immemorial nesting grounds become overcrowded, as in the case of the fulmar at St. Kilda. With the nesting comes the desire of the young to return to their birthplace, and so is built up a new nesting territory of the fulmar in the most logical fashion imaginable: a splendid example of how simply the evolutionary forces at work in the avian world produce desirable results.

The fulmar is not the gull-like bird I pictured before seeing him. In close flight his dove's head seems large out of all proportion to his plump, cylindrical body and narrow wings, which are unexpectedly dark, a patterned sooty-gray in strong contrast to his snowy head and breast, and very straight and angled at their tips, like a gannet's. Planing interminably over the bay, he beats his wings at irregular intervals, with the quick motion of a swift or a shearwater, in between long bouts of gliding and soaring. The grace of his flight grows upon me, until it becomes a beautiful and essential part of the seascape. He seems in perpetual motion—I wonder to what purpose, for, since he feeds only at night, there is nought in his ceaseless circling and planing but pleasure. But fulmars slanting athwart the colossal white crests of the surf-breakers are as vital to the perfecting of their beauty as gannets plunging into tempestuous seas; and always they return to the irresistible lure of the cliffs, planing round and round and soaring up and down to them: again, like swifts to their nesting eaves. Leaving their haunts, I have always with me the memory of their ceaselessly slanting planing over stormy seas.

To write that the first fulmar petrels come back to their nesting territories on or about Christmas Day savors, perhaps, of ornithological heresy, of a species regarded, I believe, as almost exclusively pelagic. More revolutionary still, I have to record that they begin their primitive courtship immediately on returning; nor does this become a whit more passionate, its ritual any more complex, during eight succeeding months on the nesting ledges, which they do not quit finally until September: this pelagic species!

In the first days of the New Year only two or three pairs are back at the cliffs, but by the beginning of February there are some fifty fulmars planing round and round and up and down to the cliffs, and as many as twenty-five at a time are sitting awkwardly on the turfy ledges. Lying on the extreme edge of the cliff, I can watch four nesting pairs at a distance of nine feet, and various other fulmars farther along. Although so early in the year, these four are already paired up and courting vigorously. And this of a bird reputed to return to its nesting territories in May! Indeed they are already paired up on Christmas Day, and take up then the nesting sites on which they are still sitting eight months later. How alone and infinitesimal is a fulmar petrel on a ledge of some colossal stack over the vasty deep!

There is a theory that when the sexes of brightly-colored birds, such as shelducks, kingfishers, or oyster-catchers, are similarly plumaged, male and female pair for life. And this would explain to a certain extent why the female should share the male's brilliance, because, once monogamy replaced polygamy and two birds could pair for life, the male would have no need to impress a female with his especial beauty every spring. But I know this to be wrong, because every bird enacts his courtship afresh each year—stimulated by the regrowth of the generative organs—and even before each coition: making the most of his charms, whether or not they differ in pattern from the female's.

That such as oyster-catchers and shelducks do pair for life seems to me almost certain, but no less true of other species. And by this I do not necessarily infer that male and female remain together all the year, but, circumstances being favorable, mate again a second year. The lodestone of mating spot or nest is perhaps the strongest influence in a bird's life. It has been unduly stressed by many authorities that it is the male bird who is especially attracted to the nesting territory;

but the female is no less faithful. This is particularly notice-able among waders such as oyster-catchers, who are obvious birds. These quite certainly pair for life, for if the female loses her mate, she still nests with her new mate on that same shingle-beach on which she has nested for years past, and not in a territory chosen by the male. Conversely, a male who loses his mate brings his new partner to *his* territory, because in either instance the new mate is almost bound to be a young bird without territory, older birds being already mated. I remember, too, that female roseate tern who, return-ing from West African coasts without a mate, paired with a common tern and laid her single egg on her exact nesting site of the previous year. The nests and nesting sites of small birds are transient monuments, and their tenants live but a short while. This is no place to give chapter and verse details from my notebooks, though I could produce a hundred cast-iron instances proving my case; but, always excepting polyga-mous species, I do not question that a majority of birds pair for life, or so long as the stress of their small lives permits, because both male and female tend to return to the same ter-ritory year after year, in the manner of these fulmar petrels. . . .

Here on these cliffs in the opening days of February are the pelagic fulmars sitting in pairs or units all along the ledges, on those rare calm sunny mornings when the first larks are singing over the banks. Every now and again a pair break into the quack-cawing of a mallard duck: crescending into the "flap-wing" quack at moments of intense excitement. One fulmar in particular, a solitary sitter, ejects to two or three feet streams of dark yellow viscous oil: freely spattering his neighbors, who seem not able to reply in kind, although most of their curious bills have perpetual dewdrops of this oil at their bulbous amber tips. These oil drops add, no doubt, to the enjoyment of the occasional brisk nebbing of married pairs, who are just as likely to caw at each other with wide-open bills and barking heads, like herring gulls, as at a neighbor. Although stray bents are lying on the ledges no bird ever attempts to mandibulate one. The fulmar is less conscious of any nidificatory obligations than any British bird I can call to mind. Here they just sit, each at his appointed spot, their dark brown eyes full of bewilderment and soft reproach to some avian god at their imprisonment on the ledges, gazing up and about them with waving heads bent back on one side, in soft, unknowing foolishness—"They're no wise!" the islanders say.[1]

Yet they are pleasant birds to look at, with the soft, well-fed sleekness of pigeons; at rest, the big curved head resumes its artistically correct size in proportion to the compact body and well-filled crop. Looking down on them over the edge of the cliff, along which they float just under my eyes, the lovely patterning on the mole-gray of their almost straight wings—straightest of any bird I know—is a dark violet, and the slanting shafts are beautifully laced in white gold.

To lie on top of the cliffs when a whole gale is blowing off the North Sea, with the fulmars sailing past inches from my face, is one of the most splendid experiences Nature has to offer me. They sail in a continual circle along the face and edge of the cliffs and out over the bay, slanting down athwart the great breakers and swooping almost vertically up to the

---

[1] I have to apologize to the fulmar, for I have since, one May 21, been wonderfully interested to watch an old friend, in her exact nesting site of the previous year, excavating a nest hollow: deliberately rounding a hollow with half-drooping wings pressed forward, down, and outwards at the shoulders. With their aid she rubbed away the loam with a circular motion of her body, rounding the hollow with her breast, and scratching back with her webs. This was no fortuitous posturing, but deliberate excavation. Better still, she took up small stones in her beak and dropped them backwards at her side, in familiar fashion. Moreover, she tugged deliberately at some she could not move. When she struggled off, finally aware of my presence, there was, quite a deep hollow beneath her. She was, incidentally, heavily stained on cheeks and head with the yellow oil of her mate or of a neighboring male. The next day she was laying. Thus, after all, the fulmar is not so primitive as I had thought. Alas, shall we ever be able to say of a single species: "This is final: there is no more to be learnt about this bird"?

cliffs again. What an incomparable poetry of motion is theirs! Floating on top of an up-current, their fanned tails, paler at the tips, are pushed up in a convex bow, the stiffer outer quills pressing down most strongly against the updraft; their smoothly-armored wings, shaded with brown, lifting in their centers, or sinuating unexpectedly; their pale pink legs hanging free with open webs, to maintain their sailing equilibrium, so wonderfully buoyant and imponderable; hanging, too, when they strive to alight, with sideways motion against the gale, hovering with quickly fanning wings, heads lower than tails.

In an onshore gale they have considerable difficulty in alighting on the ledges with their beautiful upward swoops: their feebly paddling shanks slipping back down the turf or rock of the cliff face, despite beating wings. One secures a perilous lodgment half on and half off a sloping ledge, holding his place by depressed, spread tail, and feebly head-waving, as if wondering what he is doing there: only to half turn and slip away into space with that glorious three-hundred-foot downward swoop I have thrilled to so many times, flattening out over the water.

Only once in fifty times does a fulmar attempt an actual landing. For the most part he is content to sail past his nesting ledge, as the swift past his hole in the eaves. When making a perfect landing he alights on straight, wide-spaced legs, to move in a step or two thus, or to sink forward onto the length of his pale lilac webs and shanks (black on the hind and undersurface), and finally to settle down with splayed webs curved away and out sideways—I can end an unnecessary but age-old controversy by stating that the fulmar *can* both stand and walk upright for several seconds.

Each new hoverer or alighter at the ledges is an invariable cause of excitement between rival pairs, or even between two birds of a pair, provoking an immediate outburst of wide-beaked cawing, which sometimes leads to oil-squirting, with much contorting and "snaking" back of heads. These primi-

tively organized birds are stimulated to sexual and jealous excitement by provocations apparently unconnected with either
of these fundamental sensations—a phenomenon to which I
return later. Observing how this is the invariable reaction of
those sitting on the ledges whenever another fulmar, swooping up, hovers above them, I cannot but incline to the opinion that this head-waving (one of the main features of their
courtship) may have arisen out of this watching and fending
off of rival hoverers and alighters—so intricately interwoven
are all the reactions and actions of birds.

In their continual planing athwart the cliffs, which I tend
in time to regard as an instance of perpetual motion, I am
suddenly aware that there are no longer any fulmars sailing
past and that the cliffs are deserted. They return, as miracu-
lously, from nowhere. At such times they are to be located
sitting on the waters half a mile out to sea: not feeding—I
have never seen a fulmar feeding by day—just bathing, and
cawing, and idly swimming. And in the early months of their
residence on the ledges they sometimes vanish for days at a
time. I have not full proof, but my evidence suggests that,
during these absences, they return to the cliffs at night. This
change in habit is due, perhaps, to some disturbance of their
planktonic food supplies by heavy seas.

I try hard to read the instincts of these fulmars; but this
early return to nesting territory seems a purely mechanical,
organic action. They have no conscious awareness of why
they plane all day about the cliffs or sit upon the ledges.
Three things rule them—Strong jealousy of their nesting site
to be: just as much ledge as they can sit upon. Spasmodic an-
tipathy to their prospective nesting neighbors (often touching
them): periodically expressed by a sudden barking and actual, or attempted, oil-ejecting, which is the supreme consummation of a bout of barking. (I have often watched a rook
going through all the actions of cawing, without producing
the caw; so the fulmar, much more often than not, goes
through all the actions of barking, without in the end produc-

ing any oil; and the gradually increasing tension of the forceful jerking and constricting of the head indicates that the actual ejection of oil is a matter of considerable physical effort.)

Third ruling emotion is a vague affection between paired
couples, hardly to be differentiated from the jealous anger of
rival pairs: except that the affectionate actions are a shade
gentler, though at all times the nebbing is very brisk, with
the bills often intertwining fiercely. The oil is undoubtedly a
powerful sexual stimulus, for there is, invariably, a great
smacking of mandibles after beak-intertwining, and the female always nebs her partner's beak provocatively when he
gets excited to the stage of ejecting, or after he has had a
bout of "oiling."

It is interesting to find that, thus early in the year, some
pairs have already established the habit of one bird replacing
the other on the nesting site, the sitting bird launching forth
directly its mate comes in; while other pairs sit amiably side
by side; and a third bird cantankerously by itself.

In February it takes a sunny day to attract the fulmars to
the cliffs; on cold, stormy days none settle on the ledges, although some sail past. But by the beginning of March there
are sixty fulmars sitting on the ledges, and some on other
parts of the island. The comedy continues all through March
and April: attendance at the ledges with unaltering ritual of
behavior on comparatively fine days; planing over the sea
and island on stormy days, of which there are a great number
on this gale-swept coast. By May they are sufficiently attached to the cliffs to sleep on them during the day with
heads tucked back into scapulars. And only then do I see the
actual mating.

On a turfy headland—where there is not the faintest
chance of their single eggs escaping the greedy fingers of island urchins or wealthy collectors—the male jumps onto his
partner's back, without any of the preliminary blandishments
of other birds, in the usual half-standing position; but beyond
rubbing his head on hers makes no attempt to hold her with

his beak, nor is there any excited vibrating of wings—indeed the cock of another mating pair sat back indifferently and waved his head bewilderedly! The mating is not consummated for two and a half minutes, and only at the critical moment do I see the fulmar for the first time as a bird of real sensibilities, and not just a superbly beautiful doll-bird. I cannot but be acutely struck by the extraordinary parallelism of emotion that runs right through the animal world. To judge by physical reactions, physical sensations can vary little from one genus to another. I feel compassionate for the poor fish—perhaps without justification.

The mating consummated, the male more or less falls off his partner's back, apparently exhausted. At a second mating of this same optimistic pair practice is making perfect. This time the male croons softly the while, and the female, uttering an occasional *cok-cok*, draws back her head to caress him in the most affectionate manner. The mating is of the usual duration, but now I am surprised to find a third bird alighting by them—on this turfy headland sixty or seventy yards from the communal nesting cliffs. Of him the mated pair take no heed during the actual mating, but two or three minutes later turn on him with gaping, oil-ejecting cawing, but without an ejection.

After a lengthy period of watching, I began to be aware that male and female fulmar have certain physical distinctions, which have not, I think, been recorded. The male's head is much bigger and bluffer, and typically masculine in its contours; he has also a bigger bulbous tip to his beak, with a distinct mauve tinting, whereas the female's is plain yellow-amber; this tip is demarcated from the remainder of his greenish-yellow beak by a black, or darkish, margining—for in these primitive birds the beak is still segmental; the inside of his beak is a deeper mauve, and the mauve along the outer edges of the mandibles is more extensive. This mauve buccal cavity is a nice instance of sexual selection: for constantly waving wide-open bill at his mate, the mauve interior is very conspicuous. And, finally, his gape is wider, and his throat baggier during the cawing. . . .

The intruder at the marriage bed is a male. Two-thirds of the fulmars at a nesting territory are non-breeding birds, which explains the nesting pair's comparative tolerance of their immediate presence by their nests—for fulmars recognize no territory except the actual nest hollow, eight or nine sitting on a square yard of cliff in complete amity, until some new arrival upsets them all and provokes an outburst of cawing and "oiling." Few sea birds—or for that matter wildfowl and larger birds generally, according to my observations—breed until their third or fourth year;[2] it is thus in no way surprising to find fulmars obeying analogous rules.

Towards the end of May, after these long months of unprogressive courtship, the fulmar lays her only egg—nor does she lay a second time if this is taken—the cock tending to sit most of the day and the hen at night, sitting hunched up low against the earth, position unchanged for hours at a time, with no visit from the respective partner. By this time the nesting sites, from long sitting, are hollows worn away in the sandy loam beneath the gray rock, and the ledges are bright with dark green thrift and its pale pink flowers. Inanimation reigns in the sleepy rookery, while the surf thunders at the base of the cliffs.

By June the fulmar are planing, not only over the island, but as far as two miles inland from the slakes: five miles inland from the island, that is to say. And out of more than one hundred birds about the island there are only fifteen nesting pairs, although sixty or seventy birds will be sitting at one time on the nesting cliffs. As befitting so primitive a bird, the fulmar's egg is shapeless (like a cormorant's), roundish, and

[2] In the greater black-backed gull I observe five separate plumages: the familiar first-winter mottling; second winter, light gray with black stripings; third winter, black mantle, grayish wings; fourth winter, brown-black and shaggy, and with black instead of red daub on bill; fifth winter, familiar full plumage.

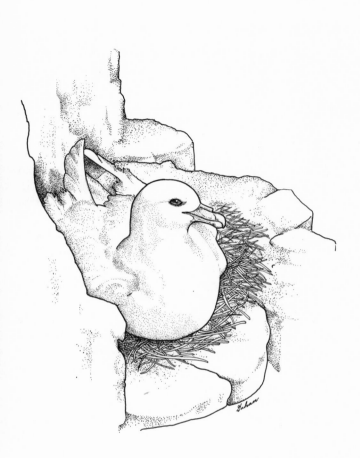

Fulmar nesting on a sea cliff ledge

as big as a pullet's, with the yolk showing through the rough white shell. Most of the eggs are taken from the island cliffs, but still the bereaved owners sit hard and patiently on stones or bare hollows, their pale breasts horribly stained with red-brown loam. They continue to caw with unflagging energy and pass away long hours in open-eyed sleep, trying my patience to the uttermost.

Incubating for sixty days, they are still pathetically sitting on or beside their eggs or pebbles at the beginning of July, screwing their heads backwards and forwards, looking up at me, half afeared. I know few pleasanter things than to sit on the cliffs on a perfect summer evening after tempest, watching the fulmars. White crests of surf break over the brown reefs with a thunderous roar, and the fulmars, riding the swell, dive through the breakers and even *fly* into them and through them for the pleasure of it! Silver Sandwich terns hawk over the gray-green waters of the bay, with strident *krooeech;* jackdaws beat out from their nesting holes in the cliffs, wretchedly feeble in comparison with the fulmars sailing strongly at some hundreds of feet on this fine evening; the same old pair of starlings chitter backwards and forwards over the bay with food for their young, and a lark sings just over my head. At the foot of the cliffs, a hundred feet below, the shallows are crystal clear, revealing the sand and rocks on the bottom. The fulmars, daintily striking the pellucid waters with pink and black webs, seem almost too heavy and material for so limpid a sea, despite the delicate motion with which they continually refresh themselves with little sips— when drinking, nearly the whole of the head is immersed for a considerable period. They bathe with delightful energy, dipping their heads well under and working the whole body with shuffling wings and depressed tails. After a vigorous flapping of wings, they run over the water on pattering webs (their normal method of breaking into flight), and shoot at females or rival males, with cawing *ga-ga-ga-ga:* the assaulted bird plopping forward, with an urgent *urg-urg* of protest.

Even in mid-July, when the sitting birds are already moulting, sexual excitement is still intense: whether darting about the water at each other, or barking on the ledges. And they are still at their splendid trick of sailing along the cliffs in the teeth of a northwest gale, and then floating with it on half-cocked wings and convex, fanned tail. At the end of July, the chick hatches: a bundle of white fluff, with black eye, steel-blue tubular beak, and (already) the lavender gape; it bobs up and down, with gaping beak, just as the adults do when barking and oil-ejecting, the male answering it with a caw, as he does his mate. . . . He has not the faintest idea what to do with it; in fact he is definitely uneasy at its stumbling approach, although the female gets as far as cosseting it. But at this time, though both parents may be with the chick in the early morning, the male normally tends it all day alone, the female feeding it at night. And again I see that remarkable, deliberate turning around of the chick from facing the sea to facing the cliff, in order to eject its yellow excreta clear of the nest over the cliff edge: an action common to such widely different species as swallows, sparrow hawks, and cormorants.[3]

In less than two weeks the chick is in gray fluff, showing a few quills, and the blue-white tip to the bill and prominent black tubular cavities (retained in the adult), sticking out like naval guns, are particularly noticeable.[4] The cocks continue to be as helpless as ever, sitting feet away from their chicks, who pant continually with the heat, particularly those in unsheltered nests on pebbles and rocks; but as they also pant on cold, cloudy days, I am forced to assume some ulterior cause than heat.

By the beginning of August the non-breeding fulmars have gone; the chick grows very fast, still being fed at night, and the ledges are often deserted by adult birds during the day. By the middle of August the chick is three-quarters the size of its parents, with tail and wings appearing and quills coming on head. And at the end of the month it is full-sized and has lost nearly all its down. At this time it is fed at all hours of the twenty-four with the inevitable oil that plays so conspicuous a part in the everyday life of a fulmar.

[3] The adult fulmar sitting on the water excretes upwards, clear of the water, to a considerable distance.

[4] In the mature fulmar the sheath of the nostrils is gray in some birds and black in others, but this seems to have no constant sexual significance.

The more I watch birds the more obvious it becomes that all their emotions—fear, jealousy, affection, hunger, anger, pleasure—are interrelated, and that all are fundamentally purely organic in their inspirations. Studying the courtships of different species in the field, I have seen how, time and time again, a bird reacts spontaneously and instinctively with antics of display to all these emotions; or that into the pattern of his display are woven gestures of fighting, nest-building, hunting, or feeding. Nature is constantly serving two purposes with one weapon, and the bird has no clear concept of what action serves what purpose: one bird reacting in one way only to a number of different emotions. The display-fight of the gray crow, for instance, is identical to that he uses when flapping to a height to drop molluscs on the shingle. When the shelduck, accompanied by her drake, returns to her burrow in the sand dunes, she enters it, as I have written earlier, with spread tail depressed as in courtship—the sexual mood full upon her. Thus it is that she smoothes the sand, leaving no trace of her webprints. Great-crested grebes and mute swans employ waterweeds in courtship, to build nests and to feed upon.[5] The fulmar feeds his young on oil, squirts it in anger at rivals, and passes it on to his partner in affectionate nebbing. . . .

At the beginning of September the chick leaves the ledges, and by the middle of the month it is rare to see a fulmar anywhere in onshore fishing grounds. Watching fulmars day in and day out for eight months in the twelve impresses me with the truth that here is the bird which most expresses the purely instinctive organism and habits of all birds. To the fulmar life is purely organic. Though I am fully of the opinion that no wild bird ever acts with tertiary intelligence—that is to say, ever forms a rational mental image—most at least have that vivacious, alert demeanor which I can designate as intelligent-looking. The fulmar appears daft and vacant. As he sits on his ledge, waving his foolish head from side to side,

[5] See Appendix B.

like a fat pigeon, or caws mightily with "snaking" neck, finally to squirt his amber oil in indeterminate direction, I look in vain for the slightest spark of awareness of his surroundings. He lives in a state of pathetic bewilderment, with no more intelligence than the banded snail clinging to a bent on top of the nesting cliffs. Courtship and mating to a fulmar are organic routine, though in the final stages of coition there are slight signs of animation. . . .

What matter! My memory is not of his foolishness, but of his free sailing over the sea. That is a glory I cannot forget: which will endure long after my defamatory writings of him are dust.

XVI

NESTING SEA BIRDS: AN IMPRESSION

An hour's sail out to sea is a three-mile half-moon of jagged reefs and precipitous islands: some submerged at high water, the wicked fangs of others seen and hidden in the swell, some rearing hundred-foot cliffs against the pounding seas. Over and around and betwixt them surge and swirl the most treacherous currents off British coasts. At high summer dense fogs come down over the islands, and hour after hour the foghorn moans twice every forty-five seconds seven miles over the blanketed sea. On black nights of tempest the eighteen-mile beam from the lighthouse quarters the compass. A ten-thousand-ton German liner once piled herself up high and dry across one of these reefs. Incredible!—If I had not seen the colossal swell surging eighty feet over the stacks.

These tempestuous islands yet harbor hundreds of thousands of sea birds in summer: some nesting on the turf-strewn larger islands, others on cliff ledges and the flat summits of sheer-faced pinnacles rising seventy-five feet from the sea, others again on the naked rock of black reefs drenched by the flung spray of the breakers. Many thousands roost on them in the winter. More thousands alight there on spring and autumn passage.

A mile downwind of the most landward reef the southerly breeze is tainted in the summer with a strange odor of decay. . . . It is the cormorants nesting on a flattened crag of black rock: more than a thousand purple-black caricatures of birds. Clearly they are more suited to wear leathern collars and catch fish in China seas than to nest on an English reef. A constant stream of hundreds of avian gargoyles pass and repass (as pterodactyls must once have passed and repassed) on their way to and from the reef, trailing nine-foot streamers of gelatinous oarweed—for they are continually adding to their nests, which by the end of the season are imposing, cylindrical stuctures. They alight beside their mates with croaking *guorwor*. Hundreds more stand uneasily beside their great drum-nests of shriveled, blackened weed, with their mates perched, spike-tailed, on their summits. They stand in their customary attitude of perpetual surprise: livid-cheeked, shaggy heads cocked at questioning angle to the heavens, black tar-brush tails flat on the sloping rock as a sitting dog's. Their beauty lies in the black-pupiled green irises with their turquoise-speckled lips, and in the exquisite white aigrettes of delicate plumes at their thighs, which they wear only in the breeding season: a wonderful instance of the workings of sexual selection—for see, of many pairs that are courting, the males, first flapping their wings, stand with "wired" pinions outstretched and bent at the elbows as those of an eagle on a lectern. The white plumes cannot fail to excite the females.[1]

How grotesquely uncouth are these great seafowl. *Wallch-gorr-gorr-wallch* they croak, wrinkling the bare skin of their chrome-salmon gular pouches. See the females responding to the amorous advances of their mates . . . crouching upon the

[1] In Chapter I the cormorants are "wired" on stakes: probably as an aid to digestion—yet another bird-action fulfilling more than one operation: the two obviously arising the one out of the other. But see footnote page 100.

Cormorant pair with its large seaweed nest

rocks, with necks snaked back into shoulders, hooked bills pointing skywards, and tar-brushes spiked over backs, heads and tails nearly meet in tensile bows . . . suddenly released with electric charge, as they bound forward, both webs together. Here is wonderful material for the evolutionist and student of animal behavior, if eye and brain are perfectly attuned.

The reef is fetid with sickening stench of rotten, half-digested fish and liquid guano streaming between the hundreds of pile-nests into sinks in the rocks—God forbid that I slip up here! Yet out of this corruption, beneath shapeless, stained, chalk-noduled exteriors, I can scrape clean with a knife exquisite pale-blue shells: lovely cradles for the blind and naked slate-gray monsters that emerge from them!

Ceaselessly harried by the fishermen, at the objurgations of their wives—for what cake is worth the eating that is not made with cormorants' eggs?—the cormorants are still feeding their white-bellied young in the last days of August. All day long little packs are streaming across the sea from the salmon river nine or ten miles to the north, their pouches so full that they fly with open beaks. When the convoys pass no more during the day, but larger packs of twenty or thirty cormorants, with closed beaks, come down only in the evening, then I know that the young are independent, and that these evening packs are flighting to roost after their day's fishing, as they will continue to do throughout the autumn and winter.

The slender, crested shag is a rare summer bird on this coast, but one or two pairs nest on broad ledges half way up dark chasms ever murmurous to the strange, wild music of the surging tide. It is as if this melancholy, croaking, prehistoric seafowl, with hooked, gamboge bill and superbly brilliant eyes as deep a green as the sea over which she brings forth her young, is sensible that her wave-washed, caverned eyrie is her ideal setting. Uneasy she stands, with her brown-eyed, dusky young on either side of her, half in shadow, half in misty sunrays playing on her bronze-green plumage and black tar-brush jauntily spiked upwards, while all about her echo the wailing cries of herring gulls nesting on the flat crag of an adjacent stack: *ullōa/ullōa/ullōa*.

With the cormorants nest some black-backed guillemots, who hop from crag to crag, webs together, like little white-bellied penguins. But on a seventy-five-foot columnar pinnacle is the miracle of thousands of these small divers massed together on its flat top so densely that the cloud of alighting birds must buffet others out of their way before they can find rock space. Eggs are constantly knocked into the sea in the turmoil; how so many survive long enough to hatch into chicks is hard to understand: a mystery not explained by the egg's pear shape. In every cranny and on every narrow ledge down the face of the cliff, too, is a guillemot sitting on her colossal egg: rough in texture as a cat's tongue, yet exquisitely colored pastel green or turquoise or rose-pink, black and brown scrawled. Others stand over dark chicks, keeping between them and the sheer drop to the sea, their mates in attendance. Above the thunder of the swell I am conscious of a dull, grating roar of drawn out caws, like the barking of sea lions.

Among these thousands are some of the "bridled" variety, grayer-hued than their congeners, with remarkable white rings to their eyes and white grooves curving back and down from their eyes across their cheeks. Here is another splendid instance of sexual selection (I have a multitude of confirmatory instances of this interrelationship of courting-gesture and plumage-coloration), for these circlets and grooves are also present in the ordinary guillemot, in whom, however, the white inlay is absent. The significance of this is of paramount interest, for here I see a species in the act of splitting on a matter of sexual selection by utilizing the obvious opening for specific change in these hitherto unexploited grooves—just as chiff-chaff and willow warbler split on the comparative advantage of one set of call-notes over another—or have I reversed the process, and is the "bridled" bird the degenerate? However this may be, I can trace this particular line of specific sexual selection through a whole family: the little auk with his white spot over the eye; the razorbill smartly distinguished by four china-white grooves in his stubby black beak and head, the grooves remaining but the white fading after the breeding season; and the remarkable puffin, with, amongst other head and bill finery (all the divers being great head- and bill-wavers during courtship), an indefinite groove running back from his obliquely-rimmed, peach-stone eye. . . .

On the guano-whitened cliffs Tommy Noddy puffins stand very upright on tiny vermilion or tangerine webs, their tails only just projecting beyond their short wings, or run along gracefully and speedily over the roof-tops of the rabbit burrows in which their mates are sitting in the pitted turf a few yards back from the cliffs. Fascinating little fellows they are: so confident that I may study them at a distance of six feet. I am minded to play with the words of sententious Dr. Boteler: "Doubtless God could have made a better beak, but doubtless God never did." Jutting, hawklike, from white face and perfectly shaped gray-black tonsure is a huge, triangular coulter-neb sheathed in vermilion and split from its gray-blue base by an orange band: a perfect sexual adornment falling away after the nesting season, exposing the coral-brown bill of winter seas. Intensifying the uniqueness of this ornate bill is the dark brown eye, ruby-ringed, with a triangular black slot above it and an intensely black bar beneath, and that indefinite groove running back to give it an oriental slant; on the white cheek is an orange-yellow raised disk, and beneath it a gray smudge. Yet all this extravagance of color springs from the sober black and white plumage of the bird of the year, with his short black bill and black shanks: a pathetic little creature, and, like all young animals, so helpless in the hands of Man, not knowing what to do, blinking in the sun, scuttling back to his burrow.

Very pleasant it is to sit upon the cliffs seventy feet above the cool green depths over the purple rocks, with little black-collared puffins continually whirring up and past me on tiny, quick-beating paddles, with a loud, soft-sounding vibrance. Brilliant coral-red webs are constantly in evidence for steering and braking: turned up flatly and spread wide either side the tail in the whirring up past the cliffs, stretched out flat behind in straight flight, pushed forward widely in the alighting. Cruising beneath them are packs of thousands of their fellows, humming with indeterminate cawing. I lack the exact words to express their peculiar charm, but I know that, given the opportunity, I could lie for hours at a time watching them, and never wish to bother myself with notes.

Over all is the undying clangor of the gulls. On a reefy knoll, a hundred or two yards square, nest a thousand lesser

black-backs. It is a grim, desolate place of naked rock dis-
eased with yellow-green lichens, of a little turf festooned with
creeping bunches of a sickly white weed, and of deep green,
noisome pools stagnant in rock hollows. Scattered over rock
and turf are the stained nests, with their magnificent owners
standing by, barking, with heads well thrown back: *ugg-ugg-
ugg:* a deeper cry than the herring gull's—a few pairs of
whom nest with them—without the beautiful wailing echo of
that gull. Wheeling in hundreds over my head they cry a
ceaseless *eeyaw/eeyaw,* which might be more appropriately
rendered, *get-off/get-off,* quickening to a yelping *eeyow-ee-
yow-eeyow.* They stoop at me with a vicious spattering, and
the threatening *wach-wach* of the black head. Wonderfully
handsome gulls these: the male far huger[2] and blacker of
mantle than his mate, the bloody stain on his powerful beak a
brighter red, brilliant yellow-brown shanks and dark amber
eyes rimmed in vermilion, in superb contrast to gray-black
mantles splendidly clean-cut against snowy cowls, breasts,
and flanks. Their nesting place so arid, I retain the impression of an almost barbaric splendor of color.

Outnumbering and out-crying all others are kittiwakes:
such silent and inoffensive gulls at other seasons. Every niche
and ledge on the cliffs has its nest or several nests of kittiwakes, cheek by jowl with guillemot and black razorbill,
waving brilliant gamboge buccal cavity at his noisy neighbors. Nature knew no color restriction in her plumaging of
sea birds: black and china-white superbly set off by a gamboge varnish; purple-black, sea-green and turquoise; gray-
black and white, bright yellow and scarlet.

The nests of the pale-plumaged kittiwakes are hollowless
drums of compressed guano and grasses, six or nine inches
thick. How the one, or two, white-downed chicks stick onto
their flat platforms, precariously wedged into their crannies
or on narrow ledges, is another mystery to me: some must get

[2] I think it is true to say that in every species of gull and tern the
male is considerably larger than the female.

Bridled guillemots.
Unlike most other birds, they walk and stand
on their shanks rather than their toes.

pushed off. The parent bird, soft of dark brown eye, stands over her cheeping nestlings on brightly-varnished, dark brown shanks (like that pastel green of the eider, an unique coloring). She squawks continually, with vividly painted scarlet gape wide open: the scarlet oozing from the base of her greenish-yellow beak.

Thousands of kittiwakes are at their nests; thousands are sailing to and fro the cliffs in pale gray and white clouds, which produce an hypnotic effect on me, looking down from above; thousands ride in packs on the sea at the base of the cliffs, with puffins and guillemots. And all the world is full of the ceaseless, deafening clangor of their childlike mewing *kittiwāā-aa*/*kittiwāā-aa*—an unusually deep note for so small a gull—echoing sadly in the chasms and caverns, reverberating from the cliff face, *kittiwāā-aa:* a cry that I cannot forget, which to think upon brings welling up sadness, that distant memories, however happy, always bring . . . perhaps because there is no surety that I can experience them again . . . the wailing of the kittiwakes and the moaning of the great gray seals.

End Note. In summer the razorbill is almost black, the tiny puffin shaggily black-brown, and the guillemot black-brown with a grayish sheen in some lights. Young guillemots are fawn, with the winter-white cheeks of the adult. At a distance on winter seas the guillemot appears black; closer, brown; in the hand, grayish-brown. One October day there was a guillemot sitting on the sands of the bay who seemed grayer than the ordinary run of guillemots. Distance, always a deceiver, had not prepared me for a lovely mole-gray plumage, with a gray line running down and back from his dull black eye across his white cheeks. I picked him up—he doing no more than open wide his long dagger-bill, with head cast back: protesting the while with deep *guorwor,* that reminded me of the croak of the shot heron. My sense of beauty always dominant, I let him go—when no doubt, in the interests of science, I should have despatched him (when no doubt, too, his beautiful plumage would have faded to some quite other shade), and preserved him for examination elsewhere. Though he progressed very feebly on land with the aid of spread flippers, he yet paddled out to sea quite happily and I saw him no more. All I could gather from the authorities was that guillemots were very gray in winter. They are, but nothing approaching a silver-gray. There not being, so far as I am aware, any gray species of guillemot, I have seen in this instance, perhaps, how in time the exception might prove the rule, and the brown guillemot, in whose plumage I can detect gray coloring-matter in certain lights at all seasons, become the gray guillemot; just as the black Arctic skua may become the cream Arctic skua.

XVII

PASSAGE OVER AUTUMN SEAS

On a July day, when young terns are essaying their first flights and the old birds are fishing in the shallows at low water, a black bird with long-shafted tail drifts in from sea, with disdainful flicker of sharp wings beating high over his back. There is sudden commotion among the terns and a tumultuous, anguished screeching, for the black stranger has singled out one with a whitebait drooping from his scarlet bill and given chase. Twisting and turning, stooping and soaring in vertical, flapping flight—as a gull does when mounting in the air to drop mussels on the shingle, but with the keenness of the pursuit imparting a decisive edge to the evolution—the pirate follows hard on the tail of the tern with grim persistence, not to be shaken off by the sharpest move. And then the victim lets fall his fish, and his pursuer stoops to seize it before it drops into the sea.

Spring and summer's northerly flow of bird life is ebbing, and this is the first Arctic skua to respond to his far-ranging southerly impulses of autumn. From now on to December the summer birds of the seas give way to birds on passage to warmer waters, and others coming in from north and east to winter off English coasts. Cruising anywhere within the ten- or twelve-mile limit of the onshore fisherman, the signs of the season are plain.

Arctic skuas, though nesting in the north of Scotland, are essentially birds of passage off British coasts from the middle of July to the end of October, which is approximately the migratory period of various species of tern, whose constant companions they are. And a few days after that first encounter, a pair of skuas are robbing the terns far out over the sands. Although they often hunt in pairs, threes and single skuas are just as common. There is no more concertedness of purpose in two hunting together than in two or more rooks harrying a starling; rather is it likely that the Arctic skua is another instance of a species that is paired up throughout the year—which I am inclined to think is usual among far-flying sea birds.

Arctic skuas are passing down the coast almost every day in September and October, and more than once I espy them sitting on a grassy headland, from which they rise to fly west inland for as far as my binoculars can follow them—a strange and significant action of so pelagic a species, and one that I have also observed of great skuas. So graceful in flight, they are ungainly on the ground, their heads seeming tiny, out of all proportion to their unexpectedly massive bodies: an oddity accentuated by their comparatively small bills and neat black crowns—about the only part of their plumage that is invariable from skua to skua. For, while some are jet-black in entirety, other Arctic skuas are white on neck, breast, and shoulders, and others cream on their bellies and chocolate on their backs; and most interesting: black and piebald paired off together. Edmund Selous recorded fifteen intermediate patternings of browns and buffs. Here is remarkable evidence of sexual selection actually in the melting pot: the original one-color patterning surrendering to specific influences in favor of some more salient patterning of advantage to the species in its stimulus to reproduction.

It is August before the first great skua beats leisurely southwards with slow, regular wing-beats and intermittent glides: careening like a gannet athwart the troughs of the waves, the extremities of his wings sloping sharply back, a silver band across his tail; and he stays in Northeast fishing waters right through into December. Individual variation in the size of both species of skua is so great that it is not easy to differentiate between them at a distance, for the immature Arctics have not the characteristic, long central tail-shafts; nor are the dull silver triangles at the elbows of a great skua's wings an infallible distinction, for the wings of some Arctic skuas are just as silvered.

In strong pursuit of an adult herring gull whining pitifully like a young bird, a great skua (of a size with his victim) chases him right into the harbor, and dropping to retrieve the fish, with dull gleam of silver belly, settles on the water, and allows himself to drift out to sea with the ebbing tide: sitting with pale head and neck hunched back into shoulders darkly mottled in brown. But not always is a skua successful in his piracy. I have often observed both terns and gulls mobbing skuas who have robbed them, or have attempted to rob them, of their fish. I have watched a great skua mobbed by a greater black-backed gull, and ridding himself of this nuisance, harry a common gull, only, in turn, to be chased by another common gull. Does a skua chase any gull or tern, or does he sense a full-fed quarry—for not always has the victim a fish in his bill—just as small birds seem to know when a hawk is satisfied, and ignore his at other times feared presence. Unsuccessful pursuits are much more numerous than successful. Some terns are not always to be harried into dropping their whitebait or sand eels for the skua to retrieve, and some gulls do not react so easily to the emotion of fear that causes their fellows to disgorge. Most, perhaps all, birds that feed their young by disgorging also disgorge when frightened or provoked—the heron is perhaps the best-known instance.

Let me stress once more, because it is perhaps a fact the significance of which is not generally appreciated, that several different stimuli can produce a like organic effect upon a bird. Any sufficiently strong provocation or fear causes a gull to disgorge, just as a parental stimulus causes him to disgorge to his young: a herring gull disgorges to a great black-back. So, again, skuas, accustomed to robbing their fellows, just as gull robs gull, and profiting by this tendency to disgorge, came in time, quite naturally, to feed only in this way, sensing perhaps which of their potential victims were full fed. I arrive at the remarkable state of affairs that a nestling great skua is fed mainly on food that has twice been disgorged: once by a gull and once by its parents!

The impulse to chase another bird is universal, and especially prevalent among terns and gulls, whose fish prey it is not always practicable to swallow at a gulp, and therefore hangs obvious from their bills: an incitement to their fellows to seize it. It is not hard to conceive that skuas, themselves of the gull stock, should, by the usual processes of natural selection, have evolved in time solely as chasers of others of their kind: just as some black-headed gulls and rooks seem to be tending that way, with peewits and starlings as their victims.

Skuas are not the only southing birds in July. There was a night in that month when I was shaken from my bed by the shattering boom of the coastguard's rocket-gun. Dashing out, I found it nothing more momentous than the Trinity tug wanting a pilot to bring her up the twisting channel into the harbor. Lying out on the shingle-beach off the castle point, I watched her skirt the bar on, I think, the loveliest night I have known on this northern island, with the brightest of moons shimmering on the waves. When she moved in across the ruby lights of Bamburgh and the Stag, the tug's bluff lines were slimmed to a destroyer's in the moon's softening light. Her black and midnight form was relieved only, and superbly, by her green navigation light, when she cut in so smoothly and swiftly. The night was quiet, but for the solemn clangor of her impatient hooter, and scattered cries of curlew, gulls, and stone-runners.

Once out of bed, it seemed foolish to go back on so lovely a night, and I lay out till morning. At dawn, on the calm waters of the slakes, I picked up the familiar figures of great-crested grebes, unexpectedly black and white against their vast background of sea and distant, rising mountains: their black cobra-heads, white cheeks, and slender necks endowing them with a grace and delicacy of form delightful to see.

Tiny grebes are constantly on the slakes in spring and autumn—black-necked and horned: the former with uptilted bill, the latter with marked black cap. In the spring, although so many hundred miles south of their nesting territories, they court on the slakes with characteristic screeling laughs: rearing up in the water before each other, with silvery flash of bellies as silky of texture as thistle plumes, in brilliant contrast to their intensely black mantles.

Cruising around a mile out to sea on a morning later in the autumn, through a motley company of guillemots and razorbills, splendid black and silver long-tailed duck ("sea pheasants" we call them in the north, because of their spike-tailed rocketing flight over the waves), gannets, shearwaters, shags, plump velvet scoter with distinctive white triangles on their wings, and large divers, the purring coble suddenly alarms more than one hundred large black-and-white grebes scattered over the mirrored waters of the great bay; at the boat's silent approach, with engine throttled down, they run along the surface with threshing white-slotted wings, and dive repeatedly: red-necked grebes, as silvery under as all their kind, with chrome-yellow beak slots slashing the sides of their heads.

An astonishing number of large divers pass along Eastern coasts in autum and in spring, when they wail lugubriously; I have seen as many as twenty great northern divers in a morning, and twelve in a pack in full breeding plumage, very fine

with their thin black heads. As his name betokens, the great
northern is a bird of considerable majesty, and his huge size
is usually apparent; in a good light I can distinguish the hallmark of black patch at the side and paler stripe down the
back of his neck; when he rolls in the sea to preen, he dis-
plays more white than the smaller divers; but the dominant
impression I retain is of the snowy whiteness of the long
neck, and of an attenuated greater black-backed gull, very
white at either end, flying low above the waves with typical
diver flight (that is to say, after the manner of a kingfisher),
his long, thin, black-bordered wings set very far back.

The smaller, shorter-necked red-throated and black-
throated divers are hard to differentiate at sea at this autumn
season, but the former is white speckled on the back and his
bill is upturned, while the latter has a habit of raising himself
in the water and flapping short grayish wings, with dagger-
beak pointing skywards.

More stable elements in northern seas are the pelagic duck;
indeed throughout the summer there are packs of hundreds of
non-breeding scoter, scores of long-tails, and tens of velvet
scoter, in the great bay; but in autumn and winter these are
increased tenfold. It is August before there are signs of this
augmentation of the non-breeding scoter, who stick very
closely to the waters of the great bay, with characteristic
glimpse of a line of sixty, one hundred and forty, three
hundred black duck, a mile offshore, flying low at great speed
one behind the other, with sea serpent sinuosity: for the line
undulates, skimming low above the waves, and individual
members of the flight are continually closing up into dark
bunches and opening out into line again—I can forgive au-
thoritative gentlemen for writing to the papers that they have
observed sea serpents traveling at one hundred miles an hour
off the East Coast. Closer, the line disintegrates into its component parts of sable-black drakes and dark maroon ducks
with light cheeks, often one behind the other right along the
line. A single duck may fly with twenty odd drakes, and

while they change from *V* to line and back into echelon again, she remains in the van: the coulter of the wedge, the spearhead of the line; just as a single duck of any species always leads her drake in flight.

The black-throated diver is a fast flyer despite its bulky appearance and relatively short wings.

It is but rarely that scoter come close inshore, but sometimes a little swarm of ducks and drakes go rushing about the shallows in great excitement, with softly croaking *goggog/gog*, chasing marine game in some creek or little bay: riding very high, and elevating tails, as spiky as pintails'. At such close quarters the drake is a delightful little duck: coalblack in entirety but for the orange base-half to his greenish upper mandible, so light in color that at a distance it often seems white—which is sometimes true of the extremity of his undertail-coverts. His brown duck's beak is a greenish-blue, and—according to my notes—both duck and drake have a lumpy protuberance at the base of the beak. Breaking into flight at my approach, the drakes whistle shrilly, presumably —like sheldrake or goldeneye—with their wings, although the whistling begins so instantaneously with the break into flight that I *have* thought it to be a vocal sound.

On a gray day in September, with a northerly gale threatening: gray clouds and rain mists scudding over the bare, gray Cheviots, bowing the wind-swept trees that lean always to the southwest: a day bringing the grim blood of the Border to me, my thoughts back in the past with the cruel forays of the hard-riding moss troopers, back in the ballads of Douglas and Percy—we go out to sea to retrieve what lobster creels we may before the swell smashes them beyond repair, and run into hundreds upon hundreds of Manx shearwaters feeding with gannets and gulls on one of those stupendous masses of sand eels we encounter so often at sea. I espy them a mile away, as I have espied them in Devon seas and off the Western Highlands: straight-winged birds silverly hovering and falling at one moment, slipping sideways, blackly gliding at another, with constant sideways cutting of black wings shaped like reversed assegais. Later, they are all about the boat, sitting dark-backed on the sea: seeming tiny divers, but for the prominent nostrils of their slender, hooked bills; and then, with short, characteristic petrel run and white flash of snowy underparts, they break into tireless gliding flight, with wings beating as rarely as a fulmar petrel's.

And, again, on a perfect October morning of moonlight— with the castle on the rock standing up like some fantasy from Scott: so dimly seen, yet so clearly black in the radiance; the silent priory half in shadow, half revealed: Wordsworth this; the moon ripple-mirrored on the sea, flooding it with silver-gold: a tithe of the Western Isles—we chug away to the line fishing. At dawn seven skylarks come out to sea from the island. Circling leisurely, occasionally chasing one another, and even stopping to hover and sing a few notes, they proceed on their way southeast to the open sea—surely a strange method of embarkation for migration! And then out of the gray gloom of dawn comes a black bird, nearly as large as the herring gulls about the boat, hawking like a nightjar low over the water with short glides and slow beats: straight, slender wings almost meeting over his back. Straightly skimming the waves, he comes skating along the surface of the sea at great speed, with wings still out-stretched (whitish on their undersurface), making skis of his widely-splayed pink legs and webs slanting outwards slightly. He skids over the surface, runs off into flight, slashes a breaker, or cuts under a wave in imperceptible dive with wings still open: emerging in the same manner. His agility on the water is astounding. With superlative energy and dash he angle-turns and "dives" with his spoils from under the very beaks of the herring gulls, with shrill, ill-natured, gull-like scream: a staccato, file-rasping *zewt*. He strikes me as essentially an ill-tempered bird. No other bird I have seen bears any likeness to this "foxy" plumaged great shearwater, with his white throat and breast, rather slender black bill hooked and nostriled like all petrels, black eye, and wings white-slashed at the elbows when they close.

He follows us to within half a mile of the shore, continually skating up, after short rests, to filch the flung guts among the screaming, slashing gulls. When he sheers off, I look back over the tiller, watching him sail away with his airy, gnatlike flight: finding it a strange thought that he is more than six thousand miles north of his birthplace in lonely Tristan da Cunha. Though this is nothing, if it be true that the Chatham Isles in New Zealand seas are the only nesting territories of the sooty shearwater, who is a comparatively common bird off this coast—a plumper, duskier bird than the Manx shearwater, though shorter-winged, and not to be met with in packs.

Each new day brings with it some characteristic sign of the season, which while of great interest to me on the spot would make but tedious reading if set out in detail. Ten miles offshore on a fine November morning, returning northwest to harbor, a fine cock snow-bunting comes up suddenly from the northeast to alight on our decked bows. After a peck round, he perches on the gunwales and tucks his head into his scapulars, keeping a weather eye open. Half an hour later he takes off with the intention of resuming his southerly passage, but chased by the greedy herring gulls, he turns back northeast and finds refuge on a southerly-going trawler. Despite his long sea passage, he is strong on the wing, and throws up successfully from the vicious stoops of the gulls.

Half a mile offshore, a dusky-white little bird, with black eye and sharp black bill, intermediate in size between knot and dunlin, for whom I at first mistook him, gets up from the sea with sibilant cry: a gray phalarope. And riding high on the calm waters of the bay, diving with spatter of coral paddles, are four very white little divers: black guillemots, who pass north again in the spring, gaily plumaged in black and scarlet, sooty wings white-slotted. And always there are magnificent gannets: for while August, September, and October are their passage months, there are mature gannets in our fishing grounds the winter through. Indeed, from the first days of

June onwards through the summer there is a continual procession of gannets down the Northeast coast from the Bass
Rock: five hundred birds an hour planing south, close inshore, the horizon never clear of them. At first I imagined
that some abnormally early southward migration was in progress; but after some days of watching from a headland, I
saw also that, all and every day, there were gannets going
north a mile or so out to sea—the precise distance depending upon conditions of weather and tide—whose mode of
flight was quite other than that of the southerly goers. For
whereas the latter sailed abandonedly south just offshore in
small scattered flights, checking their progress south from time
to time to circle and stoop for fish—each bird working on
his own, or attracted by the stoopings of others—those going
north, with the wind on their flanks too, flew in file or irregular
V, gliding and wing-beating in perfect rhythm, without checking to circle or dive for fish. My impression was that, having
exhausted the possibilities of the herring shoal they had previously been following south, they were now returning to those
fishing grounds at which they had first located the shoal. It
was not until I was among them in the smack that I saw what
should have been apparent long before, that these were all
immature gannets circling the fishing grounds and breeding
territories of their nesting brethren in a great ellipse: just as
the immature fulmar petrels are present at the nesting cliffs
of their kind.

Before moving off on migration, as already noted, gulls and
owls soar higher and higher, drifting gradually in the direction of their eventual line of flight. I deem it probable that
such species as gannets, who depend for their existence upon
migrating shoals of herrings and mackerel-guard—following,
in their turn, sand eels—travel south in this circuitous manner, often flying directly north, but always completing an
overlapping circle farther to the south than the previous
one: reacting to the normal southerly *pull* in autumn.

In big seas gannets, slanting down with a lovely motion of

tensely-sprung pinions, half close these in a rigid W only a
few feet above the waves, and I thrill to the sudden acceleration of the stoop before the clean-cut plunge. In such
weather, too, they make their dives a part of their normal
flight, and shoot into the breakers almost flat. Diving from so
low an altitude they are soon gorged, and sit upon the waves;
or rise from them only with difficulty in heavy, slow-flapping
flight; or not at all, even after disgorging two hundred sand
eels at a gulp.

On calm days they plane two hundred feet over cobalt
seas, ever searching the waters beneath them—diving at intervals, stooping as steeply as peregrine, with half-open wings
until the moment of impact, when, with pinions folded tight
to the side, the diver hits the water with terrific impact, amid
a four foot cascade of spray, that I can hear three hundred
yards away two seconds after he has vanished. Looking over
the sides of the smack into clear water, I can see that the
diver plunges almost perpendicularly down into the water
and out of sight. Although a considerable interval elapses before his reappearance, he comes to the surface some yards
distant from his place of entry flatly, with a bob so resilient
as to suggest that his emergence is the final act of a single un-
checked movement, which usually includes the swallowing of
the fish under water. On emerging from these steep dives, he
may ride the waves for a short space, but invariably flies a
hundred yards or so just above the surface of the water before beginning to climb to a height once more. When the
shoal of fish is small the sea boils with the cascades of gannets plunging headlong one after the other. It is remarkable
that they can see the fish from such a height, and that they
can dive at sufficient speed to capture those they espy. More
probably the gannet dives into a shoal with sufficient impetus
to capture a fish or fishes as the shoal dart away. This would
also be true of terns. Relative to the terrific impetus of his
plunge, I note two details of a gannet's structure: first that he
has no external nostrils, and second that the many folds of

*The gannet—a powerful bird
with a six-foot wing-spread*

loose skin at his breast are inflated before diving, to form air
cushions against the force of his impact with the water.

Stooping a few feet from our smack, an immature gannet is
a creation of the devil: black of spearing beak, and a mottled
purplish-gray of plumage, with an ashy-white bar across his
tail. I have known myself, momentarily, to confuse one of
these young gannets flying at a distance over gray seas with,
respectively, cormorant, great northern diver, and gray goose.
But a mature gannet diving is magnificent: a superlative bird

with his wing-spread of more than six feet, black wing-tips sloping sharply back from the unusually straight, long pinions dwarfing those of great gulls; and that pale-blue dagger-bill streamlined into narrow, ocher-washed head; and those webbed feet with their pale-green tendons! Is it merely coincidence that the gannet is in the habit of covering his eggs with his *feet* during incubation? The most impressive bird over English seas, in strong sun a mature gannet is distinct from a gull at a mile and a half by reason of the dazzling whiteness of his plumage. When storm clouds bank over the mountains, with the sun still shining upon the sea, the silver purity of gannets stooping athwart their intensely black background is incomparable.

On wild autumn days—gray, clear days, with the smell of the sea over all the island: with the sea slate-gray and green, white-crested, broad-surfed on sands and reefs—mighty silver gannets are forever sailing south: planing across a northeast gale, gliding at an angle athwart the troughs of the breakers at vicious speed, seeming to cut the crests with the sharp tips of their wonderful ski-shaped wings. God help all fishermen! But to see the gannets in such weather is to know the sea conquered.

XVIII

THE GULLS' WAY

I wake with a start to a heavy rattling of the windows, conscious of a hail from outside: "Hullo there! Four o'clock and a fine morning!" . . .

The cobbled streets of the sleeping village echo to the dull thud of heavy sea boots. . . .

By Heaven! But it's a lovely night!—No morning, this! Glittering stars and white, refulgent moon light the shining roofs and the rippling sea, the black cliffs and the castle high on its rock, with unearthly radiance. Curlew shriek wildly at my coming to the little bay. Rowing out to the coble, we leap aboard into a jumble of fishing gear and boxes, masts and floats. The engine chugs at the first turnover, and we sweep round and away to sea.

Our fishing grounds this morning lie out at the base of a broad stream of wave-dancing moonlight. East is the white-flashing light of the Longstone, south the ruby glow of the Stag Light, back of us the castle looming up blackly, shapeless in the moonlight.

Full speed ahead, and a dry passage with an ebbing tide.

How far away can they hear the throbbing of our engine in the night stillness? Red and white lights of a tramp-steamer pass across our bows. For an hour we chug steadily on a gentle swell, talking little: the other three coiling tow-ropes and joining the three lengths of line, I at the tiller. Vague, ghostly figures drift up on the chill breeze: soft *kit-kit* betrays the little kittiwake; larger forms are those of herring gulls and greater black-backs—for it is winter, and at that season the open sea belongs to the gulls, and to a lesser degree the small divers. Within half a mile of the shore there may be many sorts of birds: beyond that, other than these gulls and divers there are only occasional gannets and shags and more rarely still shearwaters and petrels. This is the gulls' way, where the wind's like a whetted knife, and I quiver with the numbing cold.

In the gray light before sunrise the two ruins on the islands come into line, and we are approaching our fishing grounds. On the black reef, where the cormorants nested in the summer, more than a thousand shags roost—who of late years have taken to drifting down the Northeast winter coast in droves of hundreds. Among them are some white-breasted, pale-buff individuals, aberrant birds of the year: with pale-buff webs, too, they are strange objects. At our passing they jump reluctantly off the reef into the swirling surf, diving and swimming in packs with their fellows.

Only a seal can rival the beautiful diving of a shag, who, shooting almost vertically from the sea in a sinuous curve, with spatter of webs behind bluff tail depressed, arches a bow, and dives in again almost vertically with throw up of square tail: a delicious motion. His dives average sixteen seconds, and the fish is well titillated in his bill, before it is swallowed with a jerking gulp, and a second gulp to complete the operation satisfactorily; but it is no uncommon thing to see both shag and cormorant wrestling with a large flatfish for minutes together, pouched throats visibly distended. Never was a bird's perfect physical response to exter-

Kittiwake gull with her chick on the nest,
on a narrow ledge high above the sea

nal stimulus more wonderfully illustrated than in the lightning dive of a shag at the flash of a gun thirty or forty yards
distant: he beats the pellets every time!

On these islands, too, the gray seals are suckling their
young at this season, yet here are three cows courting one
huge bull, for, somewhat strangely, this is also the season of
the rutting. Rearing up in the water, they nuzzle his mighty,
anvil head all at one moment, and then play, or display,
about him, with grunting barks, threshing the sea with their
leapings. The bull's polar-bear head is twice the size of the

shapeless cow's and mighty ugly, but perfectly shaped for swift submarine progress. It is authoritatively stated that these monsters are likely to be eleven feet in length, seven feet in girth, and weigh fifty stones. Yet they dive with that same grace and agility of the shag, leaping clear of the breakers with a lovely, tensile curving of sleek, water-shining body; shooting through the sea's filament with the sinuous swiftness of a salmon. They continually stand in the water, and seem able to ride a breaker so without losing position, their massive necks yellow-mottled like a sea leopard's (or a London plane tree). And then they sink slowly, elevating bristly snout, closing large dark eyes, opening and shutting wide nostrils which sink last of all so that I have constantly in view what looks like the vertical fluke of a killer whale, as the conical snout gradually vanishes.

When the engine is throttled down beyond the islands, I can still hear their weird cries . . . the mellow mooing of a calf, a child's wailing, a dog's howling. A lovely sound: a seawater wistful moaning in caverns, very sad and haunting . . .

Over goes the red flag, with its three sky-blue floats, and the coils of eighty fathom of tow-rope jerking out the line with its dependent hooks. For half an hour the line whips from three coracle-shaped, wicker swills over the roller on the boat's gunwale, mussel-baited hooks flickering from their grass bed at one end of the flat cradle. Sometimes a kittiwake plops into the water, with excited small-gull screech, plucking at a baited hook, getting himself hooked in the process, before the lines sink to the bottom. At this season he bears a black and gray smudged yoke over his neck; while his lovely young have broad purple marginings to the front edges of their wings, black collars, and black bands across square white tails. The only small gull at sea—for rarely do common or black-headed gulls go out many miles from the shore—the charming kittiwake meets every fishing coble coming out of harbor; accompanying us to and from the fishing grounds.

On the two and a half miles of our line there are three

thousand six hundred hooks, which will lie upon the sea floor at thirty or forty fathoms. When the last of the three swills is empty and another red flag and its blue floats hoven aboard, we put about. Far to the west, the green, rounded Cheviots are lovely against a pink sunrise, with rose-colored, feathery wisps of cloud stretching across a translucent sky of ethereal blue—foretelling a gale later. For three-quarters of an hour we ply aimlessly in great circles about our float, waiting for the bait to take: free to observe what bird life there is.

Little bundles of guillemots and razorbills and, less often, puffins or little auks, whirl away in orbicular flight downwind at astonishing speed, their tiny paddles beating as fast as those of a partridge. At this season the guillemot is the commonest diver, and after him the razorbill, for it takes heavy seas to drive many puffins and little auks within the ten-mile limit. Maintaining their reputation for humor, the coral-brown-beaked puffins bounce over the sea before the boat for a hundred yards, bounding resiliently off bright coral paddles stretched out behind them, flat and widely splayed: a delightful touch of color! After every series of bounds, they dive straight into the sea, to bob up and sip water—as all sea birds do when nervous or excited—and shoot along through the surface of the sea, neither out nor in, before setting off on their comical, bounding progress again.

There is no mistaking little auks at sea, for they whir around in slanting circles, and dive constantly, without any preliminaries, remaining down for inordinate periods. With typical diver contour of squat bodies, blunt heads, and up-tilted beaks, they are, so small, pleasing little birds: with black chin straps and black caps well down over white cheeks. Smaller than song thrushes, it is remarkable that they can live through the terrific gales at sea during autumn and winter, which must render feeding an impossibility for days at a time; yet perhaps not more than once a year do I encounter them in numbers close inshore.

For three days of terrific gales and blizzards I have

watched them ceaselessly passing south offshore, hour after hour. Standing out on the far point of a reef, with a blizzard of snow cutting into my back and blown spume from the colossal breakers drenching me, bundles of little auks, three or four or ten at a time, would come whirring up over my head or a foot or two to one side. Hardly able to beat up against a howling southwesterly gale, they continually plop into the sea to rest, diving straight under the breakers on alighting, only to be up again and on. . . . Poor little devils, they seemed to have small chance of survival under such weather conditions—and yet no corpses were washed up on the shore.

At sea the gray-brown guillemot looks much larger than the razorbill, who swims very high in the water, in a dumpy attitude accentuated by his stubby beak and spiked tail, and dives for lengthy periods, covering extraordinary distances under water. At any distance on the sea a guillemot is a strange-looking creature: the black line slanting back across his white cheek creating the illusion that his bill is uptilted, whereas, in reality, it is slightly hooked at the tip. In my hand, this illusion is dispelled, and is perhaps accounted for by a habit of carrying his head hunched back into his scapulars.

Files of gannets, magnificent in their silver plumage, sail up to us, their wings beating in perfect time, and glide athwart the boat, as we turn once more to our fishing. Catching our flag with a boat hook, we throttle down and begin to haul in the lines over the wooden roller, balancing on two fish boxes, and straining at the thin horsehair line, with fingers protected by strips of felt wound around them. (A hell of a job, this, in choppy seas!) When unhooking the catch, the kittiwakes hover within reach of our hands, alert to snap up loose bait or half-fish chopped by shark or sucked by octopus.

Almost a third of the first line is heaped in its cradle before a fish is landed: a great-headed codling, barbed of lower jaw. Fish come well on the second line, and slacken again on the third: codling, none heavier than five pounds; little purple-brown haddocks, unbelievably beautiful compared to those hideous yellow-smoked gloves usually associated with the name of haddock, St. Peter's thumbmark in purple-brown at the sides of their heads; silvery whiting tinted with pink and brown; small flatfish, still kicking; bronze-purple gurnards spined to cut our hands to the bone, and, like them, but unspined, sea bream; green-spotted dragonets, stingers, like miller's-thumbs; and a monstrous angler fish, with enormous mouth and terrible teeth, amber-eyed, leathery-skinned.

At the hauling I love to see the greater black-backed gulls barking. There are always three or four swimming a few feet from the boat. Throwing their massive heads far back, with great hooked bills opened wide (their profile exactly that of a dog howling to the moon), they let rip: *uggha-uggha-uggha-uggha*—especially when they are hungry and there is a good prospect of an early gorge on fish guts. Their deep crying affords them such obvious satisfaction that I cannot but smile. And before each bout of calling they sip a little water— which is a thing all gulls and many other sea birds do so often that I can only surmise that they actually drink salt water. On the wing they cannot lift their heads very high, but they do so slightly, constricting their necks and calling with considerable effort; while the mottled, gray young, black-striped, swoop, with squeaky calls, after another of their kind —a bird in his fourth winter, with black daub instead of red on his yellow beak, struggling to gulp down a two-pound codling which has floated off a hook.

Their deep "laughing" and the thin cries of the young bring back memories to me. In the Hebrides, pairs of great gulls are far up over the mountains, in menacing, slow-beating, purposeful flight: their torpedo bodies majestic in silver contrast to their mighty sable wings, white-edged. From time to time they sound impressive, deep-toned *aw-oo* or growling *urr*. Their young stand pink-legged on the black-and-white chimneys of the fishermen's cots, wheezing squeakily with penny whistle pipings. At low water they quarrel on the edge of the stone quay, or in the dry bed of the harbor, over the offal thrown out from the slaughterhouses. In their blue eyes in unconscious malevolence. The sea bird is different from other birds: in him is the spirit of the ocean. In the wailing cries of the gulls sounds the stress of storm-tossed breakers. Sure in their powers of riding out the fiercest tempest, a calm indifference to the elements and the affairs of men is clear in their cold, far-seeing eyes.

We hook strange beasts on our forty-fathom line—lobsters, unbelievably beautiful, with dark blue armor-plating flaked with orange, and scarlet antennae; burnt-orange edible crabs with giant claws; and stone crabs: spidery beasts in red armor; sea anemones glued to stones; red and yellow starfish, a foot across; and tiny octopuses: gelatinous, clammy messes. Let a fair-sized octopus but affix itself firmly to my skin with its sucker-disked tentacles, and it is likely to come away with skin and flesh down to the bone; drop it onto the floor of the boat, and, by some remarkable instinct, it makes for the sides and clambers over the gunwales into the sea. Red cuttlefish are hoisted, discharging streams of black ink from their torpedo bodies; but when they fall from the hooks into the water, they shoot down from a swirling cloud of *brown* ink, accelerating nine feet, with extraordinary swiftness, at single expulsions of water from the pipes within their bodies; though they are just as likely to shoot backwards, directed by their tail ailerons.

Today we have an easy haul: no section of the line fouling the bottom—to be cut, perhaps, after an hour's struggle and grappled for, probably vainly. In two hours all the line is in. We have three boxes of fish: fifteen or sixteen stone—it might be worse! Many of the boats have been landing only four or five stone this season. But it takes twenty-five stone a haul to make a living at this game. Before the War,[1] before the trawlers had swept the seas clean, it was not unusual to average sixty and seventy stone a day, for weeks at a time.

[1] World War I. (*Ed.*)

Puffin

Putting about for home, we rig a tiny brown sail to steady the boat in the half-gale now blowing against the tide. For an hour, before chugging into the smoother waters of the bay, through the splendid packs of black and silver eider, we plunge through a perpetual flam of water that penetrates my oilskins and lashes my eyes with its stinging salt. There are seconds when the bows of the massively-built, thirty-two-foot coble plunge down so far into a trough that it does not seem possible that she shall come up again . . . only to smash down upon the crest of a lower wave with an appalling dull thud —not with the proverbial shivering of timers . . . to drown us with great flukes of water flung by her terrific impact.

During this hour's homeward drenching we gut and pack our catch for the carrier, and the kittiwakes are joined by a screaming pack of two hundred greater black-backed and herring gulls swooping down upon the guts tossed overboard: accompanying us into harbor, or until the gutting is ended, when they go streaming back to the wheeling cloud over another coble a mile astern. To have scores of these grand birds, with wings spanning five and six feet, and snowy tails spread like fans, sailing over my head and alongside within reach of my hand, gives me the greatest possible pleasure. The ability of gulls to plane with motionless wings about a boat buffeting her way into a gale is consummate. No part of their bodies impedes their aerial progress, for their shanks are stretched back beneath their tails; indeed, they are often hidden in their undertail-coverts.

It is the herring gulls who filch most of the guts. They are far too quick on the wing for the great gulls, who are content to harry them, swooping down fiercely, five or six in a screaming, savagely-fighting smother in the sea. At this season the herring gulls are in their winter plumage, their heads and necks thickly striped and freckled in yellow-brown—as are the lesser black-backs before they go south in November. The eye of an adult herring gull is a strangely cold brown-amber: his plumage otherwise so pale a gray and white, this freckling about the head and neck gives him a sinister charm, which like that of a reptile, both fascinates and repels me. Nevertheless, he is especially dear to me because of his wild barking cry. I see one now standing on a reef in the Hebrides; he wails awhile—*gerwy-yer/gewy-yer*—then, throwing back his head, and pointing wide-open beak to the skies, he howls *gerwyer/gerwyer/ger-ger* and many more resounding *ger-gers:* a grand sound, with mountains rising steeply from the sea to send back a far echo. When he wails that mournful *gerwy-yer* to the winter moon over the slakes, it is the crying of a lost spirit: the saddest sound in Nature: the sound of the sea.

APPENDIX

A.

A NEW THEORY OF ECLIPSE IN DRAKES

In no species of duck are the sexes identical in plumage or coloring. I am apt to conclude that a close resemblance between the plumages of duck and drake is exceptional, for, in the British Isles, only sheldrake and duck are similarly plumaged: though even in this instance the drake is brighter than the duck, and the swanlike knob on his carmine beak is much larger—nor do I regard the shelduck as a true duck. However, *marked* differences in the plumage of duck and drake are less common generally over the world than is a fairly close similarity. Where the plumage of the drake is notably bright in color, the duck's being dull, I maintain that the plumage pattern of the duck is accurately reproduced by the drake. A brilliant rectangular marking on the drake, say, represents in every case a brighter shade of the same section of the duck's prevailing dullness—as in the case of an eider duck's darker brown belly corresponding to the intense black of the drake, or the widgeon's golden crest replacing the pinker crown of his duck. Sexual selection has built up the attractive color scheme of the drake piece by piece from the pattern of the duck. This faithfulness to generic pattern culminates in the extraordinary "stenciled" plumage of mandarin drakes, vividly, but strictly, adhering to the penciled outlines of the plumage pattern of the ducks.

There is parallelism in the color evolution of various species of ducks, of which the commonest properties are speculum, plain-colored head, and sharp distinctions in color of breast, back, and belly. Here and there occur individual selective characteristics: the tiny curled feathers of a pintail, the superciliary stripe of a garganey, the curious markings on the head of a teal, or the white cheek-spot of a goldeneye; but the pattern scheme runs true to form in the main essentials. Even in the eccentric markings of the rare buffel-headed and harlequin drakes, it is clear that the plumage pattern of drake and duck has a common groundwork.

In many species of duck this evolution of a bright plumage for purposes of display and stimulation had as its corollary the eclipse. It can be defined as the assumption of an abnormal plumage pattern by the drake, during the period of a simultaneous moulting of the flight-feathers after the courtship.

Thus drakes moult three times in the year: an abrasion in the early spring (when some of the females moult even their down feathers); the eclipse in the summer; and a full moult in the early autumn.

I maintain that in every species the eclipse plumage of the drake resembles closely the ordinary plumage of his duck. In such as the gadwall the resemblance is complete down to the color of the beak, and in the American merganser down to the adoption of the duck's crest.

In addition to the metamorphosis of plumage, a phenomenon of the eclipse is that the drakes *are said to* desert their ducks and ducklings, relegating to their ducks the entire responsibility for the incubation of the eggs and the care of the ducklings—yet I have seen drake and duck mallard "feinting" with young on June 6.

In general—the rare exceptions I note later—there are certain invariable rules associated with the adoption of an eclipse. First, it is peculiar to the drakes of those species, such as mallard and eider, in whom there is a marked distinction between the plumage colorings of duck and drake; but the drake's plumage need not necessarily be conspicuous. The brown drake gadwall has an eclipse.

Conversely, there is no eclipse when the plumage of a duck and drake is similar, even if the species is brightly colored.

Secondly, the phenomenon of eclipse is peculiar, or nearly so, to drakes breeding in the Northern Hemisphere. American and British ornithologists differ on this point: the former stating that no drakes eclipse in the Southern Hemisphere, the latter asserting that some do. But what is important is this fact that a majority of eclipsing species breed north of the Equator.

Relative to this fact, there is remarkable and repeated evidence that non-eclipsing drakes breeding south of the Equator evolve an eclipse, after a lapse of some years, when domiciled north of the Equator. The American cinnamon teal, breeding in both hemispheres, is a case in point. The drake of this species is brightly plumaged in scarlet, the duck in brown, with the spatulate bill of a shoveler, to whom he is related. In North America, true to rule, the drake teal eclipses, but not in South America; but teal transported from south to north eventually begin to eclipse. Australian southern-breeding eclipsing species react in the same way when domiciled north of the Equator.

And, thirdly, during the period of the eclipse the drakes *are said to be* unable to fly, and are thus defenseless. Therefore, Nature, according to the majority of observers, has evolved another of her popular protective devices: the helpless drake replacing his conspicuous plumage by the obscure eclipse, which will serve as a camouflage while the new flight-feathers are growing.

Superficially, this "protective" theory is as plausible as a host of other such lightly promulgated ornithological theories. On close examination its bottom falls out. If the eclipse is protective, why is it not found (or only as an exception) among drakes of the Southern Hemisphere? Do conditions of life south of the Equator render such camouflage unnecessary? What about those brightly-plumaged ducks, whose drakes moult their flight-feathers, yet have no eclipse? The eclipsing gadwall cannot well put on a more inconspicuous plumage than his breeding brown.

Most damning, a protective eclipse is superfluous. On the one hand, there is the mallard—how far can predatory beast or hawk, or gunner for that matter, penetrate into the dense reed-beds of the marshes into which the drakes retreat to moult? How many drakes do I put up in eclipse? How many museums in the British Isles possess complete series of skins or specimens of mallards in eclipse? Brightness or dullness of plumage is immaterial: at this season the drakes are virtually unapproachable.

On the other hand, there is the eider. The drake's eclipse is a dark drab, with white patching on the back, more obvious on a marine background than his normal green, white, and black plumage. To counteract this conspicuousness, the drakes *are said to* retreat far out to sea; but, on the contrary, feeding only over a rocky floor at this season, the drakes pack about the reefs and rocky bays for the whole period of the eclipse, and are loath to move away from their especial resting ground. If the object of the eclipse is protective, then how foolish it is for the helpless eider to pack about the reefs at the mercy of any predatory beast. At this season, probably owing to their bodily weakness, they are more approachable than at any other time of the year; but, whatever may be the case with other species, the eider, while not liking to do so, seems able to fly at every stage of his eclipse, although his tiny pinions, stripped of their feathers, would seem to prohibit flight entirely. And, as we have seen, while probably taking no actual part in the nesting, eclipsing drakes mix up impartially with ducks and ducklings in great packs. I have also suggested why it is not impossible for the eider to fly at this season. If migrating godwit from the Arctic can fly several thousand miles with but two flight-feathers in each wing, there is, after all, nothing very wonderful in this eclipse flight of the eider.

For a less vulnerable theory of the significance of the eclipse I have to look to the past. Differences in the plumages of duck and drake have been evolved by generations of female stimulation by certain singularities in the plumage of the males. Broadly speaking, the brighter the coloring of the drake, the more closely the eclipse plumage reverts to that of the duck or immature drake.

Those comparatively primitively organized ducks, the scoters, in whom plumage distinction between duck and drake is obvious but not startling—brown to black—have no eclipse, or but a slight modification of their normal plumage. In the long-tailed duck plumages, distinction between duck and drake is more marked, and the color gap between the drake's full and eclipse plumages is greater. Finally, where full-plumage distinction between duck and drake is most marked, as in mallard and eider, the resemblance of

the eclipse plumage to that of duck or immature male is very close
—so close, that there are few ornithologists who could correctly
identify eclipsing and immature drake mallard and eider in the
field.

Considering these facts, I infer that the eclipse is solely an organic phenomenon: a reversion by the drake to his original color
pattern—which was also that of his duck's—after the courtship and
mating, when the specially evolved breeding plumage, having
served its purpose of display and stimulation, is no longer of value
to the species. The cessation of sexual impulses, once the mating is
consummated and ovulation begun, and the drain on his virility
during the months of display, added to the organic effects of the
coming moult, impose a severe strain upon the drake's constitution,
depressing his vitality to its lowest ebb.

It is natural that so fundamental and long-established an organic
function as the simultaneous shedding of the flight-feathers, in itself
a severe operation, should have as its adjunct this reversion by the
drake to his original plumage pattern, which is still the suit of the
immature drake and the duck. With the weeks of rest and the
growth of new flight-feathers, fresh reserves of vitality are accumu-
lated in readiness for the full moult, and the assumption once again
of the characteristic male plumage. I observe a similar loss or dull-
ing of breeding plumage in all male birds whose plumage is
brighter than their mates.

Thus there are no direct, and wholly unnecessary, protective
implications attached to this phenomenon of eclipse; it serves no
special, vital purpose; rather is it a natural organic reversion to generic pattern, apparently associated with residence in the Northern
Hemisphere. This cannot be purely a matter of climatic influence,
for many southern zones have complementary climatic areas north
of the Equator. I know, however, that all species of birds, with the
possible exception of the penguins, originated north of the Equator. It seems more than probable that those southern drakes, which
evolve eclipse plumages when domiciled north of the Equator, are
reacting to generic machinery lost, for some obscure reason, during
the eras of their residence in the Southern Hemisphere—machinery
likely to be connected with the hours of daylight or the apparent
north and south passages of the sun: factors that play so important
a part in the migrations and breeding of birds.

Note: There appears to be one outstanding exception to the normal rules governing the eclipse: the ruddy duck of North America. The drake's plumage is scarlet, with a somewhat rudimentary fan-shaped tail of blue; the duck inconspicuous; but there is no eclipse. This is particularly strange, inasmuch as the ruddy duck belongs to the family of stiff-tailed ducks, among the most primitive of the *Anatidae*. Some readers may have theories to account for this apparent anachronism.

B.

THE INTERRELATION OF DIVERSE EMOTIONS

The courtship of the great-crested grebe is as illustrative of the interrelation of diverse emotions as any. In the spring both sexes of grebe develop their "ears" of feathers and grow frills around their necks. It is significant that in this species, male and female share not only the singularities of plumage but also those of display. On a sunny day in March there booms across the waters of the lake the sonorous *kraa-oo* of the male grebe: one of the most impressive sounds of the English countryside. Rushing through the water— prowed Roman galleys—their necks stretched out in line with their bodies, male and female rear up at meeting to their full height, with frills spread wide, displaying to consummate advantage their dazzling silver breasts water-shining in the sun. Then they fence lovingly with their bills and shake their heads vigorously. They dive to reappear with trailing weeds dangling from their bills, with which they tilt at one another playfully, dropping them idly, inconsequently. At a stage in their bill-caressing both, of a sudden, coil back their sinuous necks until their rich chestnut tippets are hunched back upon their brown backs, in the posture of young bitterns, whose heads and spearing bills are drawn into their shoulders to strike upwards against the threatening pearl-gray harrier. The male dives beneath his mate with up-pointed bill, as he does with intent or menacing pretense to spear a rival male. He approaches her with head depressed, frill closed, and "ears" lolling like a turkey's wattles. He rolls his body in the water, as when preening, the better to display his satin undersides. After a bout of courtship, male and female ride motionless, side by side and head to tail, bobbing peacefully up and down on the waters, so closely that no light slips between them.

As a striking display enacted against the obvious background of an open sheet of water, it is easily seen that this courtship of the great-crested grebe is as common after mating as before. Courtship may be the prelude to the pairing of male and female, but it also precedes any subsequent coitions. The physical display of the male bird, the beauty of his plumage, and possibly, to a lesser degree, the vigor of his song or the inspiration of his joy-flight, are all vital factors in maintaining at fever-heat the sexual ardor of the female, so that not only her interest in the first brood, but her energy to undertake additional layings is constantly stimulated. Once the mating has been accomplished, this is one of the most important duties of the male bird. Before the nidificatory operations preparatory to a second brood, the male re-enacts his display in full: liberating that abundant reserve of vitality he has stored up during the sexless autumn months, and inciting afresh the ovulationary instincts of the female.

The nesting site of a pair of mute swans is, more often than not, a favorite mating spot. Thereabouts tends to accumulate a heap of reeds plucked by the courtng birds at successive matings: for, like grebes, a phase of the courtship of swans is the idle culling, throwing, dangling, and offering to one another of waterweeds and reeds. The nest itself consists partly of these accumulations, partly of scattered reeds loosened in their courtship on other stretches of water, which drift down with the current, but mainly of material which the pen gathers in to her from the back-sweepings of the cob, while she is *in situ* on the mating spot, which is also her rudimentary nest. Swans, like terns, have not yet progressed to the evolutionary stage of deliberately fetching material from a distance for the nest: not even the loose material that they uproot in their courtship elsewhere.

In his courting days, before the pen begins to sit on a pile of weed, the cob sweeps offerings of waterweed back to her with his long neck, without turning his body. When she begins to sit, and long after her eggs are laid, he continues to plunge his long neck under the water, rip up a great bunch of weed, and sweep it back in her direction, which is also the direction of the nest. He goes on doing this mechanically, hour after hour, and day after day, ir-respective of how far away he is from the nest: though a great quantity of his uprootings are eventually added to the nest-heap by the pen who, while she is sitting, gathers into her all that she can reach. Occasionally, just to prove how unintelligent is his action, the cob sweeps his offerings in the wrong direction from the nest: the object of his affections apparently forgotten, though the instinct to "sweep" is still dominant. The nest of a pair of mute swans is, clearly, purely the instinctive and natural complement of their courtship.

But I need not go farther afield than the garden to observe courting blackbirds or dunnocks tearing up moss in their ecstasies, or tossing twigs and straws about them. Even barndoor fowls be-have in this manner. If this is a part of the courtship of grebes and swans, in the majority of birds—especially the female—this idle throwing of appropriate nesting material seems as unthinking as the insensate posturing of courting ruffs before sticks and stones. Of the same ancestral stock as reptiles, it is not unreasonable to conclude that primitive birds laid their eggs in mud, and later in a mound of vegetation, as the brush turkey does, to hatch by the natural heat engendered by its decay. Many birds cover, or at-tempt to cover, their eggs when leaving their nests: the dabchick is the most oft-quoted instance. This action is usually attributed to protective instincts; but rather do I think that such "coverers" are still reacting to the old instinct of covering the eggs with vegeta-tion as a means of hatching them.

As the reawakening of sexual passions impels the male birds to display, so in the females is born again the instinctive desire to pluck and pitch, particularly over their backs, the grasses and peb-bles about them: for what reason they know not. Thus, in that early practice of covering the eggs, Nature implanted the germ of nidificatory architecture, and sexual impulses were associated with the use of nesting materials. The nidificatory instinct seems to be germane in every species of bird. Guillemots, for instance, lay their single eggs on bare rock ledges of steep cliffs. But here is a guille-mot who picks up material blown from the nearby nest of a kitti-wake, and twiddles it affectionately in her sharp bill, and there an-other who lays down a feather beside his mate brooding her egg. Great skuas are but breast-hollow nesters, but one, a female, drops grasses before her mate in courtship. Once again I must emphasize that a bird is born with instincts of courtship and nest-building, fighting and feeding, ready to respond to the appropriate internal or external stimulus; but in his mind is no clear perception of their right use: for a Montagu's harrier, returning to her eggs and finding them observed, drops to the ground, and nervously picks up a twig here, dropping it idly there. With the instinct to build still strong upon her, although the eggs are laid, her emotion of jealous anxiety at the presence of an intruder near to the nest and eggs is partially confused. To equip the bird adequately for the many different emergencies with which he has to cope during his existence, Nature has so fashioned his organism that although one instinct (say, the nidificatory) is dominant, it may yet, at the same time, respond to another (that of fear, perhaps). A good instance of this is the complex emotions and reactions of a shelduck with young when danger threatens.

Nor is the nidificatory instinct only in the female of the species. We have seen how two mated terns bow forward in their courtship and pivot on their breasts in the sand or shingle, fashioning hollows. The environs of a ternery are pitted everywhere with these depressions, of which only a small percentage will contain eggs. Lapwing and ringed plover, and no doubt a multitude of other ground nesters, behave in like manner. The ways of oyster-catchers are more complex, for the cock-bird strews his cup with broken cockle and mussel shells, as his mate does hers at a later date. It is not only the wren, an arboreal and master craftsman, who builds several "cock" nests every spring: some perfect save for the lining of feathers, others never completed. When cygnets leave the nest, the female mute swan broods them on one of the accumulations of reeds about a mating site. The water hen covers her fledglings at night in a "cock" nest, and a parent bird occupies one during the winter months. Golden eagles tear up food for their young on a superfluous eyrie, sometimes using another as an alternative residence.

But it would be wrong to argue back from these instances of "cock" nests put to useful purposes, implying that they have been built with intent. Swans' nests are, so far as the cob and pen are concerned, fortuitous: born of the reed-plucking instinct of courtship. The tossing about of grasses at the breeding season is not restricted to hen-birds, and, with grebes, the dangling of weeds and offering them to the female is a part of the courtship of the male. Courtship, mating, and nesting are all inspired by the sex impulse; they react one upon the other so closely that the male is as likely to expend some of his excess vitality in fashioning a nest as the female: an action associated in his sensory being with the pleasurable emotions of courtship and mating. Many male birds are efficient in their care of the young, and in extreme instances, such as the red-necked phalarope, it is affirmed that the male does most of the incubating. When any hen-bird is sitting on her eggs, she will pluck the grasses about her and throw them in deliberate manner over her back, as though seeking to make herself a part of the nest and the promise of life it holds. Perhaps, too, she is incited by an unconscious motive of concealment: an unfulfilled desire to complete the nest above and around her: an ambition achieved only by those birds that build domed nests.

Nor was it so great a step, once the progressive rhythm of nest-building was set in motion, from a bare hollow as nest to a lining of grasses, and later, in an arboreal existence, to the deliberate gathering of materials for so wonderful an edifice as the nest of a long-tailed titmouse. Here is a spheroid of cunningly woven and felted green moss, single strands of sheep's wool, and threads of spiders' silk, faced with lichens so that it resembles the black and white crustations of the tree in which it rests. It is so strong that it withstands the buffetings of all weathers and the jostlings of twelve nestlings, a brooding mother, and a roosting father, with inordinately long tails; so malleable that the daily increasing bulk of the young birds in no way strains its capacity; so compact that it contains more than two thousand warm feathers and yet maintains a perfect ventilation. Doubtless many millenniums of bitter trial and error, and the failure of generations of unsuccessful builders, went to achieve this perfect heritage: for Nature has ever been ever more thoughtful for the species than the individual, while striving to endow both with the genius of her acquired wisdom. Yet it has been accomplished, and every spring bears witness to the consummate artistry of perfected evolution.

Once it was fortuitously discovered that a ramage of branches offered as secure a foundation for a nest as the ground, arboreal architecture could progress on its evolutionary adventure. (Like Huxley's monkeys experimenting on their typewriters, the jackdaw painstakingly dropping twigs down a hollow tree-trunk is surely its classic Sisyphus.) In the course of time such master-builders as the golden-crested wren even found it possible to undersling their minute hammocks of moss and cobwebs beneath the topmost branch of a fir.

Naturally, with the development of arboreal architecture, the building of the nest on the exact mating site became difficult or impossible. But rooks, who return to the same nesting-tree every season, and often renovate a previous year's nest or build a new one with the material of the old (the phoenix arising from its ashes) and twigs filched from their neighbors, usually mate within the nest. It is not altogether fanciful to regard the rook as a link with England's past: for his rookery testifies to the centuries-old unbroken perpetuity of his race. Each spring a clutch of green, brown-mottled eggs is the promise that his tradition lives and will continue to live.

INDEX

A complete summary of references to behavior in the text is alphabetically indexed under the following headings:

479